T0358185

### IN FINANCE
### AND ECONOMICS
#### A Beginner's Guide

# IN FINANCE
# AND ECONOMICS
## A Beginner's Guide

## Abhay Kumar Singh
Edith Cowan University, Australia

## David Edmund Allen
University of Sydney, Australia

 World Scientific

NEW JERSEY · LONDON · SINGAPORE · BEIJING · SHANGHAI · HONG KONG · TAIPEI · CHENNAI · TOKYO

*Published by*

World Scientific Publishing Co. Pte. Ltd.
5 Toh Tuck Link, Singapore 596224
*USA office:* 27 Warren Street, Suite 401-402, Hackensack, NJ 07601
*UK office:* 57 Shelton Street, Covent Garden, London WC2H 9HE

**Library of Congress Cataloging-in-Publication Data**
Names: Singh, Abhay Kumar, 1958–    author. | Allen, David E., author.
Title: R in finance and economics : a beginner's guide / Abhay Kumar Singh
    (Edith Cowan University, Australia), David E Allen (University of Sydney, Australia).
Description: New Jersey : World Scientific, 2016.
Identifiers: LCCN 2016032485 | ISBN 9789813144460 (hc : alk. paper)
Subjects: LCSH: Finance--Software. | Economics--Software. | R (Computer program language)
Classification: LCC HG1709 .S59 2016 | DDC 330.0285/5133--dc23
LC record available at https://lccn.loc.gov/2016032485

**British Library Cataloguing-in-Publication Data**
A catalogue record for this book is available from the British Library.

Copyright © 2017 by World Scientific Publishing Co. Pte. Ltd.

*All rights reserved. This book, or parts thereof, may not be reproduced in any form or by any means, electronic or mechanical, including photocopying, recording or any information storage and retrieval system now known or to be invented, without written permission from the publisher.*

For photocopying of material in this volume, please pay a copying fee through the Copyright Clearance Center, Inc., 222 Rosewood Drive, Danvers, MA 01923, USA. In this case permission to photocopy is not required from the publisher.

Desk Editors: Dipasri Sardar/Alisha Nguyen

Typeset by Stallion Press
Email: enquiries@stallionpress.com

Printed in Singapore

# About the Authors

### Dr Abhay Kumar Singh

Dr Abhay Kumar Singh is a Lecturer in the School of Business & Law at Edith Cowan University (ECU), Perth, Australia.

He has a Bachelor of Technology degree in Information Technology and an MBA from the Indian Institute of Information Technology & Management Gwalior, India (2009). He completed his Ph.D. in Finance from Edith Cowan University, Perth, Australia in 2011 and was awarded the University Research Medal for an outstanding thesis.

He is a big believer in open source software and has been using R for statistical computing including quantitative research methods for over four years. He has over five years' experience in Financial Risk Modelling & Research. He started his career as a Research Associate at ECU in 2009 and has since co-authored over 20 journal publications, 16 book chapters and several conference papers on a range of topics including, finance, investments, econometrics, machine learning, data mining and multivariate statistics.

### Professor David Allen

Professor David Allen is an Adjunct Professor in the Center for Applied Financial studies at the University of South Australia and a Visiting Professor in the School of Mathematics and Statistics at the University of Sydney.

He has an Honours degree in Economics from St. Andrews University in Scotland (1970), an M.Phil in the History of Economic thought completed at Leicester University in England (1976) and a Ph.D.

in Finance from the University of Western Australia (1996). He is a Fellow (F. Fin) of the Financial Services Institute of Australia, The Modelling and Simulation Society of Australia and New Zealand (FMSSANZ) and a Fellow of the International Institute of Engineering and Technology (FIET). He was a member of the executive of the Australian Research Council funded Financial Integrity Research Network (FIRN) for the original five years from its inception in 2005, when it was funded by the ARC.

He has been employed in a number of Universities, these include: De Montfort University in Leicester, England, in the Faculty of Business and Law, as a Lecturer in economics and finance (1975–1979). The University of Edinburgh, in Scotland, in the Business School as a Lecturer in Finance (1979–1986). The University of Western Australia, in the Business School, as a Lecturer/Senior Lecturer in Finance (1986–1992). At Curtin University as the Challenge Bank Professor of Finance (1992–1996) and Edith Cowan University where he was the Foundation Professor of Finance from 1996 to July 2013.

He has published three books and monographs, co-authored 38 book chapters, and over 100 refereed journal publications on a diverse range of topics covering business economics, finance, investments, risk analysis, time series econometrics and statistics.

# Preface

This book is designed as an easily accessible and useful practical guide to getting started with the statistical software tool R for applications in Finance and Economics. There are various open source or commercial software packages available for statistical computing. R is not just used for statistical modelling in business analysis, socio-economic analysis, etc., but is also gaining popularity among students and researchers in academia in the fields of Economics and Finance. R is currently one of the most popular software packages available. Its popularity is partly driven from the fact that it is a free resource for users and its great versatility in a variety of applications. The unique strength of R is that it has a multidiscipline base with packages being supplied from a wide spectrum of disciplinary contributors from science, mathematics, computing and operational research, plus a broad spectrum of the social sciences.

The design of this book has been greatly influenced by introductory courses in R that have been run by the authors at Edith Cowan University in Western Australia, Southampton Business School at the University of Southampton in the UK and in the Edinburgh Business School at the University of Edinburgh in Scotland. In these courses, it was found that beginners have considerable difficulty in setting up R and RStudio, in the importation of data, and in the writing of code. The book addresses these issues in a simple way to understand while more advanced books that are available on R do not do so. Yet, these courses were run for postgraduate students and university staff members, but most seemed to struggle at first.

This book is specifically targeted towards early career researchers or research students who have some exposure to basic statistical methods used in quantitative research. Although the first author of the book has over eight years of computer programming experience and over four years of experience with R, the text is designed in such a way that people with even limited knowledge of computer programming can benefit. The second author's experience with computing stretches back to working with mainframes, in the late 1970s, at the University of Edinburgh in Scotland, before switching to personal computers in the 1980s at the University of Western Australia. The bulk of his more recent research experience in finance and econometrics was with menu-driven econometrics programs. He did not have exposure to Matlab and subsequently R until he was in his 60s. This reinforced his awareness of the importance of appropriate data import, formatting, and manipulation. The intention is to make this book useful for people with computing experience as little as recording a macro in MS-Excel up to writing codes in C++/MATLAB/R/S or other programming languages.

"R in Finance and Economics — A Beginner's Guide" provides an introduction to the statistical software R and its application with an empirical approach in finance and economics. We believe that the methods and procedures outlined in the book are likely to be of use to researchers from various fields beyond the ones of focus here. The major objective of the text is to get the reader started with R by making the reader familiar with the concepts and techniques required. We do not develop any R package via this book but use various packages which are available and are useful for research to sustain the applied nature of this text. The easy to follow text, provides examples and applications of econometric and statistical analysis techniques to central methods in economics and finance.

The book covers topics ranging from introduction to the R environment to advanced topics like multivariate Vine Copulas. Chapter 1 provides an introduction to R and overview of the RStudio interface which is the primary R GUI/IDE used in the book. Chapter 2 discusses some of the most common data types and structures used in statistical analysis using R followed by various methods to import, export and preprocess external data in Chapter 3. Chapter 4 provides a brief overview of some important programming concepts including program control flow and creating functions. Almost all empirical problems in Finance and Economics require a robust preliminary data exploration with summary/descriptive statistics and exploratory plots which are discussed in Chapter 6. R is gaining popularity among the data analytics community not just because of its statistical prowess but also due to advanced data visualisation capabilities. Chapter 7 discusses various methods available to create various types of graphs in R including a short introduction to the *ggplot2* package.

Chapters 7 and 8 present Regression Analysis; one of the most widely used tools in quantitative methods. Chapter 7 provides an overview of linear regression (OLS) and Quantile Regression along with an empirical example illustrating the use of linear regression to evaluate multifactor models in finance. Panel Regression and Logistic Regression are two other statistical tools used in empirical finance and economics along with OLS and Quantile Regression. We discuss these two regression tools in Chapter 8 and provide an illustrative example on how to use Panel Regression in applied economic problems. After regression analysis, Chapter 9 provides an overview of widely used Autoregressive and conditional autoregressive time series models in Financial econometrics. We also discuss an example of modelling and forecasting Value at Risk (VaR) using a GARCH model in R.

Chapter 9 introduces Extreme Value Theory (EVT), which is used in risk quantification in finance and actuarial studies. We discuss EVT for financial risk and EVT for bivariate tail dependence along with an empirical example. The last chapter, Chapter 10 of the book focusses on multivariate dependence using Copulas. Chapter 10 presents some widely used bivariate copulas and also introduces the recently developed multivariate Vine Copulas, which are more flexible than bivariate copulas. The example in Chapter 10 demonstrates how to estimate portfolio VaR using Vine Copulas.

The book is designed with due consideration for the difficulties which a beginner programmer can face. The text contains illustrative examples and code is provided in the text itself. The examples are reproducible using the open source R and RStudio programs. The following are the key strengths of this book:

(1) Short and Concise: The book will follow a minimalistic approach in teaching how to use R. The discussions will focus primarily on easy to follow methods which are mostly used by beginner and intermediate users. There will be a discussion for more advanced users but that will be included in separate chapters.

(2) Easy to follow: The contents in the book will be kept to the level of a beginner or intermediate R user so it will be easily understood by both early career researchers and research students (Ph.D., Masters by Research, etc.).

(3) Examples: Every method explained in the book has a detailed following example with tips and tricks. The code used for the example is given in the book itself so that the user can copy it to reproduce the results (when using an ebook).

(4) Reproducible Codes: R codes (scripts) are provided for all the chapters in the book.

(5) Practical applications: Research based examples are included which will include the most widely used statistical and econometric applications such as linear regression, econometrics (GARCH, etc.). This will enable beginners to get started and produce sound results. These examples will include applications to similar problems to those addressed in the research papers by the authors of this book and thus will be current and state of the art.

(6) Reproducible Research: The examples and case studies in the book will follow step by step procedures which will enable the reader to reproduce them. The data is provided with the book on its companion website.

To summarise, the book demonstrates the latest research methods in finance and economics with applications featuring linear regression, quantile regression, panel regression, econometrics, Extreme Value methods and copulas using a range of data sets and examples.

*A. K. Singh and D. E. Allen*

# Supplementary Material

All the R code examples, data sets and generated figures used in this book are available for download at http://www.worldscientific.com/worldscibooks/10.1142/10151-sm

# Contents

*About the Authors*                                                    v

*Preface*                                                            vii

*Supplementary Material*                                              xi

1. Introduction                                                       1

   1.1   Why Should We Learn R? . . . . . . . . . . . . . . . . .   2

   1.2   R: Getting Started . . . . . . . . . . . . . . . . . . .   3

       1.2.1   Installing R on windows . . . . . . . . . . . . .   3

       1.2.2   RStudio: A better way to run R . . . . . . . . .   4

       1.2.3   Installing RStudio for windows . . . . . . . . .   4

       1.2.4   RStudio GUI/IDE . . . . . . . . . . . . . . . .   5

   1.3   Proxy Setup . . . . . . . . . . . . . . . . . . . . . . .   6

   1.4   R Packages . . . . . . . . . . . . . . . . . . . . . . .   7

       1.4.1   Installing packages . . . . . . . . . . . . . . . .   8

   1.5   R Core Packages . . . . . . . . . . . . . . . . . . . .   8

   1.6   Task Views in R: Introduction and Installation . . . . .   9

   1.7   Getting Help . . . . . . . . . . . . . . . . . . . . . .  10

       1.7.1   Getting help from the web . . . . . . . . . . .  13

   1.8   Summary . . . . . . . . . . . . . . . . . . . . . . . .  14

2. Data Objects in R                                                 15

   2.1   Introduction . . . . . . . . . . . . . . . . . . . . . .  15

   2.2   Data Types . . . . . . . . . . . . . . . . . . . . . . .  15

       2.2.1   Double . . . . . . . . . . . . . . . . . . . . . .  16

       2.2.2   Integer . . . . . . . . . . . . . . . . . . . . . .  16

       2.2.3   Complex . . . . . . . . . . . . . . . . . . . . .  16

       2.2.4   Logical . . . . . . . . . . . . . . . . . . . . . .  17

       2.2.5   Character . . . . . . . . . . . . . . . . . . . . .  17

    2.2.6    Factor . . . . . . . . . . . . . . . . . . . . . . .    18
    2.2.7    Date and time . . . . . . . . . . . . . . . . . . .    18
    2.2.8    Missing data in R . . . . . . . . . . . . . . . . .    20
2.3    Data Structures in R . . . . . . . . . . . . . . . . . . .    20
    2.3.1    Vector . . . . . . . . . . . . . . . . . . . . . . .    20
    2.3.2    Matrices . . . . . . . . . . . . . . . . . . . . . .    21
            2.3.2.1    Matrix manipulations . . . . . . . . . .    22
    2.3.3    Arrays . . . . . . . . . . . . . . . . . . . . . . .    23
    2.3.4    Data frames . . . . . . . . . . . . . . . . . . . .    25
    2.3.5    Lists . . . . . . . . . . . . . . . . . . . . . . . .    27
2.4    Summary . . . . . . . . . . . . . . . . . . . . . . . . . .    28

3.  Data Handling in R                                               29

3.1    Introduction . . . . . . . . . . . . . . . . . . . . . . . .    29
3.2    Importing and Exporting Tabular Data in R . . . . . . . .    29
    3.2.1    Reading data from a text file . . . . . . . . . . .    29
    3.2.2    Reading data from CSV file . . . . . . . . . . . .    32
    3.2.3    Reading data from excel files . . . . . . . . . . .    33
    3.2.4    Reading data from databases . . . . . . . . . . .    33
    3.2.5    Reading from data files from other statistical
             systems . . . . . . . . . . . . . . . . . . . . . .    33
            3.2.5.1    Reading SPSS data file . . . . . . . . .    34
            3.2.5.2    Reading Stata data file . . . . . . . . .    36
            3.2.5.3    Reading Matlab data files . . . . . . . .    37
3.3    Data Preprocessing in R . . . . . . . . . . . . . . . . . .    37
    3.3.1    Extracting data . . . . . . . . . . . . . . . . . .    37
    3.3.2    Combining data frames . . . . . . . . . . . . . .    39
    3.3.3    Sub-setting and logical data selection . . . . . .    41
3.4    Summary . . . . . . . . . . . . . . . . . . . . . . . . . .    43

4.  R Programming and Control Flow                                   45

4.1    Introduction . . . . . . . . . . . . . . . . . . . . . . . .    45
4.2    Control Flow . . . . . . . . . . . . . . . . . . . . . . . .    46
    4.2.1    If-else conditional statements . . . . . . . . . . .    46
    4.2.2    Using switch . . . . . . . . . . . . . . . . . . . .    47
    4.2.3    Loops . . . . . . . . . . . . . . . . . . . . . . . .    48
4.3    Functions in R . . . . . . . . . . . . . . . . . . . . . . .    50
4.4    Summary . . . . . . . . . . . . . . . . . . . . . . . . . .    52

5. Data Exploration     53

    5.1    Introduction . . . . . . . . . . . . . . . . . . . . . . . . . 53
    5.2    Summary Statistics . . . . . . . . . . . . . . . . . . . . . 53
    5.3    Example: Descriptive Statistics of Stock Returns . . . . . 59
        5.3.1    Introduction . . . . . . . . . . . . . . . . . . . . . 59
        5.3.2    Importing the data . . . . . . . . . . . . . . . . . 61
             5.3.2.1    Using the `describe` function . . . . . . . 66
             5.3.2.2    Using `stat.desc` from package
                     pastecs . . . . . . . . . . . . . . . . . . . 67
        5.3.3    Some basic plots . . . . . . . . . . . . . . . . . . 71
    5.4    Summary . . . . . . . . . . . . . . . . . . . . . . . . . . . 74

6. Graphics in R     75

    6.1    Introduction . . . . . . . . . . . . . . . . . . . . . . . . . 75
    6.2    Basic Plots in R . . . . . . . . . . . . . . . . . . . . . . . 76
    6.3    Exporting Graphics . . . . . . . . . . . . . . . . . . . . . 86
    6.4    R Graphical Parameters . . . . . . . . . . . . . . . . . . . 88
    6.5    Introduction to ggplot2 . . . . . . . . . . . . . . . . . . . 91
        6.5.1    Getting started with `qplot` . . . . . . . . . . . . 92
        6.5.2    Layered graphics using `ggplot` . . . . . . . . . . 93
    6.6    Transforming Data from Wide to Long Format . . . . . . 100
    6.7    Summary . . . . . . . . . . . . . . . . . . . . . . . . . . . 102

7. Regression Analysis-I     103

    7.1    Introduction . . . . . . . . . . . . . . . . . . . . . . . . . 103
    7.2    OLS . . . . . . . . . . . . . . . . . . . . . . . . . . . . . . 103
    7.3    QR . . . . . . . . . . . . . . . . . . . . . . . . . . . . . . 107
        7.3.1    Estimating QR . . . . . . . . . . . . . . . . . . . 110
    7.4    Example: Fama–French Factor Model and Multiple
        Regression . . . . . . . . . . . . . . . . . . . . . . . . . . 114
        7.4.1    Introduction . . . . . . . . . . . . . . . . . . . . . 114
        7.4.2    Data . . . . . . . . . . . . . . . . . . . . . . . . . 116
             7.4.2.1    Data preprocessing . . . . . . . . . . . 117
        7.4.3    OLS regression analysis of the Fama–French
             three factor model . . . . . . . . . . . . . . . . . . 121
        7.4.4    Quantile analysis of the Fama–French three
             factor model . . . . . . . . . . . . . . . . . . . . . 124
    7.5    Summary . . . . . . . . . . . . . . . . . . . . . . . . . . . 129

8.   Regression Analysis-II                                            131

     8.1   Introduction . . . . . . . . . . . . . . . . . . . . . . . . . . . 131
     8.2   Panel Data Linear Regression . . . . . . . . . . . . . . . . 131
           8.2.1   Fixed and Random effects using the *plm*
                   package . . . . . . . . . . . . . . . . . . . . . . . . . 133
                   8.2.1.1   Fixed effect estimation . . . . . . . . . 134
                   8.2.1.2   Random effect estimation . . . . . . . . 136
                   8.2.1.3   Panel or OLS . . . . . . . . . . . . . . 137
                   8.2.1.4   Fixed effect or random effect . . . . . . 139
     8.3   Logistic Regression . . . . . . . . . . . . . . . . . . . . . . 139
     8.4   Example: Economic Growth and Unemployment —
           A Panel Analysis . . . . . . . . . . . . . . . . . . . . . . . 142
           8.4.1   Data and methodology . . . . . . . . . . . . . . 142
           8.4.2   Data preprocessing . . . . . . . . . . . . . . . . 143
           8.4.3   Linear panel regression analysis . . . . . . . . . 145
     8.5   Summary . . . . . . . . . . . . . . . . . . . . . . . . . . . 151

9.   Time Series Analysis                                               153

     9.1   Introduction . . . . . . . . . . . . . . . . . . . . . . . . . . 153
     9.2   Time Series-Some Properties . . . . . . . . . . . . . . . . 153
           9.2.1   Stochastic process . . . . . . . . . . . . . . . . . 153
           9.2.2   Stationarity . . . . . . . . . . . . . . . . . . . . . 154
           9.2.3   Autocorrelation function (ACF) . . . . . . . . . 157
           9.2.4   White noise . . . . . . . . . . . . . . . . . . . . . 159
     9.3   Autoregressive Moving Average Model (ARMA) . . . . . 159
           9.3.1   Fitting an ARMA model . . . . . . . . . . . . . 161
     9.4   Volatility Modelling using Generalised Autoregressive
           Conditional Heteroskedasticity (GARCH) . . . . . . . . 166
           9.4.1   Fitting a GARCH(1,1) model using the *rugarch*
                   package . . . . . . . . . . . . . . . . . . . . . . . . . 167
     9.5   Example: Modelling and Forecasting Daily VaR
           using GARCH . . . . . . . . . . . . . . . . . . . . . . . . . 175
           9.5.1   Data and methodology . . . . . . . . . . . . . . 175
           9.5.2   VaR forecasts . . . . . . . . . . . . . . . . . . . . 178
     9.6   Summary . . . . . . . . . . . . . . . . . . . . . . . . . . . 182

10.  Extreme Value Theory Modelling                                     183

     10.1  Introduction . . . . . . . . . . . . . . . . . . . . . . . . . . 183

10.2 EVT and Financial Risk Modelling . . . . . . . . . . . . 183
    10.2.1 GPD and POT methods . . . . . . . . . . . . . . 185
        10.2.1.1 Sample mean excess plot . . . . . . . . 186
        10.2.1.2 Estimation of GPD . . . . . . . . . . . 187
        10.2.1.3 VaR and expected shortfall . . . . . . . 191
10.3 EVT and Tail Dependence . . . . . . . . . . . . . . . . . 195
    10.3.1 Measures of tail dependence . . . . . . . . . . . 195
        10.3.1.1 Asymptotic dependence — the
              conventional approach . . . . . . . . . . 197
        10.3.1.2 Asymptotic independence — an
              alternative measure of dependence . . . . 198
    10.3.2 Estimating $\chi$ and $\bar{\chi}$: nonparametric
        method . . . . . . . . . . . . . . . . . . . . . . . 202
10.4 Example: EVT VaR — A Dynamic Approach . . . . . . . 204
    10.4.1 Data and methodology . . . . . . . . . . . . . . . 206
    10.4.2 VaR forecasts using dynamic EVT model . . . . . 207
10.5 Summary . . . . . . . . . . . . . . . . . . . . . . . . . . 209

11. Introduction to Multivariate Analysis using Copulas     211

11.1 Introduction . . . . . . . . . . . . . . . . . . . . . . . . . 211
11.2 Copula . . . . . . . . . . . . . . . . . . . . . . . . . . . . 212
    11.2.1 Types of copula . . . . . . . . . . . . . . . . . . . 213
        11.2.1.1 Elliptical copulas . . . . . . . . . . . . . 213
        11.2.1.2 Archimedean copulas . . . . . . . . . . . 217
    11.2.2 Copula selection . . . . . . . . . . . . . . . . . . 222
11.3 Multivariate Vine Copulas . . . . . . . . . . . . . . . . . 222
    11.3.1 Estimating R-Vine copulas using R . . . . . . . . 224
11.4 Example: Portfolio VaR Estimation using
    Vine Copula . . . . . . . . . . . . . . . . . . . . . . . . . 229
    11.4.1 Data and methodology . . . . . . . . . . . . . . . 229
    11.4.2 VaR forecasts using R . . . . . . . . . . . . . . . 230
11.5 Summary . . . . . . . . . . . . . . . . . . . . . . . . . . 234

*Bibliography*     235

*Index*     243

# Chapter 1

# Introduction

R is an open source software package and environment for statistical computing and graphics. The R language has received a lot of attention in the last five years or so particularly with its growing use by Statisticians and data miners for their empirical analysis and software development. R started as a freely available implementation of the S programming language. R was created by Ross Ihaka and Robert Gentleman, of the University of Auckland, New Zealand, and now, R is developed by the R Development Core Team. R can be considered as a different implementation of S. There are some important differences, but much code written for S runs unaltered under R.

The official R website `http://www.r-project.org/` provides the best description and explanation for R. This section and the section following in the introduction to R are majorly adopted from the R website.

According to Wikipedia, "R is a free software programming language and a software environment for statistical computing and graphics. The R language is widely used among Statisticians and data miners for developing statistical software and data analysis. Polls and surveys of data miners suggest R's popularity has increased substantially in recent years".

By design, R provides the possibility of further computations (methods) on the results (objects) of a statistical procedure. Also the graphical capabilities of R facilitate methods as simple as plot $(x, y)$ to very specific and fine control over the output. The fact that R is based on a formal computer language gives it tremendous flexibility. Other systems present simpler interfaces in terms of menus and forms, but often the apparent user-friendliness turns into a hindrance in the longer run.

## 1.1   Why Should We Learn R?

The growth in the number of R users in recent years has indicated that researchers around the world are either using R or will use it at some point. There are several advantages to using R for statistical computing other than its open source and doesn't cost anything. The benefits of R for an introductory student and instructors are

- R is free.
- R is open source and runs on UNIX, Windows and Macintosh, so it can be used on multiple platforms.
- R has an excellent built-in help system and also various online help pages including mailing lists and boards.
- R has excellent graphing capabilities which are customisable.
- R's language has a powerful, easy to learn syntax with many built-in statistical functions which are provided by default built-in packages.
- R is a computer programming language. It is easier for programmers to learn it and its intuitive enough for beginners.
- R provides specific functions bundled in user created packages for a particular field. This makes it easier for an applied researcher to use these functions rather than having to reinvent the wheel.

R follows a type inference coding structure which enables the automatic deduction of the type of an expression in R. For example, a string is identified as character and need not be explicitly declared before. R provides a wide variety of statistical and graphical techniques, including:

- Linear and nonlinear modelling,
- Univariate and multivariate statistics,
- Classical statistical tests,
- Time series analysis/econometrics,
- Simulation and modelling,
- Data mining-classification, clustering, etc.,
- For computationally intensive tasks, C, C++, and Fortran code can be linked and called at run time.

R is easily extensible through functions and extensions, and the R community is noted for its active contributions in terms of packages. R has over 8000 packages with new packages added more frequently than any other statistical software. The R command below should run with an Internet connection. We will discuss how to setup proxy on work computers later.

```
# Run to see the total number of current packages
# available to users
length(available.packages()[, 1])
```

Although R is available for Macintosh, Unix and Linux as well, we will use R on windows in this book. In most cases, the examples and codes in this text can be used for other operating system unaltered.

Other statistical packages, such as SPSS, GRETL and Minitab, provide point-and-click graphical-user interfaces (GUIs), but R is command-oriented. Although basic R is command/script based and provides a basic script editor, GUI capabilities can be added to the R interface using packages like Rcmdr. The R interface provides a basic GUI with a console to type commands and a script editor to write scripts. It also provides a few other functionalities like loading packages, clearing workspace, changing directory, etc. Users normally type commands at a command prompt in the console or as a script in the R script editor to get a desired output.

RStudio, an integrated development environment (IDE) (`http://www.rstudio.com/ide/`) is a powerful and productive user interface for R. RStudio provides various additional functionalities to the basic R interface which makes RStudio the choice of IDE in this book. We will now discuss how to get R and RStudio along with installing them on windows[1] in the following subsections while providing more details about the R Environment.

## 1.2 R: Getting Started

### 1.2.1 Installing R on windows

The latest version of R can be downloaded from the CRAN page `https://cloud.r-project.org/bin/windows/base/`. CRAN is a network of ftp and web servers around the world which store identical, up-to-date versions of code and documentation for R. The list of available CRAN mirrors can be found at `http://cran.r-project.org/mirrors.html`. The page also provides some instructions and FAQs on R installation. The R-base is an executable package which can be easily installed on a windows machine with Administrative privileges. As stated earlier R comes with a basic GUI, which has a basic source code editor and a console window for command input.

---

[1] A 64bit version of R installed on Windows 7 is used to run all the codes and examples in this book.

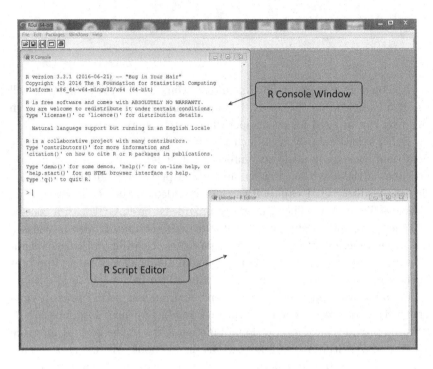

Figure 1.1: R GUI (Windows)

The R GUI in windows looks like as shown in Figure 1.1.

### 1.2.2 RStudio: A better way to run R

RStudio is an IDE and is a powerful and productive user interface for R. It is freely available, and works on Windows, Mac, and Linux. RStudio also comes in a server version that can be used to run R on a remote web server. In that case, RStudio's interface will run in your browser, RStudio provides, a highly advanced text editor, R's help system, workspace and history view along with the console to write and view results. RStudio offers many facilities that make working reproducibly a lot easier.

### 1.2.3 Installing RStudio for windows

RStudio and R both work together, so both have to be installed. Go to http://www.rstudio.com/ide/download/desktop to download RStudio for desktop, an executable which can be easily installed by clicking on the application and following the instructions. The default installation settings work for most cases. As R is constantly evolving RStudio also gets updated, a periodic check for updates from www.rstudio.com is highly recommended. RStudio also provides "Check For Update" in the Help drop down of the RStudio desktop. We will only use the RStudio desktop version, hence from here on, RStudio will refer only to the desktop version.

### 1.2.4 RStudio GUI/IDE

RStudio is an advanced IDE for R and is highly customisable providing functionality for reproducible research and project building. We will highlight the major useful features of RStudio throughout this book. RStudio provides various documentation on its website at http://www.rstudio.com/ide/docs/. Figure 1.2 gives a snapshot of the four major panes which are there in RStudio. These four panes are:

(1) The Script Editor and Data Viewer window to write the source code for execution and viewing data.

(2) The Console window to write direct commands and also to view results generated from the code.

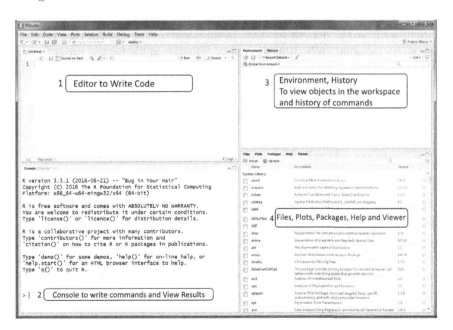

Figure 1.2: RStudio IDE

(3) The third window which gives Environment, History.
(4) The fourth window gives the Help interface along with files (working directory), List of Packages and recently generated plots (available in the workspace).

This description of the four panes is applicable to Windows OS, it may differ for OS-X and Linux. These four panes are also customisable to the users' requirements.

## 1.3  Proxy Setup

Students and other users may use R on University/work computers which have firewall proxies which prevent them from directly connecting to the internet. We will discuss how to setup R to use internet proxy connection before we learn how to install packages.

The instructions to install proxy on R's standard GUI can be found as an answer to R FAQs.[2] This will make R to ask for the username and password (which is same as we use to access the internet). Figure 1.3 gives the snapshot of where to add the proxy setting on windows.

Using proxy with RStudio has evolved now and RStudio is able to recognise proxy from the default browser. In cases where RStudio does not resolve the proxy automatically, RStudio reads a .Renviron file for the proxy.[3] The .Renviron file is mostly not available, this can be created using RStudio. Create a new text file in RStudio, type the following:

```
# set proxy- put this file in "Documents" folder
options(internet.info = 0)
http_proxy=http://
http_proxy_user=ask
```

and save it as .Renvrion in the default directory (~). To check the default directory (which is in most cases the user's document folder on Windows) run `normalizePath('' ~'')` from RStudio console.

This method of creating proxy for RStudio may not work in few cases on network connected work computers if they are using a roaming profile with data backed up on the servers. To resolve this, one can create the .Renviron (or name it to your liking) and place it in the default directory

---

[2]http://cran.r-project.org/bin/windows/base/rw-FAQ.html.
[3]http://support.rstudio.org/help/kb/faq/configuring-r-to-use-an-http-proxy.

Figure 1.3:   Add proxy to R

(or any directory of your choice) then RStudio can be forced to read this by the command `readRenviron("~/Renviron")`. Make sure to check the path where the file is located, here the file is in My Documents and its called Renviron.

## 1.4   R Packages

The R system allows the user to write custom built functions and packages for accomplishing specific tasks. This set of functions is called a package in R and it extends R's basic functions. The R packages also contain other R objects like datasets or documentation related to the package. There is a lively R user community and many R packages have been written and made available on CRAN for other users.

## 1.4.1   Installing packages

This section will provide details on how to install packages in R using RStudio.[4]

The easiest way to install packages is to do it via the RStudio console. The command *install.packages("package name")* installs R packages directly from the internet. Other options to install various dependencies to a package can be easily specified when calling this function. A call to this function asks the user to choose a CRAN mirror at the first instance. A proxy authentication is requested if the proxy is configured and it requires a user authentication.[5]

Run the following to install Quantreg package on R. Also use the *help* function to get the details.

```
# Opens a webpage when called from R or shows help in
# the help window in RStudio
help(install.packages)
# Install package Quantreg with all the required
# dependencies.
install.packages("quantreg", dependencies = c("Depends",
    "Suggests"))
```

Alternatively, the package can be installed by using the **Tools→Install Packages** drop down menu in RStudio. Figure 1.4 shows the snapshot of the menu generated to install packages.

## 1.5   R Core Packages

R comes with a few bundled core packages which provide various data analytic/statistical capabilities to R. The *base* package in R has basic functions and operators which are required for analytical programming, *stats* is another example of R core packages.

```
# List of R core packages
row.names(installed.packages(priority = "base"))

#  [1] "base"      "compiler" "datasets"  "graphics"
#  [5] "grDevices" "grid"     "methods"   "parallel"
```

---

[5]After this section, we shall use solely RStudio which runs base R as the backbone.

[6]Windows users should run the R Session as Administrator to install packages to avoid errors in some cases.

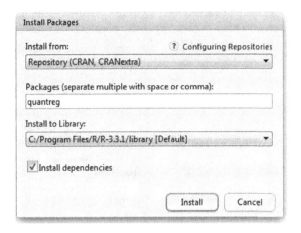

Figure 1.4: Install packages using RStudio GUI

```
#  [9] "splines"   "stats"     "stats4"    "tcltk"
# [13] "tools"     "utils"


# Use help() to get details of functions in any of the
# packages
help(package = "base")
```

The above command should give a help page similar to the one shown in Figure 1.5, which gives selectable help pages for various functions in R's base package.

## 1.6 Task Views in R: Introduction and Installation

Task Views in R provide packages grouped together according to a generalised task they are used for. Table 1.1 gives the name of Task Views available. This list of available Task Views can be found at http://cran.r-project.org/web/views/.

For example, the Finance Task View in R contains the list of packages which provide functions for empirical finance. Task Views are a helpful tool as all the packages required for a particular field can be installed at once using CRAN Task View (ctv) package. The following commands install the package *ctv* and then Finance task view (here, the function library() is used to call a package).

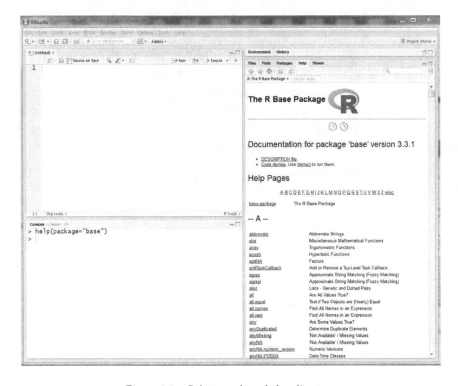

Figure 1.5:   R-base package helps directory

```
# install package task views
install.packages("ctv")
library("ctv")
# install Finance task view
install.views("Finance")
```

## 1.7   Getting Help

As R is constantly evolving and new functions/packages are introduced every day, it is good to know sources of help. The most basic help one can get is via the *help()* function. This function shows the help file for a function which has been created by package managers.

```
help("function name")
```

Table 1.1:  Task views

| CRAN task views | | | |
| --- | --- | --- | --- |
| Bayesian | Bayesian inference | Multivariate | Multivariate statistics |
| ChemPhys | Chemometrics and Computational Physics | Natural Language Processing | Natural Language Processing |
| Clinical Trials | Clinical Trial Design, Monitoring, and Analysis | Official Statistics | Official Statistics & Survey Methodology |
| Cluster | Cluster Analysis and Finite Mixture Models | Optimisation | Optimisation and Mathematical Programming |
| Differential Equations | Differential Equations | Pharmacokinetics | Analysis of Pharmacokinetic Data |
| Distributions | Probability Distributions | Phylogenetics | Phylogenetics, Especially Comparative Methods |
| Econometrics | Computational Econometrics | Psychometrics | Psychometric Models and Methods |
| Environmetrics | Analysis of Ecological and Environmental Data | Reproducible Research | Reproducible Research |
| Experimental Design | Design of Experiments (DoE) & Analysis of Experimental Data | Robust | Robust Statistical Methods |
| Finance | Empirical Finance | Social Sciences | Statistics for the Social Sciences |
| Genetics | Statistical Genetics | Spatial | Analysis of Spatial Data |
| Graphics | Graphic Displays and Dynamic Graphics and Graphic Devices and Visualisation | Spatio-Temporal | Handling and Analysing Spatio-Temporal Data |
| High Performance Computing | High-Performance and Parallel Computing with R | Survival | Survival Analysis |
| Machine Learning | Machine Learning and Statistical Learning | Time Series | Time Series Analysis |
| Medical . Imaging | Medical Image Analysis | gR | gRaphical Models in R |

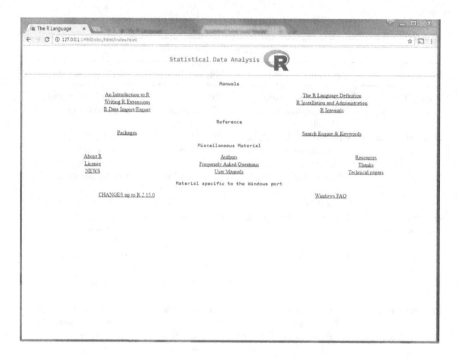

Figure 1.6:   Help browser

Alternatively, on most R installations help is available in HTML format by running the following

```
help.start()
```

which will launch the default Web browser that allows the help pages to be browsed with hyperlinks. Figure 1.6 gives a snapshot of the help browser in Mozilla Firefox.

RStudio provides a two way search facility in the help browser. The help can be searched for a topic and then the topic can be further searched. Figure 1.7 shows the two search bars in RStudio.

The following can be used to search for a function, etc.

```
#Replace the 'search string' with the expression you want to search
??search string
```

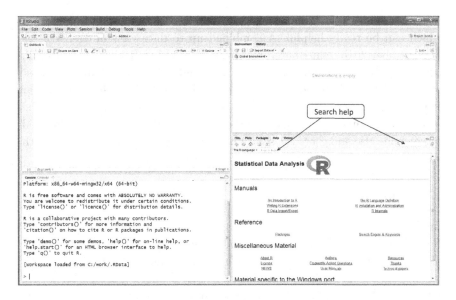

Figure 1.7:   RStudio helps browser

## 1.7.1   Getting help from the web

All the R packages (with few exceptions) have a user's manual listing the functions in a package. This can be downloaded in PDF format from the R package download page. For example, reference manual for quantreg package is at `http://cran.r-project.org/web/packages/quantreg/quantreg.pdf`. R also provides some search tools given at `http://cran.r-project.org/search.html` The R Site search is helpful in searching for topics related to the problem in hand.

RSiteSearch function can be used to search for a keyword or a phrase about R. This function gives results from the R Site search (the same as given on the R website) and displays it on a browser. Try

```
RSiteSearch("key phrase")
```

Stack Overflow (`http://stackoverflow.com/`) is a searchable Q&A site oriented toward programming issues. The Statistical Analysis area on Stack Exchange (`http://stats.stackexchange.com/`) is also a searchable Q&A site which is more oriented towards statistics. The R Journal, at `http://journal.r-project.org`. also provides good articles about R packages and functionalities.

Other than these various sites good R related blogs are on the internet which can be really helpful. A combined up to date view of over 573 (as of November 2016) contributed blogs can be found at R-bloggers.[6] Overall, there is quite a big community of R Users and help can be found for most of the topics. Last but not the least, a simple google search for a particular R issue can provide various help topics and related mailing lists, etc. The probability is that the problem you are facing has already been encountered by someone else and there is a solution available unless you are working with your own package or a relatively new topic/package.

## 1.8 Summary

In this chapter, we introduced R. We also learned how to obtain and install R on Windows OS. We discussed the major advantages of R and importance of R in research and data analysis. We also introduced RStudio along with its installation procedure, which is the IDE of choice for this book. We introduced R packages and Task Views and also discussed how to install them. Finally, we provided some useful details into how to obtain help while using R.

The next chapter is going to introduce different data types and how to import data into the R environment to use it for analysis.

---

[6]Go to `www.r-bloggers.com`.

Chapter 2

# Data Objects in R

## 2.1 Introduction

In this chapter, we will discuss the different aspects of data types and structures in R. We will focus primarily on the data types and structures which are most commonly used in statistical analysis. In quantitative analysis and research, the data can be obtained from external sources (databases like Bloomberg, Thomson Reuters, World Bank, etc.) or it could be collected by researchers using surveys, etc. In both cases, for efficient data analysis, it is imperative to learn the data types before we learn how to import those data files in to R data objects. Examples of objects in R are sequences of numeric (real) or complex values, sequence of logical values and groups of character strings.

According to R's official language definitions, in every computer language, variables provide a means of accessing the data stored in memory. R does not provide direct access to the computer's memory but rather provides a number of specialised data structures we will refer to as objects. These objects are referred to through symbols or variables. In R, however, the symbols are themselves objects and can be manipulated in the same way as any other object.

## 2.2 Data Types

There are various common data types available in R and most of them are automatically inferred by the R environment. In the following example, $=$ or $<$- are called assignment operators in R and they both have the same function of assigning a value to a variable (in this case x). It is up to personal preference to use $=$ or $<$-, we will use $=$ in the remaining text.

```
x = 10   #here x is a double as 10 is a numeric value
# x<-10 is the same as x=10
```

```
typeof(x)   #to check the type of data

# [1] "double"
```

The function typeof() in the example above returns the data type of a variable or data structure. We will now discuss major data types.

## 2.2.1  Double

Doubles are numbers like 5.0, 5.5, 10.999, etc. They may or may not include decimal places. Doubles are mostly used to represent a continuous variable like serial number, weight, age, etc. In R all the numbers, whether whole number, counting numbers or fractional numbers with decimals are double by default.

```
x = 8.5
is.double(x)   #to check if the data type is double

# [1] TRUE
```

## 2.2.2  Integer

Integers are natural numbers. Integers are mostly used for counting variables. By default, all the numbers are mostly double in R and hence a simple assignment always results in type double.

```
x = 9
typeof(x)

# [1] "double"
```

The following specifically assigns an integer to x

```
x = as.integer(9)
typeof(x)

# [1] "integer"
```

## 2.2.3  Complex

Complex in R represents complex numbers of the sort x+yi which are commonly used in financial analysis when dealing with eigenvalues and eigenvectors. The following example calculates the square root of $-1$ using complex numbers.

```
# double
x = -1
# complex
y = -1 + (0+0i)
sqrt(x)   #results in an error

# [1] NaN

sqrt(y)

# [1] 0+1i
```

### 2.2.4 Logical

A variable of data type logical has the value TRUE or FALSE. These objects are used for conditional statements to indicate if they are true or not. These objects are usually the results of logical expressions. For example

```
x = 11
y = 10
a = x > y
a

# [1] TRUE

typeof(a)

# [1] "logical"
```

To perform calculation on logical objects in R, the FALSE is replaced by a zero and TRUE is replaced by 1.

### 2.2.5 Character

Characters represent the string values in R. An object of type character can have alphanumeric strings. Character objects are specified by assigning a string or collection of characters between double quotes ("string"). Everything in a double quote is considered a string in R.

```
x = "This is a string"
print(x)
```

```
# [1] "This is a string"

x = "a"
typeof(x)

# [1] "character"
```

### 2.2.6  Factor

Factor is an important data type to represent categorical data. This also comes handy when dealing with Panel or Longitudinal data. Examples of factors are Blood type (A, B, AB, O), Sex (Male or Female). Factor objects can be created from character object or from numeric object.

```
b.type = c("A", "AB", "B", "O")   #character object
# use factor function to convert to factor object
b.type = factor(b.type)
b.type

# [1] A  AB B  O
# Levels: A AB B O

# to get individual elements (levels) in factor object
levels(b.type)

# [1] "A"  "AB" "B"  "O"
```

In the example above, b.type is a factor object with individual codes; A, B, AB and O. These individual codes are called levels. The operator c is used to create a vector of values which can be of any data type.

### 2.2.7  Date and time

R is capable of dealing with calendar dates and times. It is an important object when dealing with time series models. The function **as.Date** can be used to create an object of class Date. See **help(as.Date)** for more details on date formats.

```
date1 = "31-01-2012"
date1 = as.Date(date1, "%d-%m-%Y")
date1

# [1] "2012-01-31"
```

```
data.class(date1)

# [1] "Date"

# The date and time are internally interpreted as Double so
# the function typeof will return the type Double
typeof(date1)

# [1] "double"
```

R has two inbuilt classes **POSIXct** and **POSIX1t** to deal with date and time which can be used to represent calendar dates and times. A character date or time can be converted to these two classes by calling the function **as.POSIXct** to create a **POSIXct** object. This function accepts date, time or date with time as character input and uses a format argument to specify a nondefault format. A time zone can also be specified when dealing with a specific time zone. See **help(as.POSIXct)** or **help(as.POSIX1t)** for further details. **strptime** is a very useful function to convert one format of date and time in character to another. See **help(strptime)** for the different date/time formats. For example[1]

```
date1 = as.POSIXct("2012-01-01")
datetime1 = as.POSIXct("2012-01-01 10:10")
date1

# [1] "2012-01-01 AWST"

datetime1

# [1] "2012-01-01 10:10:00 AWST"

# args can be used to see the arguments in a function for
# example
args(as.POSIXct)

# function (x, tz = "", ...)
# NULL
```

We leave the discussion of Date/Time objects here and will continue it in detail when dealing with time series data in Chapter 8, where more useful functions and time series classes will be discussed.

---

[1]**Tip:** Use **args**(*function name*) to see the various arguments in a function.

## 2.2.8   Missing data in R

Datasets available for research often have missing data. In R, missing data is represented by NA (Not Available), it can be any missing data type. Another symbol to represent missing number is NaN (Not a Number). NULL in R represents a null object of length zero or an undefined object. We also come across +− Infinite values in the models (for instance division by zero). −Inf, Inf represent negative and positive infinite values in R.

The following example shows how to detect missing values in data vector. We first create a vector using c() then create a missing value, the function is.na() is then used to check for the missing value. is.na() returns logical output.

```
m.data = c("100", "200", "missing")
# convert m.data to double will create one missing value as
# 'missing' is not a double
m.data = as.double(m.data)
# the warning message tells that an NA was inserted for a
# value which couldnt be converted to type double
is.na(m.data)    #check for the missing value

# [1] FALSE FALSE  TRUE
```

We will now discuss the most common data structures in R.

## 2.3   Data Structures in R

Every data analysis requires the data to be structured in a well-defined way. These coherent ways to put together data forms some basic data structures in R. Every dataset intended for analysis has to be imported in to the R environment as a data structure. R has the following basic data structures:

- Vector
- Matrix
- Array
- Data Frame
- Lists

### 2.3.1   Vector

Vectors are groups of values having the same data types. There can be numeric vectors, character vector, and so on. Vectors are mostly used to represent a single variable in a dataset. A vector is constructed using the function c. The following example constructs a vector of five elements which are all of type double. The same function c can be used to combine different vectors of the same data type.

```
vec1 = c(1, 2, 3, 4, 5)
vec1

# [1] 1 2 3 4 5
```

Vectors can be used in arithmetic expressions, in which case the operations are performed element by element. The symbols for elementary arithmetic operations are $+$, $-$, $*$, $/$. Use the $\hat{}$ symbol to raise power. Also most of the mathematical functions are available in R.

### 2.3.2 Matrices

A matrix is a collection of data elements arranged in a two-dimensional rectangular layout. Like vectors, all the elements in a matrix are of the same data type. The following is an example of a matrix with 3 rows and 2 columns.

$$\begin{bmatrix} 1 & 2 \\ 3 & 4 \\ 5 & 6 \end{bmatrix}$$

The function matrix is used to create matrices in R. Note that all the elements in a matrix object are of the same basic type. Let us create the matrix in the example above

```
m1 = matrix(c(1, 2, 3, 4, 5, 6), nrow = 3, ncol = 2, byrow = TRUE)
# nrow-specify number of rows, ncol-specify number of
# columns, byrow-fill the matrix in rows with the data
# supplied
m1 #print the matrix

#      [,1] [,2]
# [1,]   1    2
# [2,]   3    4
# [3,]   5    6
```

A vector can be converted to matrix using the dim function, e.g.;

```
m2 = c(1, 2, 3, 4, 5, 6)
dim(m2) = c(3, 2)   #the matrix will be filled by columns
m2

#      [,1] [,2]
# [1,]   1    4
# [2,]   2    5
# [3,]   3    6

# use dim to get the dimension (#rows and #columns) of a
# matrix
dim(m1)

# [1] 3 2
```

Function `cbind` and `rbind` can also be used to create matrices by combining two or more vectors by columns or by rows.

### 2.3.2.1 *Matrix manipulations*

For calculations on matrices; all the mathematical functions available for vectors are applicable on a matrix. All operations are applied on each element in a matrix, e.g.

```
m3 = m1 * 2   # all elements will be multiplied by 2 individually
m3

#      [,1] [,2]
# [1,]    2    4
# [2,]    6    8
# [3,]   10   12
```

A matrix can be multiplied with a vector as long as the length of the vector is a multiple of length of the matrix. Try different combinations of matrix and vector arithmetic to see the results and errors.

Mathematical matrix operations are also available for matrices in R. For instance $\% * \%$ is used for matrix multiplication, the matrices must agree dimensionally for matrix multiplication. For example

```
dim(m1)   # 3 rows and 2 columns

# [1] 3 2

# create another matrix with 2 rows and 3 columns Note the
# use of operator to create a sequence
```

```
m3 = matrix(c(1:6), ncol = 3)
m1 %*% m3

#       [,1] [,2] [,3]
# [1,]     5   11   17
# [2,]    11   25   39
# [3,]    17   39   61
```

R facilitates various matrix specific operations. Table 2.1 gives most of the available functions and operators. Use **help()** or ? followed by function name to get more details about the operators and functions.

### 2.3.3 Arrays

Arrays are the generalisation of vectors and matrices. A vector in R is a one-dimensional array and a matrix a two-dimensional array. An array is a multiply subscripted collection of data entries of the same data type. Arrays can be constructed using the function**array** (function **dim** can also be used to define an array by assigning dimensions to a vector.) for example

```
z = c(1:24) #vector of length 24
# constructing a 3 by 4 by 2 array
a1 = array(z, dim = c(3, 4, 2))
a1

# , , 1
#
#       [,1] [,2] [,3] [,4]
# [1,]     1    4    7   10
# [2,]     2    5    8   11
# [3,]     3    6    9   12
#
# , , 2
#
#       [,1] [,2] [,3] [,4]
# [1,]    13   16   19   22
# [2,]    14   17   20   23
# [3,]    15   18   21   24
```

Individual elements of an array are accessed by referring to them by their index. This is done by giving the name of the array followed by the subscript (index) in this square bracket separated by commas. We try to access the element [1,3,1] of array a1 in the following example:

Table 2.1:   Functions and operators for matrices.

| Operator or Function | Description |
| --- | --- |
| X * Y | Element-wise multiplication |
| X %*% Y | Matrix multiplication |
| Y %o% X | Outer product. XB$'$. |
| crossprod(X,Y) | X$'$Y |
| crossprod(X) | X$'$X |
| t(X) | Transpose |
| diag(x) | Creates diagonal matrix with elements of x in the principal diagonal. |
| diag(X) | Returns a vector containing the elements of the principal diagonal. |
| diag(k) | If k is a scalar, this creates a k $\times$ k identity matrix. Go figure. |
| solve(X, b) | Returns vector x in the equation b $=$ Xx (i.e. X$-$1b) |
| solve(X) | Inverse of X where X is a square matrix. |
| y $=$ eigen(X) | y\$val are the eigenvalues of X. y\$vec are the eigenvectors of X. |
| y $=$ svd(X) | Singular value decomposition of X. |
| R $=$ chol(X) | Choleski factorisation of X. Returns the upper triangular factor, such that R$'$R $=$ X. |
| y $=$ qr(X) | QR decomposition of X. |
| cbind(X,Y,...) | Combine matrices(vectors) horizontally. Returns a matrix. |
| rbind(X,Y,...) | Combine matrices(vectors) vertically. Returns a matrix. |
| rowMeans(X) | Returns vector of row means. |
| rowSums(X) | Returns vector of row sums. |
| colMeans(X) | Returns vector of column means. |
| colSums(X) | Returns vector of column means. |

```
# element in the row 1 and column 3 in the first subset
a1[1, 3, 1]

# [1] 7
```

Next we discuss the Data Frames which are the most convenient data structures for data analysis in R.

## 2.3.4  Data frames

Data frames form the most convenient data structures in R to represent tabular data. In quantitative analysis, data is often in the form of data tables. These data tables have multiple rows and can have multiple columns with each column representing a different variable (quantity). A data frame in R is the most natural way to represent these datasets as it can have different data type in the data frame object. Most statistical routines in R require a data frame as input.

The following example uses an important function str on R's inbuilt data frame "swiss". str function is used to see the internal structure of an object in R.

```
# swiss dataframe has standardised fertility measure and
# socio-economic indicators for each of 47 French-speaking
# provinces of Switzerland at about 1888.
data(swiss)
str(swiss)

# 'data.frame': 47 obs. of  6 variables:
# $ Fertility       : num  80.2 83.1 92.5 85.8 76.9 ...
# $ Agriculture     : num  17 45.1 39.7 36.5 43.5 ...
# $ Examination     : int  15 6 5 12 17 ...
# $ Education       : int  12 9 5 7 15 ...
# $ Catholic        : num  9.96 84.84 ...
# $ Infant.Mortality: num  22.2 22.2 20.2 20.3 20.6 ...
```

Data frames have two attributes namely, **names** and **row.names**, these two contains the column names and row names, respectively. The data in the named column can be accessed by the $ operator.

```
# using names and row.names
names(swiss)  #name of the columns (can also use colnames)

# [1] "Fertility"    "Agriculture"    "Examination"
# [4] "Education"    "Catholic"       "Infant.Mortality"
```

```
colnames(swiss)

# [1] "Fertility"      "Agriculture"    "Examination"
# [4] "Education"      "Catholic"       "Infant.Mortality"

row.names(swiss)   #name of the rows

#  [1] "Courtelary"    "Delemont"       "Franches-Mnt"
#  [4] "Moutier"       "Neuveville"     "Porrentruy"
#  [7] "Broye"         "Glane"          "Gruyere"
# [10] "Sarine"        "Veveyse"        "Aigle"
# [13] "Aubonne"       "Avenches"       "Cossonay"
# [16] "Echallens"     "Grandson"       "Lausanne"
# [19] "La Vallee"     "Lavaux"         "Morges"
# [22] "Moudon"        "Nyone"          "Orbe"
# [25] "Oron"          "Payerne"        "Paysd'enhaut"
# [28] "Rolle"         "Vevey"          "Yverdon"
# [31] "Conthey"       "Entremont"      "Herens"
# [34] "Martigwy"      "Monthey"        "St Maurice"
# [37] "Sierre"        "Sion"           "Boudry"
# [40] "La Chauxdfnd"  "Le Locle"       "Neuchatel"
# [43] "Val de Ruz"    "ValdeTravers"   "V. De Geneve"
# [46] "Rive Droite"   "Rive Gauche"

swiss$Fertility   #returns the vector of data in the column Fertility

#  [1] 80.2 83.1 92.5 85.8 76.9 76.1 83.8 92.4 82.4 82.9 87.1
# [12] 64.1 66.9 68.9 61.7 68.3 71.7 55.7 54.3 65.1 65.5 65.0
# [23] 56.6 57.4 72.5 74.2 72.0 60.5 58.3 65.4 75.5 69.3 77.3
# [34] 70.5 79.4 65.0 92.2 79.3 70.4 65.7 72.7 64.4 77.6 67.6
# [45] 35.0 44.7 42.8
```

Data frames are constructed using the function **data.frame**. For example, the following creates a data frame of a character and numeric vector.

```
num1 = seq(1:5)
ch1 = c("A", "B", "C", "D", "E")
df1 = data.frame(ch1, num1)
df1

#   ch1 num1
# 1   A    1
# 2   B    2
# 3   C    3
```

```
# 4   D    4
# 5   E    5
```

## 2.3.5   Lists

A list is like a generic vector containing other objects. Lists can have numerous elements any type and structure they can also be of different lengths. A list can contain another list and therefore it can be used to construct arbitrary data structures. The output from various statistical routines in R is conventionally reported in a list format. A list can be constructed using the `list` function, for example

```
e1 = c(2, 3, 5)  #element-1
e2 = c("aa", "bb", "cc", "dd", "ee")  #element-2
e3 = c(TRUE, FALSE, TRUE, FALSE, FALSE)  #element-3
e4 = df1  #element-4 (previously constructed data frame)
lst1 = list(e1, e2, e3, e4)  # lst contains copies of e1,e2,e3,e4
str(lst1)  #show the structure of lst1

# List of 4
# $ : num [1:3] 2 3 5
# $ : chr [1:5] "aa" "bb" ...
# $ : logi [1:5] TRUE FALSE TRUE ...
# $ :'data.frame': 5 obs. of  2 variables:
#  ..$ ch1 : Factor w/ 5 levels "A","B","C","D",..: 1 2 3 4 5
#  ..$ num1: int [1:5] 1 2 3 4 5
```

Components are always numbered and may always be referred to as such. Thus if lst1 is the name of a list with four components, these may be individually referred to as lst1[[1]], lst1[[2]], lst1[[3]] and lst1[[4]]. When a single square bracket is used, the component of a list are returned as a list while the single square bracket returns the component itself

```
# first element of lst1
lst1[[1]]

# [1] 2 3 5

lst1[1]

# [[1]]
# [1] 2 3 5
```

The elements in a list can also be named using the `list` function and these elements can be referred individually via their names.

```
names(lst1) = c("e1", "e2", "e3", "e4")
names(lst1)  #name of the elements

# [1] "e1" "e2" "e3" "e4"

lst1$e1  #using $operator to refer the element

# [1] 2 3 5
```

## 2.4  Summary

In this chapter, we discussed various data types and data structures used in R. We focussed primarily on data types which are most often used when getting started with R. It is imperative to learn these data structures and how to use them in various operations before we can do any analysis on the data as all data imported in R is converted in a data structure. The next chapter will introduce data handling including data import/export and conversion.

Chapter 3

# Data Handling in R

## 3.1 Introduction

Using any statistical system for data analysis requires importing of the external data. As the data for the research problem in hand can come in various formats and sizes, the task of importing this data from different file formats to do statistical analysis on them can take a lot of time and effort. In this chapter, we will discuss a few methods of importing tabular data from external file sources like, text files, comma separated (CSV) files and data files created by other statistical systems like SPSS, MATLAB, etc. We will also discuss some basic data manipulation on data frames.

R provides a manual for data import/export using the R statistical system which can be consulted for this topic.[1]

## 3.2 Importing and Exporting Tabular Data in R

### 3.2.1 Reading data from a text file

The easiest way to import data into R's statistical system is to do it in a tabular format saved in a text file. In fact, for most of the data processing and analysis, the easiest way forward is to transfer data to text file or a CSV from any other format or statistical system (SPSS, MATLAB, etc.) before importing into R. We will first discuss how to import and export spreadsheet like data, e.g. tabular data in a text file or a CSV.

To import tabular data from a text file, R provides the function read.table(). RStudio also provides GUI based support to import data, which can be helpful for importing small datasets. read.table() is the most convenient function to import tabular data from text files and can be easily used for data files of small or moderate size having data in a

---

[1]http://cran.r-project.org/doc/manuals/r-release/R-data.pdf

rectangular format. The function reads a text file into R and returns a data frame object. The arguments which can be passed to read.table() are given below.

```
args(read.table)

# function (file, header = FALSE, sep = "", quote = "\"'", dec = ".",
#     numerals = c("allow.loss", "warn.loss", "no.loss"), row.names,
#     col.names, as.is = !stringsAsFactors, na.strings = "NA",
#     colClasses = NA, nrows = -1, skip = 0, check.names = TRUE,
#     fill = !blank.lines.skip, strip.white = FALSE, blank.lines.skip = TRUE,
#     comment.char = "#", allowEscapes = FALSE, flush = FALSE,
#     stringsAsFactors = default.stringsAsFactors(), fileEncoding = "",
#     encoding = "unknown", text, skipNul = FALSE)
# NULL
```

Some of the important arguments for the function read.table are discussed below, for the rest see the help file using help(read.table).

| Argument | Description |
|---|---|
| file | The name of the tabular (text) file to import along with the full path. |
| header | A logical argument to specify if the names of the variables are available in the first row. |
| sep | Character to specify the separator type, default " " takes any white space as a separator. |
| quote | To specify if the character vectors in the data are in quotes, this should specify the type of quotes. |
| as.is | To specify if the character vectors should be converted to factors. The default behaviour is to read characters as characters and not factors. |
| strip.white | A logical value to specify if the extra leading and trailing white spaces have to be removed from the character fields. This is used when sep !=". |
| fill | Logical value to specify if the blank fields in a row should be filled. |

The example below imports a tab delimited text file. Note the use of "\t" in the sep argument for tab delimited data. The header argument is also TRUE here as our dataset has variable names in the first row. The imported data is stored as a data.frame object which can be easily manipulated in R. Note that in the example below, the working directory for the RStudio session has already been set to the destination file's directory. If the working directory is different from the location of the data file, then either the working directory should be changed using setwd or RStudio's GUI or full path for the file's location should be provided with the file name.

```
data_readtable = read.table("demo_data.txt", sep = "\t", header = TRUE)
head(data_readtable)

#       Date AAPL  MSFT
# 1 2/01/1998 4.06 16.39
# 2 5/01/1998 3.97 16.30
# 3 6/01/1998 4.73 16.39
# 4 7/01/1998 4.38 16.20
# 5 8/01/1998 4.55 16.31
# 6 9/01/1998 4.55 15.88
```

This data can be now saved into .Rdata format after importing from a text file using **save** or can be written to another text file using **write.table** as shown below:

```
# saving data as an object in .Rdata format
save(data_readtable, file = "data1.Rdata")
# saving data into another text file
write.table(data_readtable, file = "data1.txt")
```

The advantage of saving the data into .Rdata format is that it decreases the file size which makes it easier to load for further processing and it also keeps the data in its intended format. The .Rdata file can be easily loaded into the system using **load** function as shown below

```
load("data1.Rdata")    #using load to load R data
head(data_readtable)

#       Date AAPL  MSFT
# 1 2/01/1998 4.06 16.39
# 2 5/01/1998 3.97 16.30
# 3 6/01/1998 4.73 16.39
# 4 7/01/1998 4.38 16.20
# 5 8/01/1998 4.55 16.31
# 6 9/01/1998 4.55 15.88
```

Note we are still in the same working directory, if this is not the case you will have to provide the path or change the directory.

### 3.2.2    Reading data from CSV file

Some data vendors like SIRCA (Thomson Reuters Tick History and others) provide data in CSV format, which has to be imported into R for further processing. Reading data from a CSV file is made easy by the **read.csv** function. **read.csv** function is an extension of **read.table**. It facilitates direct import of data from CSV files. **read.csv** function takes the following arguments

```
# function (file, header = TRUE, sep = ",", quote = "\"", dec = ".",
#      fill = TRUE, comment.char = "", ...)
# NULL
```

As you can see, the **sep** field already has ',' as the delimiter. Here, **header** takes the default value of TRUE as it is assumed that the first row of a CSV file will have the variable names. The ... in the end refers to other arguments which can be passed to the main **read.table** function. See **help(read.table)** to see other functions provided, viz., **read.csv2**, **read.delim** and **read.delim2**, to import delimited data in tabular format. The following example imports a CSV file with the same data as previously imported from a text file.

```
# Check the working directory before importing else provide
# full path
data_readcsv = read.csv("demo_data.csv")
head(data_readcsv)

#       Date AAPL  MSFT
# 1 2/01/1998 4.06 16.39
# 2 5/01/1998 3.97 16.30
# 3 6/01/1998 4.73 16.39
# 4 7/01/1998 4.38 16.20
# 5 8/01/1998 4.55 16.31
# 6 9/01/1998 4.55 15.88
```

Similar to **write.table** data can also be written to an external csv file using **write.csv**. The following example uses an inbuilt dataset in R and exports it to a CSV. Notice the use of **row.names=FALSE** to avoid creating one more column in the CSV file with row numbers

```
data(iris)    #R inbuilt dataset
head(iris)
```

```
#   Sepal.Length Sepal.Width Petal.Length Petal.Width Species
# 1          5.1         3.5          1.4         0.2 setosa
# 2          4.9         3.0          1.4         0.2 setosa
# 3          4.7         3.2          1.3         0.2 setosa
# 4          4.6         3.1          1.5         0.2 setosa
# 5          5.0         3.6          1.4         0.2 setosa
# 6          5.4         3.9          1.7         0.4 setosa
```

```
write.csv(iris, "data_iris.csv", row.names = FALSE)
```

### 3.2.3   Reading data from excel files

Most researchers are used to working with excel for data processing and other statistical softwares like STATA, Eviews, etc., which provide direct GUI based methods to import such datasets. Although not convenient R does provide methods to import data from an excel file with the help of external packages. Overall, all the methods provided by packages like *gdata, XLConnet, xlsx* are not as efficient as transporting an excel sheet to a CSV and then importing it in R. The best work around is to transfer the data into a csv file or text file before importing in R. The packages can be of help if you want to save time and put more effort in learning to use these packages. We will not go further into reading data from excel files.

### 3.2.4   Reading data from databases

There are various packages available to import data from an external database like, *RODBC, RMySQL, RSQLite*, etc. This becomes important as there are some research datasets which can be quite huge in length and have to be processed via an external database engine like MS-Access, SQLite, etc. As this process requires some knowledge of Sequential Query Language (SQL) and is for advanced R users, we will not discuss this any further.

### 3.2.5   Reading from data files from other statistical systems

As R gains more popularity, various researchers are migrating from other statistical systems to R. When migrating from softwares like SPSS, Stata,

Matlab users might want to use the old datasets generated from these systems in R. This requires methods for importing these datasets into R. There are packages like *foreign* and *R.matlab* which provide these functionalities.

#### 3.2.5.1    *Reading SPSS data file*

The function **read.spss** provided in the package *foreign* can be used to read SPSS data files in R. The SPSS data file used in the example below is obtained from `http://ssnds.uwo.ca/statsexamples/` `SPSS/samplereadSPSS.zip`

```
# first install the foreign package
install.packages("foreign")


library("foreign")
# load the data personnel obtained from the webpage
data_SPSS = read.spss("personnel.sav")
head(data_SPSS)
```

```
# $NAME
#  [1] "Dorothy Carole Osborne  " "Lucinda Jackson          "
#  [3] "Anita Pulaski          "  "Reuben D. Cross          "
#  [5] "Peter D. Gamino        "  "Theresa P. Olden         "
#  [7] "Calvin King            "  "Sean D. McGillicuddy     "
#  [9] "Brian M. Curtis        "  "Jerri D. Mategrano       "
# [11] "Maria Provenza         "  "Billy J. Lyle            "
# [13] "Karen McAndrews        "  "Stephen S. Brown         "
# [15] "Guy J. LaVelle         "  "Jean D. Weiss            "
# [17] "Cleveland Smith        "  "Monica C. Rivers         "
# [19] "Linus Guric            "  "Bernard K. Golden        "
# [21] "Della D. Miller        "  "M. Elliot Kraft          "
# [23] "Helen K. Washington    "  "Regina K. Newton         "
# [25] "Rebecca K. Cohen       "  "Cynthia Riley            "
# [27] "Charles P. Black       "  "Linda Iverson            "
# [29] "LaDonna Akers          "  "Silvia Kudirka           "
# [31] "Polly E. Chan          "  "Nick Kozak               "
# [33] "Amanda Howell          "  "Geraldine K. Jordan      "
# [35] "Beth D. Goodall        "  "Aristotle M. Geocaris    "
# [37] "Leonard D. Cunningham  "  "Pamela Simon             "
# [39] "Soo Lin Ho             "  "Kathleen Rooney          "
# [41] "Ping Huffman           "  "Paulette Ho              "
# [43] "John C. Holcomb        "  "Jennifer K. Logan        "
# [45] "Paul Harman            "  "Marci Syms               "
# [47] "Pierre LeClair         "  "Andrea Smith             "
```

```
# [49] "Elena Lopez          " "Ruby Blair              "
#
# $EMPLOYID
#  [1]  3081  3261  3390  4381  5402  5931  6159  6241  6351
# [10]  6581  6871  7241  7911  8851 10471 10852 10891 11001
# [19] 11031 12330 12440 13480 16351 16512 16801 17412 20191
# [28] 20271 20322 21802 23811 24341 24450 26001 27402 28461
# [37] 29231 29852 30542 32512 32791 34651 35141 35461 35601
# [46] 36351 37121 39691 40331 41481
#
# $YRHIRED
#  [1] 79 79 79 74 67 76 79 79 72 79 79 80 79 77 76 78 79 70
# [19] 79 80 80 79 75 73 69 76 81 72 79 68 80 78 76 69 59 79
# [37] 78 79 80 79 75 79 78 79 48 78 78 79 79 76
#
# $AGE
#  [1] 30 33 45 49 39 31 29 28 64 29 22 54 42 48 26 47 24 49
# [19] 34 36 26 27 27 38 39 35 30 60 26 59 29 26 35 42 69 30
# [37] 33 35 23 27 51 38 33 29 61 38 27 36 23 35
#
# $RACE
#  [1] White    Black    White    Black    White    Black
#  [7] Black    White    White    White    Latino   Black
# [13] White    White    Black    White    Black    White
# [19] White    White    Black    White    Black    Black
# [25] White    White    Black    White    Black    White
# [31] Oriental White    Black    Black    White    White
# [37] White    White    Oriental White    Oriental Oriental
# [43] White    White    White    Black    Black    Black
# [49] Latino   Black
# Levels: Black A.Indian Oriental Latino White
#
# $SEX
#  [1] Female Female Female Male   Male   Female Male   Male
#  [9] Male   Female Female Male   Female Male   Male   Female
# [17] Male   Female Male   Male   Female Male   Female Female
# [25] Female Female Male   Female Female Female Female Male
# [33] Female Female Female Male   Male   Female Male   Female
# [41] Female Female Male   Female Male   Female Male   Female
# [49] Female Female
# Levels: Male Female

# convert this list into a dataframe
data_SPSS = as.data.frame(data_SPSS)
head(data_SPSS)
```

```
#                       NAME EMPLOYID YRHIRED AGE  RACE
# 1 Dorothy Carole Osborne    3081      79   30 White
# 2 Lucinda Jackson           3261      79   33 Black
# 3 Anita Pulaski             3390      79   45 White
# 4 Reuben D. Cross           4381      74   49 Black
# 5 Peter D. Gamino           5402      67   39 White
# 6 Theresa P. Olden          5931      76   31 Black
#      SEX    LOCATN82            DEPT82
# 1 Female Not Employed     Not Employed
# 2 Female      Chicago Chicago Operations
# 3 Female      Chicago Chicago Operations
# 4   Male      Chicago     Administrative
# 5   Male    St. Louis  Project Directors
# 6 Female Not Employed     Not Employed
#                 JOBCAT      PROMO82 SALARY82 RAISE82 EEO82
# 1        Professionals Not Employed       0    -999     0
# 2          Technicians           No    9840     974     5
# 3          Technicians          Yes   12328    2578     5
# 4 Officials & Managers           No   19240    2665     1
# 5        Professionals           No   25837    2438     2
# 6          Technicians Not Employed       0    -999     0
```

### 3.2.5.2   *Reading Stata data file*

Similar to **read.spss**, the package *foreign* provides the function **read.dta** to read Stata data files. The Stata data used in the following example is also obtained from the same source, see **http://ssnds.uwo.ca/statsexamples/Stata/samplereadStata.zip**

```
# import the dataset downloaded before
data_Stata = read.dta("Income.dta")
head(data_Stata)

#    income   cons
# 1 177.21 110.37
# 2 177.69 102.32
# 3 169.96 110.82
# 4 175.59 112.14
# 5 169.56 102.02
# 6 166.33  98.95
```

## 3.2.5.3 Reading Matlab data files

The package *R.matlab* can be used to import Matlab .mat data files. The function **readMat** can be used to read complicated multidimensional Matlab data files. We will not discuss an example here but leave it as an exercise for the reader. A good start would be to see **example(readMat)**.

## 3.3 Data Preprocessing in R

Real world data mostly requires some data preprocessing before it can be used for statistical analysis. The term data preprocessing is mostly used in the context of data mining but we are here using it in a generalised sense to refer to all the data cleaning and other manipulations required before it can be used for statistical analysis. The data used in a particular research problem is often not in the required format or its not up to the scratch for using it directly for the required analysis. It may take some data manipulation before the data can be used for actual statistical analysis. This chapter will discuss some methods for data manipulation to clean a dataset, combine various datasets or extract a variable from a data frame.

### 3.3.1 Extracting data

Data frames are the most used data structures in R as they offer more flexibility in the way they can handle data. Let us see some methods to extract data from a data frame. We will use the example dataset called **us_stocks.csv**. This dataset contains closing stock prices for six US stocks viz., Microsoft, IBM, Apple, McDonald Corp., Procter & Gamble and Google. Let us import it using **read.csv**

```
data_stocks = read.csv(file = "us_stocks.csv", header = TRUE)
head(data_stocks)

#        Date  MSFT     IBM  AAPL   MCD    PG GOOG
# 1 2/01/2002 33.52  121.50 11.65 26.49 40.00   NA
# 2 3/01/2002 34.62  123.66 11.79 26.79 39.62   NA
# 3 4/01/2002 34.45  125.60 11.84 26.99 39.22   NA
# 4 7/01/2002 34.28  124.05 11.45 27.20 38.78   NA
# 5 8/01/2002 34.69  124.70 11.30 27.36 38.88   NA
# 6 9/01/2002 34.36  124.49 10.82 26.88 38.60   NA
```

Notice that Google doesn't have data for all the time periods and hence it is considered as NA for those days. The function **names** or **colnames** are used to access the names of the columns (or variables) in the dataset as shown below. The function **row.names** can be used to access row names (if any) from a dataset

```
names(data_stocks)

# [1] "Date" "MSFT" "IBM"   "AAPL" "MCD"  "PG"    "GOOG"

colnames(data_stocks)

# [1] "Date" "MSFT" "IBM"   "AAPL" "MCD"   "PG"    "GOOG"
```

A specific data variable can be accessed using its name or index (column number) in the data frame. To select any column use $ symbol followed by the column name or its name in square brackets as shown in the example below

```
msft_prices1 = data_stocks$MSFT   #the data is returned as a vector
head(msft_prices1)

# [1] 33.52 34.62 34.45 34.28 34.69 34.36

msft_prices2 = data_stocks[["MSFT"]]
# the data is returned as a vector
head(msft_prices2)

# [1] 33.52 34.62 34.45 34.28 34.69 34.36

# the following returns data as a data frame
msft_prices3 = data_stocks["MSFT"]
# can also be used to access multiple columns
head(msft_prices3)

#     MSFT
# 1 33.52
# 2 34.62
# 3 34.45
# 4 34.28
# 5 34.69
# 6 34.36
```

These data columns can also be accessed like a matrix, using a matrix index. This method can return a complete row, a complete column or just an element from the dataset.

```
# MSFT is in the second column and leaving the row index
# blank returns all the rows for the particular column

msft_prices4 = data_stocks[, 2]

head(msft_prices4)

# [1] 33.52 34.62 34.45 34.28 34.69 34.36

# all the elements in row 4
data_stocks[4, ]

#        Date  MSFT     IBM  AAPL   MCD     PG GOOG
# 4 7/01/2002 34.28 124.05 11.45  27.2 38.78    NA
```

### 3.3.2 Combining data frames

It may be required to combine two data frames during a data processing. This can be done by stacking them row by row or combining them by columns using **rbind** and **cbind**, respectively. When using **cbind**, the number of rows in the columns combined must be of equal length likewise in **rbind**, the number of columns of the datasets combined should be equal. Let us see an example where we use **c** to combine two vectors and then **cbind** to add (combine) a column to the dataset

```
# First create a vector having the returns for msft
msft_ret = 100 * diff(log(data_stocks$MSFT))
# combine the vector with the data
data_stocks_r = cbind(data_stocks, MSFT_RET = msft_ret)

# Error in data.frame(..., check.names = FALSE): arguments imply
differing number of rows: 2784, 2783

# this will generate an error message different length
length(msft_ret)

# [1] 2783

length(data_stocks$MSFT)

# [1] 2784

# add one more value to vector msft_ret
msft_ret = c(0, msft_ret)
# check the length
```

```
length(msft_ret)

# [1] 2784

# lets combine now (it should work)
data_stocks_r = cbind(data_stocks, MSFT_RET = msft_ret)
head(data_stocks_r)   #shows one more column added to the data

#       Date  MSFT    IBM  AAPL   MCD    PG GOOG   MSFT_RET
# 1 2/01/2002 33.52 121.50 11.65 26.49 40.00   NA  0.0000000
# 2 3/01/2002 34.62 123.66 11.79 26.79 39.62   NA  3.2289274
# 3 4/01/2002 34.45 125.60 11.84 26.99 39.22   NA -0.4922552
# 4 7/01/2002 34.28 124.05 11.45 27.20 38.78   NA -0.4946904
# 5 8/01/2002 34.69 124.70 11.30 27.36 38.88   NA  1.1889367
# 6 9/01/2002 34.36 124.49 10.82 26.88 38.60   NA -0.9558364
```

The following example adds a row to the data frame and uses : operator to make successive selection.

```
# create two dataframes from data_stocks
data_r1 = data_stocks[1:10, ]   #first 10 rows
data_r2 = data_stocks[2775:2784, ]   #last 10 rows
data_stocks_rbind = rbind(data_r1, data_r2)
print(data_stocks_rbind)

#            Date  MSFT    IBM   AAPL   MCD    PG   GOOG
# 1      2/01/2002 33.52 121.50  11.65 26.49 40.00     NA
# 2      3/01/2002 34.62 123.66  11.79 26.79 39.62     NA
# 3      4/01/2002 34.45 125.60  11.84 26.99 39.22     NA
# 4      7/01/2002 34.28 124.05  11.45 27.20 38.78     NA
# 5      8/01/2002 34.69 124.70  11.30 27.36 38.88     NA
# 6      9/01/2002 34.36 124.49  10.82 26.88 38.60     NA
# 7     10/01/2002 34.64 122.14  10.62 26.81 38.46     NA
# 8     11/01/2002 34.30 120.31  10.52 26.34 38.60     NA
# 9     14/01/2002 34.24 118.05  10.58 26.02 39.35     NA
# 10    15/01/2002 34.78 118.85  10.85 26.20 39.82     NA
# 2775  17/12/2012 27.10 193.62 518.83 89.91 69.93 720.78
# 2776  18/12/2012 27.56 195.69 533.90 90.52 69.97 721.07
# 2777  19/12/2012 27.31 195.08 526.31 89.71 69.34 720.11
# 2778  20/12/2012 27.68 194.77 521.73 90.04 69.82 722.36
# 2779  21/12/2012 27.45 193.42 519.33 90.18 68.72 715.63
# 2780  24/12/2012 27.06 192.40 520.17 89.29 68.52 709.50
# 2781  26/12/2012 26.86 191.95 513.00 88.74 68.00 708.87
# 2782  27/12/2012 26.96 192.71 515.06 88.72 67.97 706.29
# 2783  28/12/2012 26.55 189.83 509.59 87.58 67.15 700.01
# 2784  31/12/2012 26.71 191.55 532.17 88.21 67.89 707.38
```

### 3.3.3  Sub-setting and logical data selection

Suppose we want to extract data with particular characteristics like values ranges, etc. This can be accomplished using logical statements in bracket notations. The following example illustrates (see `help("")`) to see more comparison operators).

```
# select all rows with Apple prices above 100
data_aaplgr100 = data_stocks[data_stocks$AAPL > 100, ]
head(data_aaplgr100)

#         Date  MSFT     IBM    AAPL   MCD     PG    GOOG
# 1342 2/05/2007 30.61 102.22 100.39 50.02 62.37 465.78
# 1343 3/05/2007 30.97 102.80 100.40 49.91 62.00 473.23
# 1344 4/05/2007 30.56 102.96 100.81 49.92 62.41 471.12
# 1345 7/05/2007 30.71 103.16 103.92 49.50 62.18 467.27
# 1346 8/05/2007 30.75 103.29 105.06 49.32 61.75 466.81
# 1347 9/05/2007 30.78 104.38 106.88 49.84 62.01 469.25

min(data_aaplgr100$AAPL)   #check if the prices are above 100

# [1] NA

# this give NA as the minimum which indicates that data frame
# has NA lets remove NAs from data_aaplgr100 using na.omit
# function
data_aaplgr100 = na.omit(data_aaplgr100)
# now check the minimum again
min(data_aaplgr100$AAPL)

# [1] 100.06
```

The `na.omit` function used in the example above can be used to remove all the empty values in the dataset. As seen earlier, the dataset `data_stocks` contains empty (NA) values in rows. The example below first removes all the rows with NAs for Google stock then all the rows with NAs for all the stocks.

```
head(data_stocks)   #notice NAs in GOOG

#      Date  MSFT     IBM   AAPL   MCD    PG GOOG
# 1 2/01/2002 33.52 121.50 11.65 26.49 40.00   NA
# 2 3/01/2002 34.62 123.66 11.79 26.79 39.62   NA
# 3 4/01/2002 34.45 125.60 11.84 26.99 39.22   NA
# 4 7/01/2002 34.28 124.05 11.45 27.20 38.78   NA
# 5 8/01/2002 34.69 124.70 11.30 27.36 38.88   NA
```

```
# 6 9/01/2002 34.36 124.49 10.82 26.88 38.60    NA

data_stocks_googlena = data_stocks[!is.na(data_stocks$GOOG),
     ]
head(data_stocks_googlena)   #after removing NAs

#          Date MSFT   IBM  AAPL   MCD    PG   GOOG
# 663 19/08/2004 27.12 84.89 15.36 26.60 54.48 100.34
# 664 20/08/2004 27.20 85.25 15.40 27.07 54.85 108.31
# 665 23/08/2004 27.24 84.65 15.54 26.64 54.75 109.40
# 666 24/08/2004 27.24 84.71 15.98 26.87 54.95 104.87
# 667 25/08/2004 27.55 85.07 16.52 26.95 55.30 106.00
# 668 26/08/2004 27.44 84.69 17.33 27.10 55.70 107.91

# the above can still leave NAs in other columns use na.omit
# to remove all the blank data
data_stocks_naomit = na.omit(data_stocks)
```

There can be a requirement in data preprocessing where one might have to select data in a range. The following example selects data where MSFT prices lie between 20 and 30. Here, & is a Logic operator in R see help("&") to see more details and other Logic operators.

```
data_msft = data_stocks_naomit[data_stocks_naomit$MSFT <= 30 &
     data_stocks_naomit$MSFT > 20, ]
min(data_msft$MSFT)   #check

# [1] 20.06
```

These selections can also be performed using the function **subset**. The following example uses the **subset** function to select rows with AAPL > 100. The arguments to the function are also shown in the example. Notice that we have taken arguments of subset.data.frame, as subset is a generalised function which has methods for data.frame.

```
args(subset.data.frame)

# function (x, subset, select, drop = FALSE, ...)
# NULL

aaplgr100 = subset(data_stocks_naomit, AAPL > 100)
head(aaplgr100)

#          Date MSFT   IBM  AAPL   MCD    PG   GOOG
# 1342 2/05/2007 30.61 102.22 100.39 50.02 62.37 465.78
```

```
#  1343  3/05/2007  30.97  102.80  100.40  49.91  62.00  473.23
#  1344  4/05/2007  30.56  102.96  100.81  49.92  62.41  471.12
#  1345  7/05/2007  30.71  103.16  103.92  49.50  62.18  467.27
#  1346  8/05/2007  30.75  103.29  105.06  49.32  61.75  466.81
#  1347  9/05/2007  30.78  104.38  106.88  49.84  62.01  469.25

min(aaplgr100$AAPL)

#  [1]  100.06
```

There are various other methods for data manipulation which can be helpful in reshaping data before it can be used for statistical evaluation. These methods will be discussed as and when they will be required in the text's examples. The readers can look into package *reshape* and *plyr* to gain a head start.

## 3.4 Summary

In this chapter, we discussed various methods to import external data in R and also some methods which can be used for data preprocessing. We discussed various methods to extract data based on specific criteria from a data file and also methods to import data from other software like Matlab and SPSS. We will now discuss some basic R programming methods and control flow in the next chapter.

Chapter 4

# R Programming and Control Flow

## 4.1 Introduction

R is a scripting language where you provide a set of instructions to the R programming environment. Programming refers to the process of writing a set of instructions and executing them in a logical sequence which instructs the computer to perform the desired task and tells it how to do it, in the present case statistical and graphical analysis. In the case of R, we write scripts which are mostly sequential (there can be variations in case many functions are used). All the programs written in any language have at least the steps of starting, operations and stopping. Even just one assignment operation follows this sequence. This chapter has an extended motivation as we have found that it is not easy to motivate researchers and students to make them put the effort into learning R programming. Most students take the easier route of using R extensions like RCommander to do some basic analysis.

Many R users do not want to learn R programming, they are of the opinion that basic statements (assignments most of the time) are all they want to know for their work. This particular way of learning R faces problems when you have to do more data operations and statistical analysis than you initially thought or if you do not have access to some basic functions which you want to use regularly in your research. It is always beneficial to know basic programming structures in R which makes life easier and saves a lot of time while doing research. All the researchers who do not know basic programming in any language have faced similar problems such as, the functions written by others do not perform exactly the same computations they desire or they cannot understand the basic structure of someone else's code. The choices left at this point are either to pay someone who knows how to program to write the program for you, or learn R yourself. Although it might take some time to learn R programming, it will probably save you money and valuable time in the end.

In this chapter, we will cover the basic structures of R programming, including control flow (if else) and loops (iteration routines) followed by writing our first function. We will confine our discussion to the intermediate level and more advanced concepts will be discussed in specific case studies.

## 4.2    Control Flow

All the computer programming languages require a proper controlled flow of the program from one part to the another. Control flow (or flow control) is a well-defined sequence of conditional statements, loops and statements which directs the R script (or code in generalised sense) to execute one thing or the other based on the conditions written in the program.

### 4.2.1    If-else conditional statements

We use if-else conditional statements when we want the R program to branch out in different directions based on a logical condition. The following example compares the mean of two stocks and assigns a variable with the greater mean.

```
data_stocks = read.csv("us_stocks.csv")
# remove NAs from the data

data_stocks = na.omit(data_stocks)
m_msft = mean(data_stocks$MSFT)
m_aapl = mean(data_stocks$AAPL)
if (m_msft > m_aapl) {
    g_mean = m_msft
} else {
    g_mean = m_aapl
}
g_mean   #print greater mean

# [1] 207.7967
```

The if-else also works as a function call, the if-else call in the example above can be reduced to one line as follows

```
g_mean = if (m_msft > m_aapl) m_msft else m_aapl
g_mean

# [1] 207.7967
```

Note that the curly brackets in the case of just one statement are optional. They are required in the case of a block operation. It is easy to just use them to avoid confusion.

R also has a function **ifelse** which does the same operation as in example above. See **help(ifelse)** for more details

```
# arguments to ifelse
args(ifelse)

# function (test, yes, no)
# NULL

g_mean = ifelse(m_msft > m_aapl, m_msft, m_aapl)
g_mean

# [1] 207.7967
```

## 4.2.2 Using switch

Like most of the programming platforms, R also provides another way to do conditional statements using **switch** statements. **switch** statements evaluate an expression (**EXPR**) and accordingly chooses one of the arguments. Let us illustrate using the following example

```
doit = "mean"
switch(doit, mean = {
    mean(data_stocks$MSFT)
}, median = {
    median(data_stocks$MSFT)
})

# [1] 26.91177

# try the above with doit=median
doit = "median"
switch(doit, mean = {
    mean(data_stocks$MSFT)
}, median = {
    median(data_stocks$MSFT)
})

# [1] 27.07
```

We have repeated the switch statements in this example, this can be avoided using a function call. We will explore this while discussing writing functions.

### 4.2.3   Loops

Loops are the common feature in almost all the programming languages. R provides three basic loops using `for`, `while` and `repeat`. We will use loops in various examples in this book.

**`for` *loop*

`for` loops are repetitive structures which execute a set of commands while iterating through values in a vector. These values are mostly sequences or values in a vector. The following example runs a loop 15 times by iterating through a vector having a sequence of numbers from 1 to 15.

```
# construct the loop
j = 0
for (i in 1:15) {
    j = j + i    #add i to j
    print(j)     #print the sequential sum
}

# [1] 1
# [1] 3
# [1] 6
# [1] 10
# [1] 15
# [1] 21
# [1] 28
# [1] 36
# [1] 45
# [1] 55
# [1] 66
# [1] 78
# [1] 91
# [1] 105
# [1] 120
```

**`while` *loop*

A `while` loop evaluates an expression or a function while a condition is TRUE. Let us repeat the above example using `while` loop

```
# initialise j and i
j = 0
i = 1
```

```
# one can also use i<=15
while (i < 16) {
    j = j + i
    i = i + 1
    print(j)
}

# [1] 1
# [1] 3
# [1] 6
# [1] 10
# [1] 15
# [1] 21
# [1] 28
# [1] 36
# [1] 45
# [1] 55
# [1] 66
# [1] 78
# [1] 91
# [1] 105
# [1] 120
```

## repeat *loop*

A **repeat** loop repeats the same expression till it is broken due to a condition.

```
# initialise
j = 0
i = 1
repeat {
    j = j + i
    i = i + 1
    print(j)
    if (i > 15)
        break
}

# [1] 1
# [1] 3
# [1] 6
# [1] 10
```

```
# [1] 15
# [1] 21
# [1] 28
# [1] 36
# [1] 45
# [1] 55
# [1] 66
# [1] 78
# [1] 91
# [1] 105
# [1] 120
```

Together, all these three loops can be used for iterative operations. The loops come handy when you have to iterate medium to large datasets by row or column. Next we will learn how to write functions.

## 4.3    Functions in R

In all research fields, there are a few statistical (or otherwise) calculations which are used frequently by the users, for example calculation of returns in finance research. R provides the facility for creating specific functions to evaluate a set of arguments and return an output value which are stored as R objects. This section explains how to create and use a function in R. The functions in R are created by the keyword `function` which takes the following syntax.

`function(arguments)`*body*

The arguments are the values/defaults/variables which are used in the body of the function to evaluate an expression. The body of the function is enclosed in curly braces. The function is assigned to a named object and called by passing arguments to the object. The following example illustrates by creating a function to calculate the mean for all the columns in the dataset **data_stats**

```
# the following function takes 2 arguments, x a data frame,
# dates to indicate if there are dates in the first column
cal_mean = function(x, dates = TRUE) {
    num_cols = ncol(x)  #calculate the number of columns
    # lets use a list and a loop to refresh our concepts
    m_stocks = list()  #creating an empty list
```

```
    # use for loop assign the starting value based on the dates
    # column,we skip dates column if they are present (dates are
    # basically row names to more generalised version will be to
    # check for row names)
    l = ifelse(dates == TRUE, 2, 1)
    j = 1  #starting point in the list m_stocks
    for (i in l:num_cols) {
        m_stocks[[j]] = mean(x[, i])
        j = j + 1
    }
    names(m_stocks) = colnames(x[, l:num_cols])
    return(m_stocks)
}
# lets call the function cal_mean
cal_mean(data_stocks, TRUE)

# $MSFT
# [1] 26.91177
#
# $IBM
# [1] 122.3303
#
# $AAPL
# [1] 207.7967
#
# $MCD
# [1] 58.95141
#
# $PG
# [1] 61.32512
#
# $GOOG
# [1] 469.9453

# lets call the function with no dates column
cal_mean(data_stocks[, 2:ncol(data_stocks)], FALSE)

# $MSFT
# [1] 26.91177
#
# $IBM
# [1] 122.3303
#
# $AAPL
# [1] 207.7967
#
```

```
# $MCD
# [1] 58.95141
#
# $PG
# [1] 61.32512
#
# $GOOG
# [1] 469.9453
```

This is just an example to show how to build a function. This function can be replaced by `apply` function which is easier and an inbuilt R function. We will look into details of these functions later in the book. As an exercise, construct the above function with the median in it based on user's choice. This will require an additional argument with the choice of statistics required.[1]

## 4.4 Summary

In this chapter, we covered some basic concepts of programming a routine in R. We discussed how to program a control flow using conditional routines and loops. We also discussed how to create a simple function in R which is helpful for routines which are used often. We will now shift our focus to real data processing and discuss data exploration in the next chapter.

---

[1]**Hint:** Use switch to switch between mean and median based on the choice of either mean or median.

Chapter 5

# Data Exploration

## 5.1 Introduction

This chapter describes various statistical methods to explore data. Data is not always easy to understand just by looking at it. Initial summary statistics or descriptive statistics can be used to calculate various measures from the data, which help in a better understanding of the data. In most research problems, descriptive statistics are one of the first steps in the analysis. R provides methods to calculate various statistical measures like the mean, median, etc., which are helpful in summarising data characteristics. R also provides various simple graphical methods, for example, histograms, bar charts, etc. for the initial data visualisation. This chapter will discuss various such functions. The focus of this chapter will be on functions to calculate basic statistics rather than on the details of the methods. A knowledge of basic statistics is assumed in this chapter. If you have not taken any statistics course, it is advisable to consult a basic statistics text before you begin this chapter or as you learn the functions.

## 5.2 Summary Statistics

It is simple to calculate basic summary statistics in R, as most of the functions are named according to what they do. For instance, **mean** calculates the mean of a single variable and **sd** calculates the standard deviation. Table 5.1 provides R functions for some basic descriptive statistical measures followed by an example using these functions on a dataset. See the help pages for these functions for further details. We will use a sample dataset with prices of the Dow Jones Stock index and 19 other stock prices will be

Table 5.1:    Basic statistics functions in R

| Statistics | R-function |
| --- | --- |
| Arithmetic mean | mean(x) |
| Geometric mean | exp(mean(log(x))) |
| Median | median(x) |
| Range | range(x) |
| Variance | var(x) |
| Standard deviation | sd(x) |
| Interquartile range | IQR(x) |
| Other quantiles | quantile(x) |
| Skewness | skewness(x) |
| Kurtosis | kurtosis(x) |

used to demonstrate basic summary statistics functions. The data in the file *data_fin.csv* is obtained from www.Quandl.com and is available for free.[1]

The following example demonstrates how to calculate the statistics measures in Table 5.1 for Dow Jones prices in data file *data_fin.csv*

```
# change the working directory to the folder containing
# data_fin.csv or provide the full path with the filename
data_stocks = read.csv("data_fin.csv")  #import data
head(data_stocks)

#        Date      DJI   AXP   MMM   ATT    BA   CAT CISCO
# 1  3/01/2000 11357.5 45.82 47.19 47.19 40.12 24.31 54.05
# 2  4/01/2000 10997.9 44.09 45.31 44.25 40.12 24.00 51.00
# 3  5/01/2000 11122.7 42.96 46.62 44.94 42.62 24.56 51.19
# 4  6/01/2000 11253.3 43.78 50.62 43.75 43.06 25.81 50.00
# 5  7/01/2000 11522.6 44.42 51.47 44.12 44.12 26.66 52.94
# 6 10/01/2000 11572.2 45.04 51.12 44.75 43.69 25.78 54.91
#       DD   XOM    GE    GS    HD    IBM  INTC   JNJ   JPM
# 1 65.00 39.09 49.95 88.31 65.50 115.56 43.47 46.09 48.69
# 2 65.00 38.41 48.06 82.38 61.50 112.06 41.47 44.41 47.27
# 3 67.75 40.50 47.70 78.88 61.44 116.00 41.81 44.88 46.98
# 4 71.50 42.59 48.51 82.25 60.00 114.62 39.38 46.28 47.65
# 5 71.62 42.31 50.28 82.56 62.81 113.31 41.00 47.88 48.52
# 6 70.00 41.88 50.37 84.38 63.19 118.44 42.88 47.03 47.69
#      MRK   MCD  MSFT   NKE
# 1 64.04 39.62 58.34 12.03
# 2 61.61 38.81 56.31 11.38
```

---

[1]The dataset obtained from Quandl are available for free, but it comes without any warranty for accuracy. It is advisable to use data from some reputable source for actual research problems.

```
# 3 64.22 39.44 56.91 12.03
# 4 64.75 38.88 55.00 11.97
# 5 70.97 39.75 55.72 11.97
# 6 68.89 40.06 56.12 12.17

DJI = data_stocks$DJI
DJI = na.omit(DJI)   #remove NAs as it will affect the calculations
# Arithmetic mean
mean(DJI)

# [1] 11098.12

# Geometric mean
exp(mean(log(DJI)))

# [1] 10953.39

# median
median(DJI)

# [1] 10748.8

# variance & standard deviation
var(DJI)

# [1] 3280347

sd(DJI)

# [1] 1811.173

# interquartile range and few quantiles
IQR(DJI)

# [1] 2276.25

quantile(DJI)

#       0%      25%      50%      75%     100%
#  6547.10 10063.25 10748.80 12339.50 16576.66

# skewness and kurtosis skewness and kurtosis functions are
# not available in R core library but in library e1071 (there
# are other packages which have functions for skewness and
# kurtosis try ??kurtosis or search for the function on
# RSearch.
library(e1071)
skewness(DJI)
```

```
# [1] 0.4777828

kurtosis(DJI)

# [1] 0.08404185
```

There are functions available to calculate descriptive statistics using a single call which will be discussed later in an example.

In the example above, we calculated descriptive statistics for the prices of the Dow Jones Index using individual functions. The function **summary** in R provides some basic summary viz., minimum value, maximum value, median value and quartiles for one variable or a dataset. The function **summary** can be used as follows

```
# summary of one column/variable in a dataframe
summary(DJI)

#    Min. 1st Qu.  Median    Mean 3rd Qu.    Max.
#    6547   10060   10750   11100   12340   16580

# summary of whole dataset excluding the time column
summary(data_stocks[, c(2:21)])

#       DJI              AXP              MMM
#  Min.   : 6547   Min.   :10.26   Min.   : 39.50
#  1st Qu.:10063   1st Qu.:38.31   1st Qu.: 62.55
#  Median :10749   Median :47.49   Median : 77.67
#  Mean   :11098   Mean   :46.77   Mean   : 75.78
#  3rd Qu.:12340   3rd Qu.:54.44   3rd Qu.: 85.55
#  Max.   :16577   Max.   :90.73   Max.   :140.25
#  NA's   :27      NA's   :12      NA's   :12
#       ATT              BA               CAT
#  Min.   :19.34   Min.   : 25.06   Min.   : 14.91
#  1st Qu.:25.54   1st Qu.: 44.00   1st Qu.: 28.64
#  Median :29.65   Median : 63.56   Median : 57.10
#  Mean   :31.77   Mean   : 62.95   Mean   : 56.01
#  3rd Qu.:37.22   3rd Qu.: 74.90   3rd Qu.: 79.36
#  Max.   :58.50   Max.   :138.36   Max.   :116.20
#  NA's   :12      NA's   :12       NA's   :12
#      CISCO             DD               XOM
#  Min.   : 8.60   Min.   :16.14   Min.   : 30.27
#  1st Qu.:17.68   1st Qu.:41.13   1st Qu.: 42.46
#  Median :20.43   Median :44.53   Median : 64.77
#  Mean   :23.41   Mean   :44.37   Mean   : 63.20
#  3rd Qu.:24.17   3rd Qu.:48.92   3rd Qu.: 81.62
```

```
#   Max.    :80.06   Max.    :71.62   Max.    :101.51
#   NA's    :13      NA's    :12      NA's    :12
#        GE                GS              HD
#   Min.   :  6.66   Min.   :  52.0   Min.    :18.00
#   1st Qu.:20.00    1st Qu.:  92.2   1st Qu.:31.00
#   Median :30.33    Median :116.2    Median :37.37
#   Mean   :29.56    Mean   :126.9    Mean    :40.20
#   3rd Qu.:36.03    3rd Qu.:159.5    3rd Qu.:46.23
#   Max.   :59.94    Max.   :247.9    Max.    :82.34
#   NA's   :12       NA's   :12       NA's    :12
#        IBM              INTC             JNJ
#   Min.   : 55.07   Min.    :12.08   Min.    :33.69
#   1st Qu.: 87.82   1st Qu.:20.17    1st Qu.:55.27
#   Median :106.48   Median :22.76    Median :61.30
#   Mean   :118.83   Mean    :25.21   Mean    :61.07
#   3rd Qu.:130.00   3rd Qu.:26.77    3rd Qu.:65.20
#   Max.   :215.80   Max.    :74.88   Max.    :95.63
#   NA's   :12       NA's    :13      NA's    :12
#        JPM              MRK              MCD
#   Min.    :15.45   Min.    :20.99   Min.    : 12.38
#   1st Qu.:35.66    1st Qu.:34.53    1st Qu.: 29.19
#   Median :40.20    Median :43.63    Median : 43.78
#   Mean    :40.36   Mean    :44.65   Mean    : 51.07
#   3rd Qu.:45.71    3rd Qu.:51.55    3rd Qu.: 70.36
#   Max.    :65.70   Max.    :89.85   Max.    :103.59
#   NA's    :12      NA's    :13      NA's    :12
#        MSFT             NKE
#   Min.    :15.15   Min.    : 6.64
#   1st Qu.:25.67    1st Qu.:14.56
#   Median :27.59    Median :23.25
#   Mean    :28.38   Mean    :28.01
#   3rd Qu.:30.19    3rd Qu.:36.90
#   Max.    :58.34   Max.    :79.86
#   NA's    :13      NA's    :12
```

Together with the statistical measures, there are some basic plots which are used to get a better understanding of the data. In R, various functions are available to produce several graphs such as Histograms, Box Plot, etc. Histograms plot the frequency distribution of a quantitative variable which is useful to assess the distribution of the variable. R has the function hist() to generate the histogram. The argument breaks can be used to increase or decrease the bins in a histogram which can help in a better visualisation.

We can use the following code to show the histogram of DJI prices (see Figure 5.1). R graph function `curve` can be used to plot a normal distribution over the histogram to give a better understanding of the distribution of DJI.

```
# plot the histogram of the prices (figure-5.1)
hist(DJI, prob = TRUE)   #default breaks
```

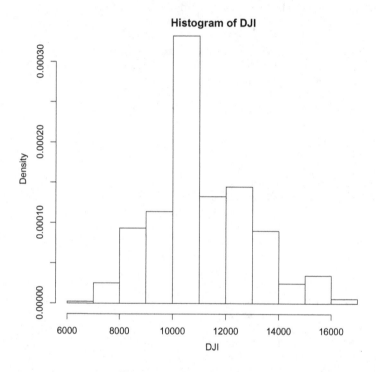

Figure 5.1:   Price histogram

```
hist(DJI, breaks = 15, prob = TRUE)
curve(dnorm(x, mean = mean(DJI), sd = sd(DJI)), col = "darkblue",
    lwd = 2, add = TRUE) # figure-5.2
```

The function **dnorm** in the example calculates the density of the normal distribution given the mean and standard deviation for DJI (see Figure 5.2[2]).

---

[2]The R code used in this book produces figures in various colours. All the figures in this book are printed in black and white, please download the coloured figures from http://www.worldscientific.com/worldscibooks/10.1142/10151-sm for a better understanding of the R code and associated output.

**Histogram of DJI**

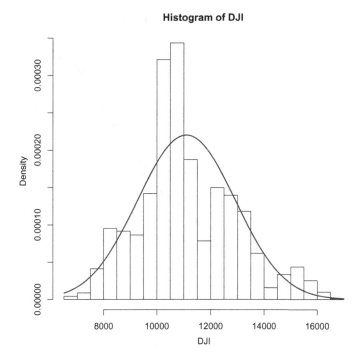

Figure 5.2:   Price histogram with normal curve

Another plot which can be used to compare the distribution of a data series is the quantile–quantile plot (see Figure 5.3). The function `qqplot` plots the sorted quantiles of one dataset against the other which helps in visual inspection of two datasets or one dataset with a statistical distribution. The following example compares the prices of DJI with normal distribution where the `qqline` function plots the quantiles from a theoretical normal distribution.

```
# plot quantiles of DJI (figure-5.3)
qqnorm(DJI)
# plot quantiles from the theoretical normal distribution
qqline(DJI, col = "red")
```

## 5.3   Example: Descriptive Statistics of Stock Returns

### 5.3.1   Introduction

Most of the empirical research requires data exploration before the data analysis. The descriptive statistics and basic graphs of the data provides

**Normal Q–Q Plot**

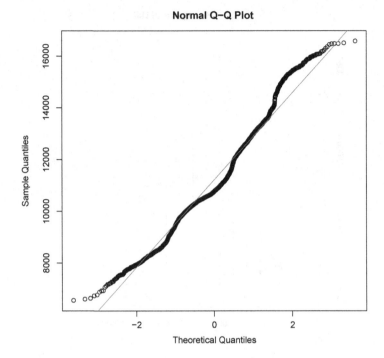

Figure 5.3:    Quantile–Quantile plot

an overview of the data used for the empirical research. As most research deals with more than one data series, calculating the statistical measures individually for all the data series can take a lot of time and effort. Luckily various packages in R provide methods to calculate basic descriptive statistics using a single function. In this first example, we will demonstrate how to use R to calculate descriptive statistics for the returns of 10 stocks in the data file **data_fin.csv**. We will also demonstrate how to generate basic graphs for data exploration. We will only demonstrate basic plots here as graphs in R will be dealt in detail in the next chapter.

The datafile *data_fin.csv* contains daily prices for 20 stocks (Table 5.2) traded in Dow Jones Industrial-30 stock index along with the daily prices of the index for the period from January 2000 to December 2013. This data is downloaded[3] from Quandl, which provides free access to publicly available data.

---

[3]The data used in this example is downloaded from Quandl via the website. This data can also be downloaded directly from R using rquandl package.

Table 5.2:   Stocks in *data_fin.csv*

| Code | Asset's Name |
|------|--------------|
| DJI | Dow Jones Industrial Index |
| AXP | American Express Company |
| MMM | 3M Company |
| ATT | AT&T |
| BA | Boeing Company |
| CAT | Caterpillar |
| CISCO | Cisco Systems |
| DD | ăE I du Pont de Nemours and Co |
| XOM | Exxon Mobile |
| GE | General Electrics |
| GS | Goldman Sachs |
| HD | Home Depot |
| IBM | International Business Machines |
| INTC | Intel Corp. |
| JNJ | Johnson & Johnson |
| JPM | JPMorgan Chase and Co. |
| MRK | Merc and Co. |
| MCD | MacDonald's Corp |
| MSFT | Microsoft Corp |
| NKE | Nike Inc |

## 5.3.2   Importing the data

We will first import the dataset into R using the `read.csv` function.

```
data_cs1 = read.csv("data_fin.csv")
head(data_cs1)   #check the imported data
```

```
#       Date     DJI   AXP   MMM   ATT    BA   CAT CISCO
# 1  3/01/2000 11357.5 45.82 47.19 47.19 40.12 24.31 54.05
# 2  4/01/2000 10997.9 44.09 45.31 44.25 40.12 24.00 51.00
# 3  5/01/2000 11122.7 42.96 46.62 44.94 42.62 24.56 51.19
# 4  6/01/2000 11253.3 43.78 50.62 43.75 43.06 25.81 50.00
# 5  7/01/2000 11522.6 44.42 51.47 44.12 44.12 26.66 52.94
# 6 10/01/2000 11572.2 45.04 51.12 44.75 43.69 25.78 54.91
#       DD   XOM    GE    GS    HD    IBM  INTC   JNJ   JPM
# 1 65.00 39.09 49.95 88.31 65.50 115.56 43.47 46.09 48.69
# 2 65.00 38.41 48.06 82.38 61.50 112.06 41.47 44.41 47.27
# 3 67.75 40.50 47.70 78.88 61.44 116.00 41.81 44.88 46.98
# 4 71.50 42.59 48.51 82.25 60.00 114.62 39.38 46.28 47.65
# 5 71.62 42.31 50.28 82.56 62.81 113.31 41.00 47.88 48.52
# 6 70.00 41.88 50.37 84.38 63.19 118.44 42.88 47.03 47.69
#      MRK   MCD  MSFT   NKE
# 1 64.04 39.62 58.34 12.03
```

```
# 2 61.61 38.81 56.31 11.38
# 3 64.22 39.44 56.91 12.03
# 4 64.75 38.88 55.00 11.97
# 5 70.97 39.75 55.72 11.97
# 6 68.89 40.06 56.12 12.17
```

The following code creates another dataset **data_cs1.1** with 10 series prices from **data_fin.csv** and then converts the date column to Date data type. The first column in the dataset is a date column giving the dates for the prices. These dates are in character format (see **help(as.Date)** for more details) which should be converted to Date format for proper date operations. We give one basic example in this case. More complex date/time conversions and operations will be addressed in Chapter 9 focussed on time series econometrics. As an example, we will first apply the **summary** function to **data_cs1.1** with dates as character and then after converting dates to Date class.

```
# selecting first 10 price series including the data column
data_cs1.1 = data_cs1[, c(1:11)]
# data cleaning-remove NAs
data_cs1.1 = na.omit(data_cs1.1)
colnames(data_cs1.1)  # see the columns present in the data

#  [1] "Date"  "DJI"   "AXP"   "MMM"   "ATT"   "BA"    "CAT"
#  [8] "CISCO" "DD"    "XOM"   "GE"

summary(data_cs1.1)  #notice the Date variable

#          Date             DJI             AXP
#  1/02/2000:    1   Min.   :  6547   Min.   :10.26
#  1/02/2001:    1   1st Qu.:10063   1st Qu.:38.38
#  1/02/2002:    1   Median :10749   Median :47.60
#  1/02/2005:    1   Mean   :11098   Mean   :46.83
#  1/02/2006:    1   3rd Qu.:12340   3rd Qu.:54.50
#  1/02/2007:    1   Max.   :16577   Max.   :90.73
#  (Other)   :3517
#         MMM               ATT              BA
#  Min.   : 39.50   Min.   :19.34   Min.   :  25.06
#  1st Qu.: 62.55   1st Qu.:25.54   1st Qu.:  44.02
#  Median : 77.67   Median :29.76   Median :  63.61
#  Mean   : 75.80   Mean   :31.79   Mean   :  62.99
#  3rd Qu.: 85.61   3rd Qu.:37.23   3rd Qu.:  74.95
#  Max.   :140.25   Max.   :58.50   Max.   :138.36
#
```

```
#       CAT              CISCO              DD
# Min.   : 14.91   Min.   : 8.60   Min.   :16.14
# 1st Qu.: 28.48   1st Qu.:17.68   1st Qu.:41.17
# Median : 57.11   Median :20.39   Median :44.58
# Mean   : 56.03   Mean   :23.42   Mean   :44.43
# 3rd Qu.: 79.50   3rd Qu.:24.18   3rd Qu.:48.93
# Max.   :116.20   Max.   :80.06   Max.   :71.62
#
#       XOM              GE
# Min.   : 30.27   Min.   : 6.66
# 1st Qu.: 42.41   1st Qu.:20.04
# Median : 64.70   Median :30.37
# Mean   : 63.18   Mean   :29.63
# 3rd Qu.: 81.70   3rd Qu.:36.05
# Max.   :101.51   Max.   :59.94
#

# check class of dates which will be factor (treated as
# factor by default)
class(data_cs1.1$Date)

# [1] "factor"

# convert dates to class Date
data_cs1.1$Date = as.Date(data_cs1.1$Date, format = "%d/%m/%Y")
class(data_cs1.1$Date)

# [1] "Date"

summary(data_cs1.1)   #notice the Date variable

#       Date                DJI              AXP
# Min.   :2000-01-03   Min.   : 6547   Min.   :10.26
# 1st Qu.:2003-07-08   1st Qu.:10063   1st Qu.:38.38
# Median :2007-01-05   Median :10749   Median :47.60
# Mean   :2007-01-03   Mean   :11098   Mean   :46.83
# 3rd Qu.:2010-07-06   3rd Qu.:12340   3rd Qu.:54.50
# Max.   :2014-01-03   Max.   :16577   Max.   :90.73
#       MMM              ATT              BA
# Min.   : 39.50   Min.   :19.34   Min.   : 25.06
# 1st Qu.: 62.55   1st Qu.:25.54   1st Qu.: 44.02
# Median : 77.67   Median :29.76   Median : 63.61
# Mean   : 75.80   Mean   :31.79   Mean   : 62.99
# 3rd Qu.: 85.61   3rd Qu.:37.23   3rd Qu.: 74.95
# Max.   :140.25   Max.   :58.50   Max.   :138.36
#       CAT              CISCO              DD
# Min.   : 14.91   Min.   : 8.60   Min.   :16.14
```

```
#    1st Qu.:  28.48    1st Qu.:17.68    1st Qu.:41.17
#    Median :  57.11    Median :20.39    Median :44.58
#    Mean   :  56.03    Mean   :23.42    Mean   :44.43
#    3rd Qu.:  79.50    3rd Qu.:24.18    3rd Qu.:48.93
#    Max.   :116.20     Max.   :80.06    Max.   :71.62
#         XOM                   GE
#    Min.   : 30.27    Min.    : 6.66
#    1st Qu.: 42.41    1st Qu.:20.04
#    Median : 64.70    Median :30.37
#    Mean   : 63.18    Mean   :29.63
#    3rd Qu.: 81.70    3rd Qu.:36.05
#    Max.   :101.51    Max.   :59.94
```

The following code converts the prices to logarithmic returns. We design a generalised function here to convert prices into logarithmic and simple returns.

```
ptor=function(data,date.pos=1,date.format="%d/%m/%Y",
log.ret=TRUE, percntg=TRUE)
{
n =nrow(data)   # number of observations
# creates a negative index in case a date is to be excluded
ndx =if (date.pos) -date.pos else 1:ncol(data)
if(percntg){ multiplicator=100}
if (log.ret) # in case of log-returns
{
#log-returns
ret =log(data[2:n,ndx]/data[1:(n-1),ndx])*multiplicator
}
   else
#in case of simple returns
{
#returns
ret=(data[2:n,ndx]/data[1:(n-1),ndx]-1)*multiplicator
}
if (date.pos) # in case some date is in the dataframe
{
#returns a dataframe with the date in R format in the first position
return(data.frame(Date=as.Date(data[2:n,date.pos],
format=date.format),ret))
}
#returns the returns, but no date is defined
else return(ret)
}
```

The above function takes a data frame as input to calculate the logarithmic or simple returns. The function can also handle dates if present in the first column which are returned as the standard R date format after the user provides the format they are passed to the function. There is also another argument to the function which helps in converting returns to percentage returns (percntg = TRUE/FALSE). Let us convert the prices in data_cs1.1 to percentage logarithmic returns.

```
data_cs1.1r = ptor(data_cs1.1, date.pos = 1, date.format = "%Y-%m-%d")
head(data_cs1.1r)
```

```
#        Date        DJI        AXP        MMM        ATT
# 2 2000-01-04 -3.2173973 -3.8487678 -4.0654247 -6.4326634
# 3 2000-01-05  1.1283720 -2.5963549  2.8501875  1.5472895
# 4 2000-01-06  1.1673354  1.8907642  8.2317122 -2.6836654
# 5 2000-01-07  2.3648905  1.4512726  1.6652359  0.8421582
# 6 2000-01-10  0.4295346  1.3861165 -0.6823304  1.4178250
# 7 2000-01-11 -0.5293883  0.9061837 -1.7165263 -1.4178250
#          BA        CAT       CISCO         DD        XOM
# 2  0.0000000  -1.283396 -5.8083911  0.0000000 -1.7548837
# 3  6.0448664   2.306527  0.3718568  4.1437190  5.2984132
# 4  1.0270865   4.964291 -2.3521195  5.3872990  5.0317510
# 5  2.4318702   3.240230  5.7136191  0.1676915 -0.6596019
# 6 -0.9793951  -3.356532  3.6536284 -2.2879123 -1.0215079
# 7 -1.8713726  -1.563754 -3.0697677 -1.8018506  1.1868167
#          GE
# 2 -3.8572275
# 3 -0.7518832
# 4  1.6838564
# 5  3.5837421
# 6  0.1788376
# 7  0.2379537
```

From this point, there are two ways to go about this case problem. We can either apply all the basic statistical functions one by one on each series or we can use functions available in R packages which calculate most commonly used descriptive or summary statistics for a data series. We demonstrate the use of two functions[4] viz., describe from package *psych* and stat.desc from the package *pastecs*.

---

[4]We assume that these packages are already installed, if not install them before running the code.

5.3.2.1    *Using the* describe *function*

The package *psych* comes with a function called describe which generated the descriptive statistics for all the data vectors (columns) in a data frame, matrix or a vector. The following code demonstrate the use of describe from the *psych* package where we use the function in its default setting, which calculates Skewness and Kurtosis for other options see help(describe)

```
library(psych)    #load the required package
args(describe)    #arguments for describe function

# function (x, na.rm = TRUE, interp = FALSE, skew = TRUE,
ranges = TRUE,
#      trim = 0.1, type = 3, check = TRUE, fast = NULL)
# NULL

# use describe to calculate descriptive stats for data_cs1.1r
desc1 = describe(data_cs1.1r[,2:11])
#note we dont pass the date
column # check the output head(desc1)

#      vars     n   mean    sd median trimmed   mad     min    max
# DJI     1  3522   0.01  1.23   0.04    0.03  0.82   -8.20  10.51
# AXP     2  3522   0.02  2.89   0.02    0.03  1.55  -19.35  18.77
# MMM     3  3522   0.03  1.55   0.03    0.03  1.10   -9.38  10.39
# ATT     4  3522  -0.01  1.80   0.03    0.01  1.22  -13.54  15.08
# BA      5  3522   0.03  2.01   0.05    0.06  1.57  -19.39  14.38
# CAT     6  3522   0.04  2.14   0.04    0.05  1.65  -15.69  13.73
#      range  skew kurtosis    se
# DJI  18.71 -0.06     7.71  0.02
# AXP  38.12 -0.01     9.14  0.05
# MMM  19.78  0.06     4.87  0.03
# ATT  28.62  0.02     6.26  0.03
# BA   33.77 -0.26     5.39  0.03
# CAT  29.42 -0.08     4.08  0.04

# the above output is in long format, we can transpose it get
# column format
desc1.t = t(desc1)
head(desc1.t)

#                    DJI           AXP           MMM
# vars     1.000000e+00  2.000000e+00  3.000000e+00
# n        3.522000e+03  3.522000e+03  3.522000e+03
# mean     1.055257e-02  1.908563e-02  3.056011e-02
```

```
# sd       1.226702e+00  2.892586e+00  1.551706e+00
# median   4.442671e-02  1.723604e-02  3.233787e-02
# trimmed  2.597511e-02  3.152635e-02  3.241946e-02
#                   ATT            BA           CAT
# vars      4.000000e+00  5.000000e+00  6.000000e+00
# n         3.522000e+03  3.522000e+03  3.522000e+03
# mean     -8.647491e-03  3.499777e-02  3.710732e-02
# sd        1.799180e+00  2.013123e+00  2.143040e+00
# median    3.018428e-02  5.279680e-02  4.291300e-02
# trimmed   9.134423e-03  5.567097e-02  4.678016e-02
#                  CISCO            DD           XOM
# vars      7.000000e+00  8.000000e+00  9.000000e+00
# n         3.522000e+03  3.522000e+03  3.522000e+03
# mean     -2.554732e-02 -5.379787e-04  2.653014e-02
# sd        2.744068e+00  1.881993e+00  1.629181e+00
# median    3.800312e-02  0.000000e+00  5.437650e-02
# trimmed  -1.339579e-04  1.469270e-03  4.883990e-02
#                     GE
# vars      1.000000e+01
# n         3.522000e+03
# mean     -1.696661e-02
# sd        2.057353e+00
# median    0.000000e+00
# trimmed   9.841473e-05
```

The descriptive statistics generated above gives the mean, median, standard deviation, trimmed mean (trimmed),[5] median, mad (median absolute deviation from the median), minimum (min), maximum (max), skewness (skew), kurtosis and standard error (se) . This can easily be transferred to a CSV file or a text file. The following single line of code transfers the descriptive statistics to a CSV file which then can be imported into a word or latex file as required.

```
write.csv(desc1.t, file = "desc1_psych.csv")
```

### 5.3.2.2   *Using* stat.desc *from package pastecs*

The *pastecs* package provides the function stat.desc which generated descriptive statistics for a data frame, matrix or a time series. Skewness and Kurtosis are not calculated by default in stat.desc but the argument norm

---

[5]Trimmed mean is the average after removing a small percentage of the largest and smallest values before calculating the mean.

can be set to TRUE to get these measures along with their standard errors. The following code demonstrates

```
require(pastecs)  # note library and require can both be
used to include a package
# detach the package pastecs its useful to avoid any
# conflicts (e.g. psych and Hmisc have 'describe' function
# with two different behaviours
detach("package:psych", unload =
TRUE) # use stat.desc in with default arguments
desc2 = stat.desc(data_cs1.1r[,
2:11]) desc2  #note no
skewness/kurtosis
```

| # | DJI | AXP | MMM |
|---|---|---|---|
| # nbr.val | 3522.00000000 | 3522.00000000 | 3522.00000000 |
| # nbr.null | 2.00000000 | 24.00000000 | 30.00000000 |
| # nbr.na | 0.00000000 | 0.00000000 | 0.00000000 |
| # min | -8.20073686 | -19.35233033 | -9.38368830 |
| # max | 10.50812264 | 18.77115508 | 10.39309228 |
| # range | 18.70885950 | 38.12348541 | 19.77678059 |
| # sum | 37.16616184 | 67.21959235 | 107.63272439 |
| # median | 0.04442671 | 0.01723604 | 0.03233787 |
| # mean | 0.01055257 | 0.01908563 | 0.03056011 |
| # SE.mean | 0.02067018 | 0.04874068 | 0.02614656 |
| # CI.mean.0.95 | 0.04052675 | 0.09556282 | 0.05126395 |
| # var | 1.50479753 | 8.36705196 | 2.40779004 |
| # std.dev | 1.22670189 | 2.89258569 | 1.55170553 |
| # coef.var | 116.24671056 | 151.55829475 | 50.77551363 |
| # | ATT | BA | CAT |
| # nbr.val | 3.522000e+03 | 3522.00000000 | 3522.00000000 |
| # nbr.null | 5.000000e+01 | 15.00000000 | 24.00000000 |
| # nbr.na | 0.000000e+00 | 0.00000000 | 0.00000000 |
| # min | -1.353821e+01 | -19.38930814 | -15.68588738 |
| # max | 1.508318e+01 | 14.37773538 | 13.73497369 |
| # range | 2.862139e+01 | 33.76704352 | 29.42086106 |
| # sum | -3.045646e+01 | 123.26213007 | 130.69198793 |
| # median | 3.018428e-02 | 0.05279680 | 0.04291300 |
| # mean | -8.647491e-03 | 0.03499777 | 0.03710732 |
| # SE.mean | 3.031656e-02 | 0.03392155 | 0.03611067 |
| # CI.mean.0.95 | 5.943979e-02 | 0.06650788 | 0.07079996 |
| # var | 3.237048e+00 | 4.05266523 | 4.59262031 |
| # std.dev | 1.799180e+00 | 2.01312325 | 2.14303997 |
| # coef.var | -2.080580e+02 | 57.52147953 | 57.75248272 |
| # | CISCO | DD | XOM |
| # nbr.val | 3522.00000000 | 3.522000e+03 | 3522.00000000 |

```
# nbr.null            50.00000000    2.900000e+01     29.00000000
# nbr.na               0.00000000    0.000000e+00      0.00000000
# min                -17.68648507   -1.202802e+01    -15.02710133
# max                 21.82385752    1.085590e+01     15.86306873
# range               39.51034259    2.288392e+01     30.89017007
# sum                -89.97765951   -1.894761e+00     93.43914618
# median               0.03800312    0.000000e+00      0.05437650
# mean                -0.02554732   -5.379787e-04      0.02653014
# SE.mean              0.04623812    3.171197e-02      0.02745205
# CI.mean.0.95         0.09065621    6.217570e-02      0.05382353
# var                  7.52990741    3.541897e+00      2.65423201
# std.dev              2.74406768    1.881993e+00      1.62918139
# coef.var          -107.41117745   -3.498266e+03     61.40870397
#                             GE
# nbr.val          3522.00000000
# nbr.null           63.00000000
# nbr.na              0.00000000
# min               -13.68410423
# max                17.98443570
# range              31.66853993
# sum               -59.75640377
# median              0.00000000
# mean               -0.01696661
# SE.mean             0.03466683
# CI.mean.0.95        0.06796911
# var                 4.23270154
# std.dev             2.05735304
# coef.var         -121.25892722
```

Additional to the **describe** function in the *psych* package **stat.desc** also generate confidence interval of the mean (CI.mean) and the variation coefficient (coef.var). The following code sets the argument **norm** to TRUE to get Skewness and Kurtosis.

```
desc2.sk = stat.desc(data_cs1.1r[, 2:11], norm = TRUE)
print(round(desc2.sk, 4)) #round the values just for display purposes
```

```
#                   DJI        AXP        MMM        ATT
# nbr.val      3522.0000  3522.0000  3522.0000  3522.0000
# nbr.null        2.0000    24.0000    30.0000    50.0000
# nbr.na          0.0000     0.0000     0.0000     0.0000
# min            -8.2007   -19.3523    -9.3837   -13.5382
# max            10.5081    18.7712    10.3931    15.0832
# range          18.7089    38.1235    19.7768    28.6214
# sum            37.1662    67.2196   107.6327   -30.4565
```

```
# median           0.0444      0.0172      0.0323      0.0302
# mean             0.0106      0.0191      0.0306     -0.0086
# SE.mean          0.0207      0.0487      0.0261      0.0303
# CI.mean.0.95     0.0405      0.0956      0.0513      0.0594
# var              1.5048      8.3671      2.4078      3.2370
# std.dev          1.2267      2.8926      1.5517      1.7992
# coef.var       116.2467    151.5583     50.7755   -208.0580
# skewness        -0.0583     -0.0067      0.0593      0.0162
# skew.2SE        -0.7065     -0.0811      0.7183      0.1964
# kurtosis         7.7143      9.1411      4.8653      6.2572
# kurt.2SE        46.7588     55.4068     29.4901     37.9266
# normtest.W       0.9188      0.8497      0.9385      0.9299
# normtest.p       0.0000      0.0000      0.0000      0.0000
#                      BA         CAT       CISCO          DD
# nbr.val       3522.0000   3522.0000   3522.0000   3522.0000
# nbr.null        15.0000     24.0000     50.0000     29.0000
# nbr.na           0.0000      0.0000      0.0000      0.0000
# min            -19.3893    -15.6859    -17.6865    -12.0280
# max             14.3777     13.7350     21.8239     10.8559
# range           33.7670     29.4209     39.5103     22.8839
# sum            123.2621    130.6920    -89.9777     -1.8948
# median           0.0528      0.0429      0.0380      0.0000
# mean             0.0350      0.0371     -0.0255     -0.0005
# SE.mean          0.0339      0.0361      0.0462      0.0317
# CI.mean.0.95     0.0665      0.0708      0.0907      0.0622
# var              4.0527      4.5926      7.5299      3.5419
# std.dev          2.0131      2.1430      2.7441      1.8820
# coef.var        57.5215     57.7525   -107.4112  -3498.2665
# skewness        -0.2605     -0.0837      0.1548     -0.1523
# skew.2SE        -3.1573     -1.0144      1.8759     -1.8462
# kurtosis         5.3924      4.0770      7.3294      5.0613
# kurt.2SE        32.6851     24.7121     44.4258     30.6781
# normtest.W       0.9550      0.9583      0.9104      0.9381
# normtest.p       0.0000      0.0000      0.0000      0.0000
#                     XOM          GE
# nbr.val       3522.0000   3522.0000
# nbr.null        29.0000     63.0000
# nbr.na           0.0000      0.0000
# min            -15.0271    -13.6841
# max             15.8631     17.9844
# range           30.8902     31.6685
# sum             93.4391    -59.7564
# median           0.0544      0.0000
# mean             0.0265     -0.0170
# SE.mean          0.0275      0.0347
```

```
# CI.mean.0.95    0.0538    0.0680
# var             2.6542    4.2327
# std.dev         1.6292    2.0574
# coef.var       61.4087 -121.2589
# skewness        0.0465    0.0110
# skew.2SE        0.5637    0.1336
# kurtosis       10.4319    7.7810
# kurt.2SE       63.2313   47.1632
# normtest.W      0.9161    0.9047
# normtest.p      0.0000    0.0000

# save the stats in a csv
write.csv(desc2.sk, "desc2_pastecs.csv")
```

### 5.3.3    Some basic plots

This part of the example will demonstrate how to plot some basic charts to get more insight into the DJIA return data. We discussed histograms and Q–Q plots earlier in the chapter. Here, we will plot simple line charts and Q–Q plots for all the 10 return series in our dataset (see Figure 5.4). As discussed, one way to draw these plots using R is to plot each individual series one by one. The following code plots a line plot for all the 10 series using the basic **plot** function in a for loop. The same concept can be used to plot other plots like Bar Plot, Histograms or Q–Q plot.

```
n = ncol(data_cs1.1r)  #calculate number of data columns
s.names = c(colnames(data_cs1.1r))  #get the names of each return
series
# generate a series of colors
clrs = seq(1:10)
# graphical parameter to plot 10 plots on one screen (2 rows
# X 5 columns)
par(mfrow = c(5, 2))
#figure-5.4
for (i in 2:n) {
    plot(data_cs1.1r$Date, data_cs1.1r[, i], type = "l", main
    = s.names[i],
        col = clrs[(i - 1)], xlab = "Date", ylab = "Return")
}
```

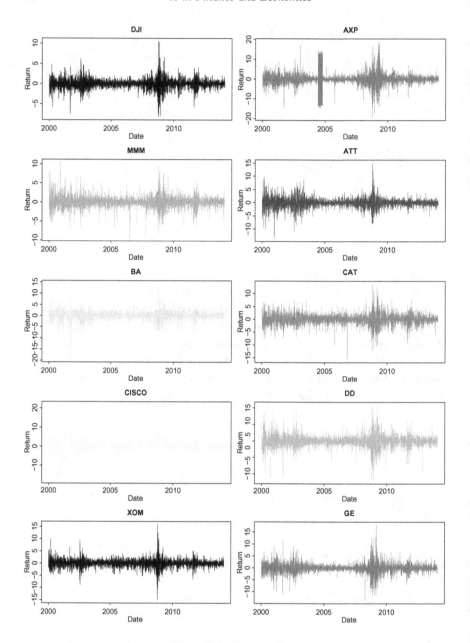

Figure 5.4:   Return plots

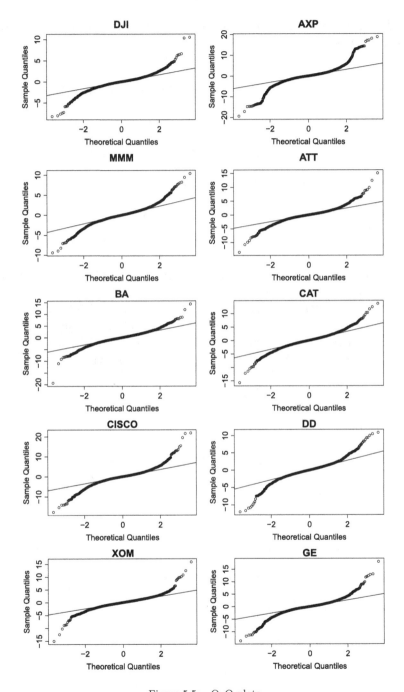

Figure 5.5: Q–Q plots

The procedure used above can be easily replicated for Q–Q plot (see Figure 5.5) as shown below

```
# graphical parameter to plot 10 plots on one screen (2 rows
# X 5 columns)
par(mfrow = c(5, 2))
#figure-5.5
for (i in 2:n) {
    qqnorm(data_cs1.1r[, i], main = s.names[i])
    qqline(data_cs1.1r[, i])
}
```

## 5.4 Summary

In this chapter, we discussed how to calculate some basic descriptive statistics using R. We also discussed how to generate some basic graphs which provide more insight into the nature of the data. This chapter also featured the first example of the book which demonstrated how to generate descriptive statistics and basic graphs for financial return data. The next chapter will discuss data visualisation or graphics capabilities in R. We will introduce ggplot2 in the following chapter and its use with examples.

Chapter 6

# Graphics in R

## 6.1 Introduction

One of the major strengths of R in comparison with similar software (SAS, SPSS, etc.) are its data visualisation capabilities. R offers an outstanding variety of graphics ranging from simple line or scatter plots to multidimensional data visualisation. R provides facilities to create simple standard graphs like a line plot or a scatter plot or to modify the graphs. The base R system provides three types of graph functions, viz., high level plot functions, low level plot functions and interactive plot functions. The high level plot functions are used to produce complete new graphs over the existing or new graphical device. These functions erase existing graphs in most cases[1] unless specified to do otherwise. The low level plot functions are used to add graphical objects to an existing plot. These objects can be an additional line, points or text. The interactive plot functions enable the user to interactively add information to an existing plot or even extract information from an existing plot. R also provides various graphical parameters which can be customised depending on the user requirements.

There are also a wide variety of packages available in addition to the base R graphics capabilities which provide advanced data visualisation procedures, *lattice* and *ggplot2* are couple of examples. In this chapter, we will first discuss some of the graphical procedures available in the base R system followed by an introduction to *ggplot2*, `www.ggplot2.org` which is a more advanced graphical package. The discussion in the chapter will be confined to commonly used plots, graphical procedures and settings. There are various text books (Chang (2012); Wickham (2009)) and online resources available for R graphics for beginner to advanced level data visualisation

---

[1] This behaviour is different in RStudio where in most cases, new graphs do not overwrite the old graphs.

in R. We will use various datasets from various R packages and data downloaded from freely available sources for examples.

## 6.2   Basic Plots in R

R provides various standard statistical plots like scatter plots, box plots,
histograms, bar plots or simple line plots. Most R plots/graphics are ini-
tiated by calling a high level graphics function. Low level graph functions
are then used to add more details to the plot. One of the most popular
and most frequently used functions to build a new plot in R is the `plot`
function. The `plot`function is a generic function in R which produces a plot
depending on the data type or class. In simplest form, it creates a scatter
plot of two input vectors. For example,

```
# Generate two random normal vectors
x = rnorm(100)
y = rnorm(100)
# plot x and y using the plot() function (figure-6.1)
plot(x, y)
```

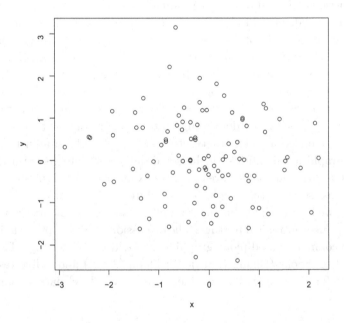

Figure 6.1:   Simple scatter plot

There are various other arguments which can be modified to change the overall presentation of the plot and even the type of plot. The argument *type* in the function refers to the type of plot, where *p* is for points, *l* is for lines, *o* is for overplotted points and lines, *b* is for points joined by lines, *s* for stair steps, *h* for histogram, *n* for no points or lines. See the help file for details on other arguments.

```
args(plot.default)

# function (x, y = NULL, type = "p", xlim = NULL, ylim = NULL,
#     log = "", main = NULL, sub = NULL, xlab = NULL, ylab = NULL,
#     ann = par("ann"), axes = TRUE, frame.plot = axes, panel.
first = NULL,
#     panel.last = NULL, asp = NA, ...)
# NULL
```

The following example uses the argument **main** in the **plot** function to include a title on the plot along with axis titles using the arguments **xlab** and **ylab**.

```
# figure-6.2
plot(x, y, main = "Figure-6.2", xlab = "Normal X", ylab = "Normal Y")
```

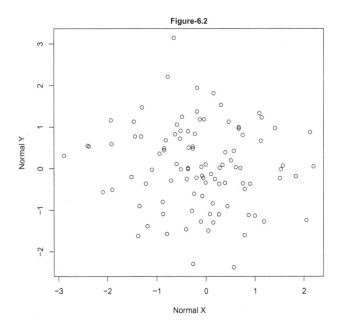

Figure 6.2: Simple scatter plot with title

In the above two examples, the plot function is used to plot basic scatter plots. We can also use the plot function to plot line plots which is useful to graph trends, time series data like stock prices, etc. The following example demonstrates how to create a line plot using Microsoft prices given in the data file **data_fin.RData**.

```
# change the working directory to the folder containing
# data_fin.csv or provide the full path with the
# filename
load("data_fin.RData")
# column names
colnames(FinData)

#  [1] "Date"  "DJI"    "AXP"   "MMM"    "ATT"   "BA"
#  [7] "CAT"   "CISCO"  "DD"    "XOM"    "GE"    "GS"
# [13] "HD"    "IBM"    "INTC"  "JNJ"    "JPM"   "MRK"
# [19] "MCD"   "MSFT"   "NKE"

# plot a line plot for Dow Jones stock index prices (figure-6.3)
plot(FinData$MSFT, type = "l", main = "Microsoft Prices",
    ylab = "Prices")
```

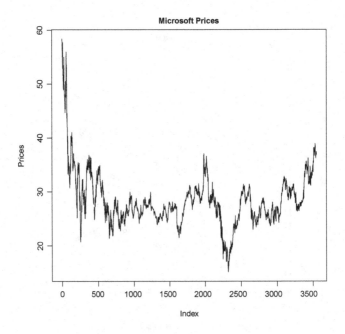

Figure 6.3:   Line chart

We can also use the $x$-axis data argument in the plot above to plot the
dates associated with the prices. As mentioned earlier, R also has low level
plot functions which are used to augment the plots created by the high level
plot function. `lines` and `points` are two such functions which can be used
to add another price series to the plot. The following example adds dates
to the $x$-axis of the plot followed by adding the stock prices using the low
level function `lines` for JP Morgan to the same plot in gray colour.

```
# figure-6.4
plot(x = FinData$Date, y = FinData$MSFT, type = "l",
main = "Stock Prices",
    ylab = "Prices", xlab = "Time")
lines(x = FinData$Date, y = FinData$JPM, col = "gray")
```

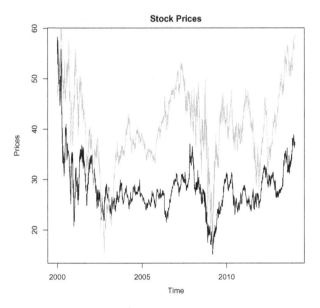

Figure 6.4:   Using low level plot functions

It is also possible to plot both lines and symbols with type $=$ "b", vertical lines with type $=$ "h", and steps with type $=$ "s".

Plot is a high level generic graphic function which depends on the class
of the first argument (usually the data object). For example, if the first
argument is of the class zoo which is a time series[2] object, the `plot` function

---

[2]We will discuss time series data manipulation in the chapter on econometrics.

will call `plot.zoo` from the R package *zoo*. This time series plot can be a
single time series line plot or multiple time series stacked plot.

```
library(zoo)
# convert data to class zoo
FinData.ts = zoo(FinData[, 2:5], order.by = FinData$Date)
# plot multiple stacked plot (figure-6.5)
plot(FinData.ts, col = gray.colors(4))
```

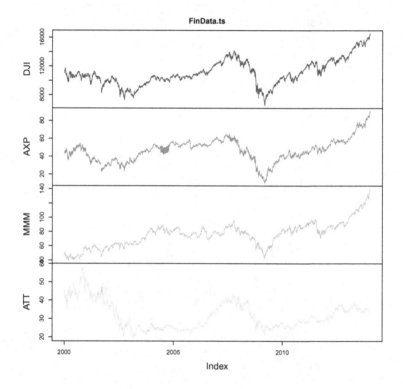

Figure 6.5:   Time series plot

There are other high level graphics functions which can be used to create
other graphs like histograms, function plots, quantile–quantile plots, bar
plots, etc. We have already discussed histograms (`hist`), function plots
(`curve`) and quantile–quantile plots (`qqplot`) in Chapter 5.

The function `barplot` creates bar graphs in R. There are various arguments available to customise bar graphs generated from `barplot` as shown
below.

```
# ## Default S3 method:
# barplot(height, width = 1, space = NULL, names.arg = NULL,
#     legend.text = NULL, beside = FALSE, horiz = FALSE,
#     density = NULL,
#     angle = 45, col = NULL, border = par("fg"), main = NULL,
#     sub = NULL, xlab = NULL, ylab = NULL, xlim = NULL, ylim = NULL,
#     xpd = TRUE, log = "", axes = TRUE, axisnames = TRUE,
#     cex.axis = par("cex.axis"), cex.names = par("cex.axis"),
#     inside = TRUE, plot = TRUE, axis.lty = 0, offset = 0,
#     add = FALSE, args.legend = NULL, ...)
```

The main data argument in this function is **height** which can be a vector or a matrix of values describing the bars which make up the plot. If **height** is a matrix, the bar graph can be a stacked graph or a juxtaposed graph with **besides = TRUE**. In the following example, we introduce a new dataset *GDP_Yearly.RData* which contains yearly GDP per capita from 1990 to 2013 of 11 countries and the world.

```
load("GDP_Yearly.RData")
#figure-6.6
barplot(height = GDP$Australia, names.arg
= GDP$Year, ylab = "GDP Per Capita")
```

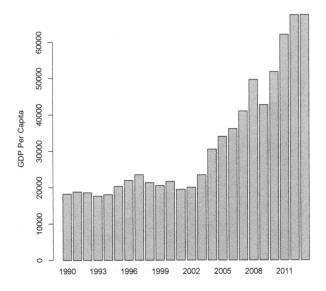

Figure 6.6: Bar graph with argument height as vector

It is also possible to create a yearly vertical stacked or yearly horizontal grouped bar plot for the GDP data. The data has to be first converted into a matrix to create stacked or grouped bar plots. The following example code creates stacked and grouped bar plots of the first five rows of the GDP data. These plots also show the legend for the years in the data, legends in the plots can be customised with various arguments (see help(legend) for more details). In this example, the argument legend specifies the names (Years) to appear in the legend and the argument args.legend specifies the position (x = "top"), alignment (horiz = TRUE) and distance from the margin (inset = −0.1).

```
# convert data to matrix
data = as.matrix(GDP[, 2:12])
# create row names
rownames(data) = GDP$Year
# plot a stacked bar plot with legend showing the years (figure-6.7)
barplot(height = data[1:5, ], beside = FALSE, col = rainbow(5),
    legend = rownames(data[1:5, ]), args.legend = list(x = "top",
      horiz = TRUE, inset = -0.1), cex.names = 0.6)
```

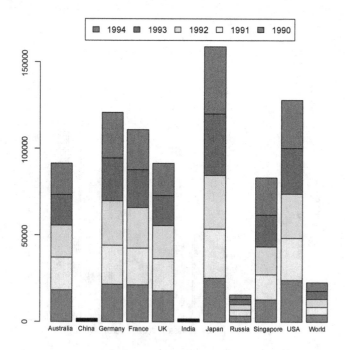

Figure 6.7:  Vertical stacked bar plot

```
# grouped barplot (figure-6.8)
barplot(data[1:5, ], beside = TRUE, col = gray.colors(5),
    legend = rownames(data[1:5, ]), args.legend = list(x = "top",
        horiz = TRUE, inset = -0.1), border = "blue", width = 0.1,
    cex.names = 0.6)
```

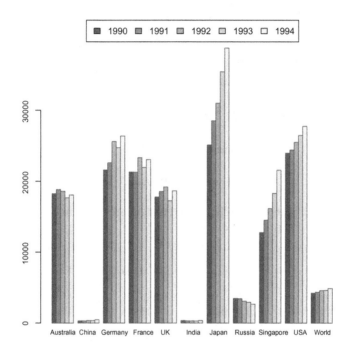

Figure 6.8: Horizontal grouped bar plot

Pie charts are an alternative to bar charts, and they can be used to show the number of observations in each category as a proportion of the total. R provides the function `pie` to create pie graphs. The following example creates a pie chart for GDP per capita in year 1990 as given in Figure 6.9. The observations for the pie chart are passed to the argument x and the labels are passed to the argument `labels`.

```
# figure-6.9
pie(x = data[1, ], labels = colnames(data))
```

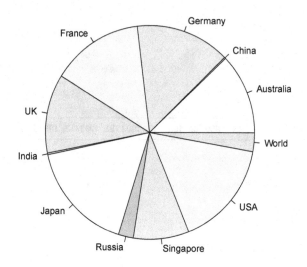

Figure 6.9:   Pie chart

Figure 6.10 plots a pie chart for Australian GDP from year 1990 to 2000.

```
# figure-6.10
pie(x = data[1:11, 1], labels = rownames(data[1:11, ]))
```

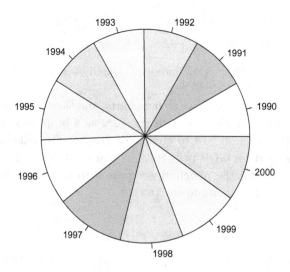

Figure 6.10:   GDP per capita (Australia)

The basic `plot` function plots a scatter plot for bivariate or univariate data. It is also possible to create a scatter plot for multivariate data using the `pairs` function. Figure 6.11 generated from the code below gives a scatter plot for first five countries in the GDP data

```
# figure-6.11
pairs(data[, 1:5])
```

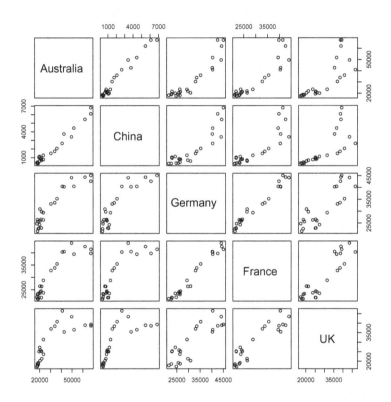

Figure 6.11: Scatter plot for GDP dataset

A subset can also be selected using formula method, for example, the following R code will generate a scatter plot with only Australia, the UK and the USA.

```
# figure-6.12
pairs(~Australia + UK + USA, data = data)
```

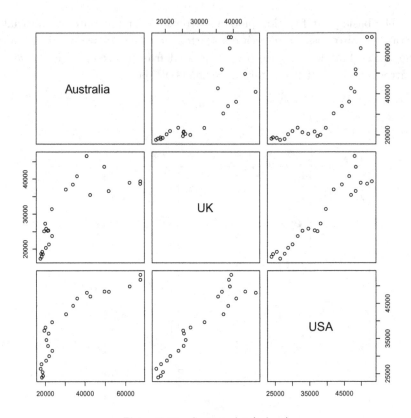

Figure 6.12: Scatter plot (subset)

R provides various other plots in addition to the ones discussed in this section. More insights into various R plots and settings can be obtained from well documented R manuals (`https://cran.r-project.org/manuals.html`) and contributed documentation (`http://cran.r-project.org/other-docs.html`).

## 6.3 Exporting Graphics

In most cases, it is required to export or save the graphs generated by R to an external file such as a pdf document file or an image file (png, jpeg, etc.). The easiest way to export graphics to a file is to use the *Export* button in RStudio (Figure 6.13) which gives options to save an image as a pdf, an image file or to copy it to the clipboard. After clicking on the required

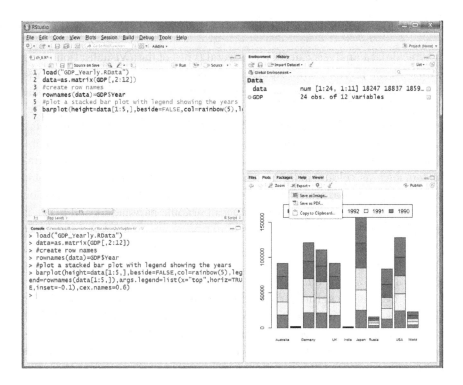

Figure 6.13:    Export graphics

export, the image can be re-sized to fit the requirements and saved to a file in a browsable location.

R also provides facilities to save the image in various file types like pdf, png, jpeg, bmp, postscript, etc. These file types have associated graphical devices with **windows** being the default device, see **help(Devices)** to see a list of available devices. To save a graph in pdf, jpeg, etc. a graphical device corresponding to the file type (e.g. jpeg for jpeg file) is first opened followed by the graph to be plotted which writes the graph on the opened device. The graph is then saved to the corresponding file once the device is switched off using **dev.off()**. The following example exports the graph created in Figure 6.12 to a png file saved in the working directory unless specified otherwise via an absolute path to the file.

```
png("Figure-6.12.png")
pairs(~Australia + UK + USA, data = data)
dev.off()
```

## 6.4 R Graphical Parameters

A typical data analysis can require several types of data visualisation along with custom presentation requirements such as different colour schemes, shapes, sizes, grouped graphs, etc. R provides a large number of graphic parameters which can be used to control all these different custom requirements. These parameters can be set individually for each graph using arguments within the function used to plot a graph or globally for all plots. The **par** function facilitates access and modification of a large list of parameters such as colour, margin, number of rows and columns on a graphic device, etc. (see **help(par)** for a list of such parameters). A modification to **par** always changes the global values of graphic parameters and hence it is a good practice to first store the default parameters in a separate object (variable) which can be later used to restore default graphic parameters. As there are numerous parameters which can be adjusted, we will discuss a few for demonstration.

The default background colour for R graphs is white (transparent) but sometimes a different background colour is desired. The background colour can be changed using the **bg** parameter in **par** function. The following example changes the background to "lightgray" after retrieving the available colours.

```
# first save the default parameters
par.old = par()
# see available colors (only top 6 shown)
head(colors())

# [1] "white"        "aliceblue"     "antiquewhite"
# [4] "antiquewhite1" "antiquewhite2" "antiquewhite3"

# change background to lightgray
par(bg = "lightgray")
# plot the bargraph (figure-6.14)
barplot(height = data[1:5, ], beside = FALSE, col = rainbow(5),
    legend = rownames(data[1:5, ]), args.legend = list(x = "top",
        horiz = TRUE, inset = -0.1), cex.names = 0.6)
```

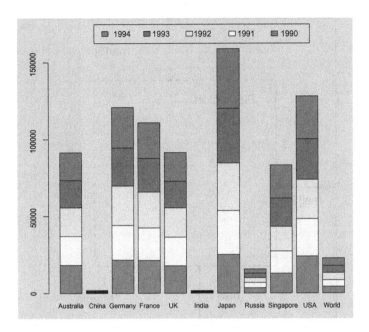

Figure 6.14: Horizontal grouped bar plot with lightgray background

```
# set parameters to default
par(par.old)
```

Occasionally, in R, default margins may not be a perfect fit for the plot in hand, for example, if custom plot or axes titles have to be added. R provides various margin parameters to tweak inner and outer margins of a graphical device. The plot region in R can be viewed as a figure surrounded by margins as shown in Figure 6.15.

These margins can be altered using **mai** or **mar** parameters with first setting the margins in inches and second in unit of text lines. Setting one of these will adjust the other accordingly. The following example changes the margins to $c(5, 4, 7, 2)$ from the default of $c(5, 4, 4, 2) + 0.1$ to accommodate a title on top of the figure.[3]

```
# first save the default parameters
par.old = par()
```

---

[3]Compare the figure from the code below with the Figure 6.14 to recognise the extra space on top of the figure added by additional margin lines.

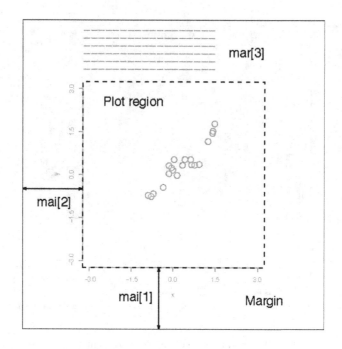

Figure 6.15: Margins in R graphs

```
# change the margins
par(mar = c(5, 4, 7, 2))
# plot the bargraph
barplot(height = data[1:5, ], beside = FALSE, col = rainbow(5),
    legend = rownames(data[1:5, ]), args.legend = list(x = "top",
        horiz = TRUE, inset = -0.1), cex.names = 0.6)
title("Bar Plot \n(with custom margins)")
# set parameters to default
par(par.old)
```

Along with altering the margins of a figure, R facilitates creation of multiple plots on one graphic device in a grid formation. A multiple plot grid can be created by altering `mfrow` or `mfcol` parameter which specifies the number of rows and columns in a grid. The following example produces a grid of four of the earlier plots in one single plot.

```
# figure-6.16 first saves the default parameters
par.old = par()
# create a 2X2 grid
par(mfrow = c(2, 2))
```

```
# scatterplot
plot(x, y, xlab = "Normal X", ylab = "Normal Y")
# time series plot
plot(FinData.ts[, 1])
# bar plot
barplot(height = GDP$Australia, names.arg = GDP$Year,
ylab = "GDP Per Capita (Australia)")
# pie chart
pie(x = data[1:11, 1], labels = rownames(data[1:11, ]))
# set parameters to default
par(par.old)
```

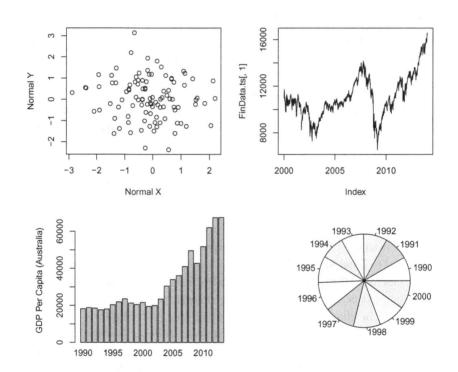

Figure 6.16:   Multiple plots in a grid

## 6.5   Introduction to ggplot2

Although R provides various in built graphical procedures, it also has
very powerful contributed packages for better data visualisation. *ggplot2*
(Wickham, 2009) is an R package which provides a large variety of plotting

functionality to enable better and highly customisable graphs. These functions in *ggplot2* are based on the *grammar of graphics* (Wickham, 2010) which is a more formal and structured way to plotting. *ggplot2* produces graphs in layers, i.e. a typical plot will start with an initial layer of showing the raw data followed by adding more layers for annotations and other customisations like statistical summaries, etc., which enables structured data visualisation. We will now discuss how to replicate the graphs in the previous sections using *ggoplot2*, for a list of various possible graphs, customisation settings and procedures see http://www.ggplot2.org.

### 6.5.1   Getting started with qplot

The quickest way to make a plot with *ggplot2* is using the function qplot. qplot stands for *quick plot* and makes it easy to produce plots which may often require several lines of codes using base R graphics system. qplot is particularly useful for beginners as they are just getting used to the plot function from the base package also the data arguments in qplot are same as in the plot function (see help(qplot) for other arguments to the function). For example, Figure 6.17 replicates the scatter plot (Figure 6.1).

```
# load the library
library(ggplot2)
# simple scatterplot using qplot (figure-6.17)
qplot(x, y)
```

Similar to the base plot function qplot also have arguments, *xlab*, *ylab* and *main* to label axes and title your plot. For example, Figure 6.18 shows a line plot of DJIA prices given in FinData dataset plotted using qplot. The argument *geom*, which stands for geometric objects drawn to represent data has to be changed to *"line"* create this line plot. Similarly there is an option to plot histograms using the argument *geom = "histogram"*. qplot can also automatically detect the required *geom* depending if only *x* is supplied (histogram) or both *x* and *y* are supplied (scatter plot).

```
# line plot using qplot (figure-6.18)
qplot(x = FinData$Date, y = FinData$DJI, geom = "line",
    xlab = "Dates", ylab = "Prices", main = "DJIA Price Timeseries")
```

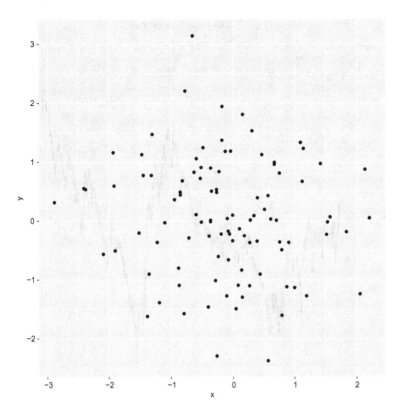

Figure 6.17:   Scatter plot using qplot

## 6.5.2   Layered graphics using ggplot

The qplot function is just sufficient for creating various plots with better presentation compared to base R plots but the true capabilities of ggplot2 are realised by the function ggplot which involves creating graphs in layers. Layering allows for additional data elements to be added to a plot which can come from a single or different dataset. In general, there are five components to a layer, viz., the data, a set of aesthetic mappings (colour, shape and size), geometric objects (geoms), statistical transformation and position adjustment. We will not discuss these elements in detail but focus on the use of ggplot function with various examples. It is important to note that ggplot function requires the data in *"long"* format and hence it is required to first transform the dataset to *"long"* from *"wide"* format as in ggplot2, groups are identified by rows, not by columns. The data used

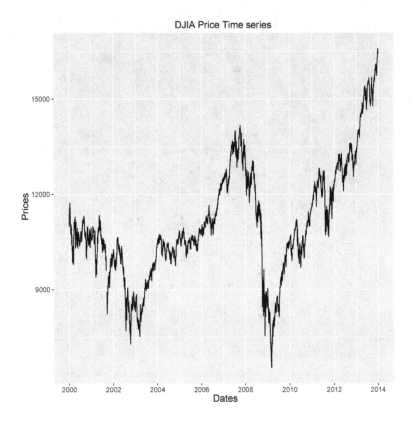

Figure 6.18:   Line plot with labels using qplot

for the examples henceforth will be in long format with a discussion on how to convert wide format to long data format in Section 6.6.

ggplot function creates the foundation of a layered plot, it does not produce a plot itself but sets its necessary aesthetic mapping. This is much like qplot where we map variables to axes from the corresponding data. Unlike qplot, ggplot base layers should be assigned to a variable so that it is easier to add layers to it. The following example first imports the GDP dataset in long format before using ggplot to create the basic aesthetics for a plot with *Country* on $x$-axis, *GDP* on $y$-axis and the colour fill automatically assigned according to the categorical variable Year.[4]

---

[4]It is also possible to fill the bars with custom colour by specifying the colour in the fill argument.

```
# Read 'long' format data
load("GDP_1.RData")
# data snapshot
head(GDP_1)

#   Year   Country      GDP          ●
# 1 1990 Australia 18247.39
# 2 1991 Australia 18837.19
# 3 1992 Australia 18599.00
# 4 1993 Australia 17658.08
# 5 1994 Australia 18080.70
# 6 1995 Australia 20375.30

# creating the aesthetics using ggplot
p1 = ggplot(GDP_1, aes(Country, GDP, fill = Year))
```

A plot can be created by adding another layer to *p1*, this second layer should generally define the geom for the plot. For example, adding **geom_bar** will create a bar plot.

```
# figure-6.19
p1 + geom_bar(stat = "identity")
```

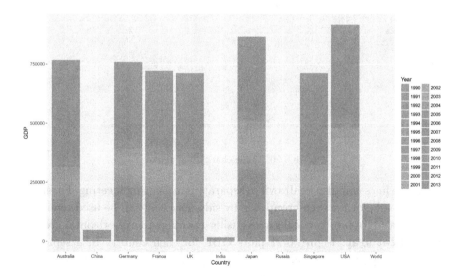

Figure 6.19:   Bar chart using ggplot function

To draw a line chart using `ggplot`, `geom_line()` is used in the second layer as shown in Figure 6.20. As our Country variable is a factor, we will also have to tell ggplot to group the data accordingly using *group = Country*. Additionally, we also use *linetype = Country* to plot each country with a different line type.

```
# change the aesthetics to show time on X-axis and GDP
# values on Y-axis, the line colour and line type
# assigned according to the country (figure-6.20)
p2 = ggplot(GDP_1, aes(Year, GDP, colour = Country, group = Country,
    linetype = Country))
p2 + geom_line()
```

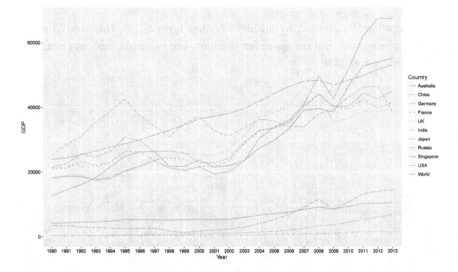

Figure 6.20:   Line chart using ggplot

These lines can also be drawn in separate panels using faceting. Faceting creates a subplot for each group side by side. Faceting can be used to either to split the data into vertical groups using `facet_grid` or horizontal groups using `facet_wrap`. Figure 6.21 plots GDP for each country in a separate subplot using grid faceting.[5]

```
# change the aesthetics to show time on X-axis and GDP
# values on Y-axis, the line colour and line type
```

---

[5]Try `facet_wrap` to plot horizontal groups.

```
# assigned according to the country (figure-6.21)
p2 = ggplot(GDP_1, aes(Year, GDP, colour = Country, group = Country,
    linetype = Country))
p2 + geom_line() + facet_grid(Country ~ .)
```

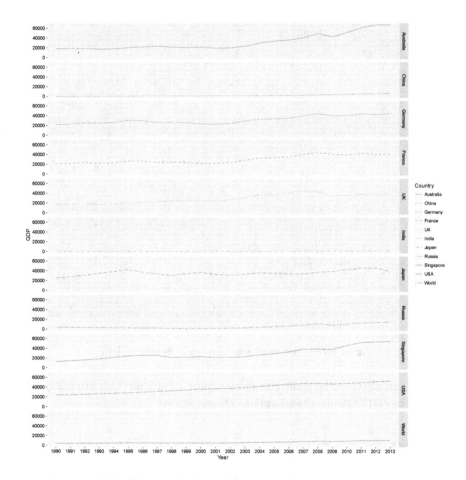

Figure 6.21:    Faceting in ggplot (line chart)

A subset from the dataset can also be used to plot just a single variable (country in this case) as shown in Figure 6.22. Specifying *group* = 1 in the aesthetics draws a single line connecting all the points.

```
# subset the dataset to Country==Australia
# the colour can be any custom colour (figure-6.22)
p2 = ggplot(subset(GDP_1, Country == "Australia"), aes(Year,
```

```
  GDP, group = 1))
p2 + geom_line(colour = 2)
```

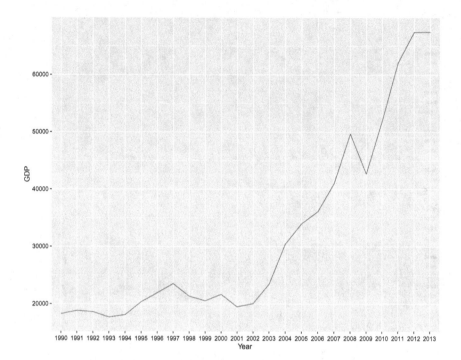

Figure 6.22:   Line chart using ggplot (Australian GDP)

We can also use the same subset to create a bar chart (Figure 6.23) for Australian GDP using **geom_bar()** as shown below:

```
# figure-6.23
p2 + geom_bar(stat = "identity")
```

Figure 6.22 plots a timeline for Australian GDP but it lacks axes annotations which are usually required for a well-informed graph. ggplot facilitates various text annotations using the same layer structure. xlab and ylab functions are used to label the axes, **ggtitle** function can be used for the graph title. Figure 6.24 re-plots Figure 6.22 with axes labels and a main title.

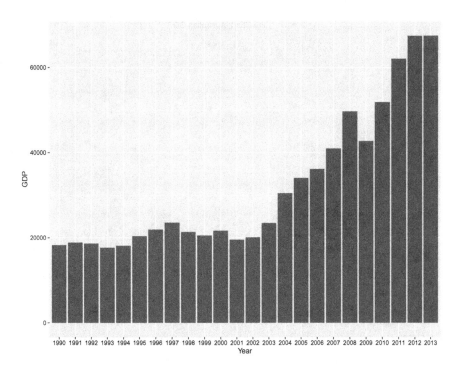

Figure 6.23: Bar chart using ggplot for Australian GDP

```
# subset the dataset to Country==Australia
# the colour can be any custom colour (figure-6.24)
p2 = ggplot(subset(GDP_1, Country == "Australia"), aes(Year,
    GDP, group = 1))
p2 + geom_line(colour = 2) + xlab("Years") + ylab("GDP") +
    ggtitle("Line Chart-Australian GDP")
```

The *ggplot2* package provides a wide library of different plots types along with highly flexible customisation capabilities for data visualisation. We will confine our discussion on *ggplot2* to this introduction as there are specialised texts available for an elaborate discussion. We will now discuss how to transform the data from wide to long format to before it can be used with *ggplot2*.

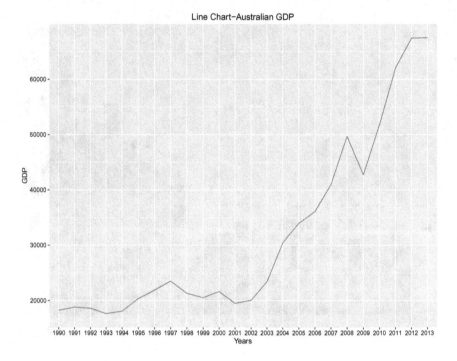

Figure 6.24:   Labelled line chart using ggplot (Australian GDP)

## 6.6  Transforming Data from Wide to Long Format

Most datasets in finance and economics are in wide format with groups identified by columns but in *ggplot2*, specially for `ggplot` function datasets have to be in long format where the groups are defined by rows not by columns. This difference in datatype is evident in the two GDP data objects used in *ggplot2* examples in Section 6.5. The dataset `GDP_Yearly.RData` was in wide format and the dataset `GDP_l.RData` was in long format.

```
# GDP_Yearly- wide format
head(GDP)

#   Year Australia    China  Germany    France       UK
# 1 1990  18247.39 314.4310 21583.84 21300.80 17805.25
# 2 1991  18837.19 329.7491 22603.62 21268.23 18571.36
# 3 1992  18599.00 362.8081 25604.73 23330.26 19211.86
# 4 1993  17658.08 373.8003 24735.62 21944.03 17270.12
# 5 1994  18080.70 469.2128 26375.85 23059.23 18664.39
# 6 1995  20375.30 604.2283 30887.87 26403.11 20349.96
```

```
#      India     Japan   Russia Singapore      USA
# 1 375.8908 25123.63 3485.112  12766.19 23954.52
# 2 310.0838 28540.77 3427.318  14504.52 24404.99
# 3 324.4951 31013.65 3095.087  16144.33 25492.96
# 4 308.5348 35451.30 2929.303  18302.37 26464.78
# 5 354.8549 38814.89 2663.457  21578.14 27776.43
# 6 383.5509 42522.07 2669.946  24937.31 28781.95
#       World
# 1 4220.646
# 2 4357.310
# 3 4591.093
# 4 4604.253
# 5 4882.079
# 6 5323.422

# GDP_1-long format
head(GDP_1)

#   Year   Country      GDP
# 1 1990 Australia 18247.39
# 2 1991 Australia 18837.19
# 3 1992 Australia 18599.00
# 4 1993 Australia 17658.08
# 5 1994 Australia 18080.70
# 6 1995 Australia 20375.30
```

This data transformation from wide to long format is not straight forward as it requires replicating column name (identifying the group) several times to match the number of observation and then inserting it into rows. Luckily the *reshape2* package in R provides a really easy to use function melt to transform wide format to long format.[6] There are three important arguments to the melt function; data for the dataframe which has to be converted, id.vars to identify the variables that measurement takes place on (Year or timeline in the GDP dataset) and measure.vars which represent the measurement (countries in the GDP dataset). The following code demonstrates how to transform the GDP dataset from wide to long format.[7]

```
# Wide to long transformation
library(reshape2)
GDP_Long = melt(data = GDP, id.vars = "Year",
variable.name = "Country",
```

---

[6] *reshape2* also provides the cast() function to reverse this process.
[7] Also see help(melt.data.frame) for more details.

```
   value.name = "GDP")
# variable.name specifies column name for variable
# (country) value.name specifies column name for
# measurement (GDP)
head(GDP_Long)

#   Year  Country      GDP
# 1 1990 Australia 18247.39
# 2 1991 Australia 18837.19
# 3 1992 Australia 18599.00
# 4 1993 Australia 17658.08
# 5 1994 Australia 18080.70
# 6 1995 Australia 20375.30
```

## 6.7   Summary

In this chapter, we introduced some of the graphics capabilities from the powerful graphical capabilities provided by R. We also introduced *ggplot2*, which is a powerful graphics package on the grammar of graphics and capable of generating high level data visualisation. The next chapter will start our discussion on statistical modelling using R with regression analysis.

Chapter 7

# Regression Analysis-I

## 7.1 Introduction

Regression analysis is one of the most widely used tools in quantitative research which is used to analyse the relationship between variables. One or more variables are considered to be explanatory variables, and the other is considered to be the dependent variable. In general, linear regression is used to predict a continuous dependent variable (regressand) from a number of independent variables (regressors) assuming that the relationship between the dependent and independent variables is linear.

We will discuss two linear regression techniques, viz., Ordinary Least Squares (OLS) and Quantile Regression (QR) in this part-I of our discussion on regression analysis using R. We will first introduce the functions available for these regression tools followed by a case study which will demonstrate how to use multiple regression analysis in empirical research. There are various statistics texts available with extensive discussion of regression analysis. As the focus of this book is on empirical implementation, this chapter provides a brief discussion of these regression techniques. The chapter will primarily focus on the implementation of these regression techniques using functions in R and associated packages.

## 7.2 OLS

Linear Regression is a basic approach for predicting the behaviour of a dependent variable based on one or more independent variables. The regression model with only one independent variable is called a simple linear regression and the model with more than one independent variable is known as multiple linear regression. If we have a dependent (or response) variable $Y$ which is related to a predictor variables $X_i$. The simple regression model is given by

$$Y = \alpha + \beta X_i + \epsilon_i, \tag{7.1}$$

where the error term $\epsilon_i$ are assumed to be *i.i.d.* and independent of $X_i$. This model describes $Y$ lying on a straight line with the slope of the line $\beta$, also called the regression coefficient and the intercept of the line $\alpha$. Here, $Y$ and $X$ are assumed to have a bivariate normal distribution. These three parameters can be estimated using the method of Ordinary Least Squares (OLS). The basic optimisation model minimises the sum of squared residuals

$$Sum_{\text{Res}} = \sum_i (Y_i - (\alpha + \beta X_i))^2. \qquad (7.2)$$

R has the function `lm` (linear model) for linear regression. The main arguments to the function `lm` are a formula and the data. `lm` takes the defining model input as a formula,[1] which is from a *formula* class. For a dependent variable $y$ and independent variable $x$, the formula will be $y \sim x$. The operator $\sim$ is basic in the formation for such models which indicates "described by". If we have more than one independent variable, the model can be written as $y \sim x_1 + x_2$. See `help(formula)` for more details. The following demonstrates the use of `lm`, we use the data file *ch7_data1.csv*, the return series data used in Chapter 5.

```
# change the working directory to the folder
# containing ch7_data1.csv or provide the full path
# with the filename
ch7_data1 = read.csv("ch7_data1.csv")   #import data
# convert dates to R date class
ch7_data1$Date = as.Date(ch7_data1$Date)
```

The above data file contains percentage logarithmic returns for the Dow Jones Industrial Average (DJIA) index and another 10 stocks traded in the DJIA. In financial asset pricing, stock returns are found to be dependent on market returns. The 'market model' regression can be represented as the following regression.

$$R_i = \alpha + \beta_i R_M + \epsilon. \qquad (7.3)$$

The following example estimates an OLS regression coefficient for DJIA and GE

```
lreg1 = lm(formula = GE ~ DJI, data = ch7_data1)
lreg1
```

---

[1] A `formula` object is also used in other statistical function like `glm`, `nls`, `rq`, etc.

```
#
# Call:
# lm(formula = GE ~ DJI, data = ch7_data1)
#
# Coefficients:
# (Intercept)          DJI
#    -0.03024      1.25757
```

The result in the above example is an lm object which can be used with extractor functions like **summary** to provide more information.

summary(lreg1)

```
#
# Call:
# lm(formula = GE ~ DJI, data = ch7_data1)
#
# Residuals:
#      Min        1Q    Median        3Q       Max
# -15.5376   -0.5606   -0.0256    0.5633   14.2294
#
# Coefficients:
#                Estimate Std. Error t value Pr(>|t|)
# (Intercept) -0.03024    0.02294   -1.318    0.188
# DJI          1.25757    0.01870   67.239   <2e-16
#
# (Intercept)
# DJI             ***
# ---
# Signif. codes:
# 0 '***' 0.001 '**' 0.01 '*' 0.05 '.' 0.1 ' ' 1
#
# Residual standard error: 1.361 on 3520 degrees of freedom
# Multiple R-squared:  0.5622,   Adjusted R-squared:  0.5621
# F-statistic:  4521 on 1 and 3520 DF,  p-value: < 2.2e-16
```

We get more information about the regression model using **summary**. For instance under "Coefficients", it produces the regression coefficient and the intercept along with accompanying standard errors, $t$ tests, and $p$-values. The $R^2$ and adjusted-$R^2$ for the regression model are also generated along with the F-Statistics for the hypothesis that the regression coefficients are zero.

There are other generic functions which can be used to get more information from **lreg1** and similar regression objects. Table 7.1 gives a list of some such functions.

Table 7.1:   List of generic functions to extract more information

| Generic function | Use |
| --- | --- |
| summary() | Returns summary of the fitted models |
| coef() | Estimated model parameters |
| resid() | The model residuals |
| fitted() | The fitted values of the model |
| deviance() | The residual sum of squares |
| anova() | An ANOVA table |
| predict() | Returns predictions |
| plot() | Used for creating plots |

The following example shows how to create plots for the lreg1 object.

```
# we first set the graphical parameter as the plot
# function for lm object creates 4 plots
par(mfrow = c(2, 2))
plot(lreg1) # figure-7.1
```

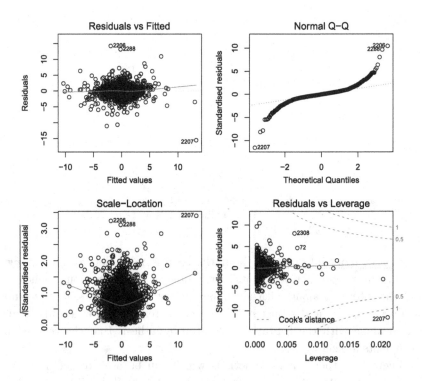

Figure 7.1:   Linear regression diagnostic plots

The upper left plot in Figure 7.1 shows the residual errors plotted versus their fitted values. The plot in the upper right is a standard Q–Q plot, which should suggest that the residual errors are normally distributed. This does not seem to be the case in the current example which can be accounted to the non-normal distribution of the returns series. The scale-location plot in the lower left shows the square root of the standardised residuals as a function of the fitted values. The fourth plot in the lower right shows each points leverage, a measure of the point importance in determining the regression result. The contour lines on the plot are for the Cook's distance, which is another measure of the importance of each observation to the regression. Smaller distances mean that removing the observation has little effect on the regression results. Only one plot out of the four can also be generated using the argument *which* in the function `plot`.

Sometimes, it is just required to plot the regression line over the data points. The following example demonstrates how to add the regression line using the function `abline`

```
# first plot GE and DJI returns
plot(ch7_data1$DJI, ch7_data1$GE)
# add the regression line (figure-7.2)
abline(lreg1, col = "blue")
```

The function `lm` can handle multiple linear regression along with simple linear regression. We will discuss multiple linear regression in the case study following QR.

## 7.3 QR

Simple linear regression or OLS provides inference about the conditional distribution of the dependent variable assuming a multivariate normal distribution between the dependent and independent variables. OLS loses its effectiveness when we try to go beyond the mean value or towards the extremes of a data set (see Allen *et al.*, 2009; Allen, Singh and Powell, 2011; Barnes and Hughes, 2002). Specifically in the case of an unknown or arbitrary joint distribution $(X, Y)$, OLS does not provide all the necessary information required to quantify the conditional distribution of the dependent variable.

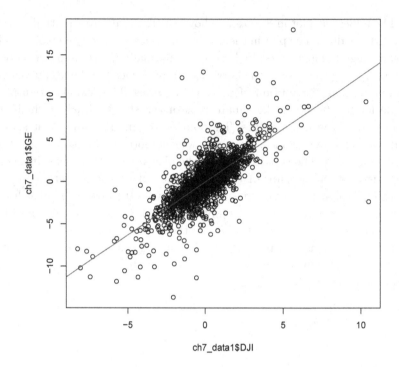

Figure 7.2:   Regression fit

Quantiles refer to the generalised case of dividing a conditional distribution into parts. The technique of QR extends this idea to build models which express the quantile of conditional distribution of the response variable as a function of observed covariates.

QR is modelled as an extension of classical OLS (Koenker and Bassett Jr, 1978). In QR, the estimation of conditional mean as estimated by OLS is extended to similar estimation of an ensemble of models of various conditional quantile functions for a data distribution. In this fashion, QR can better quantify the conditional distribution of $(Y|X)$. The central special case is the median regression estimator that minimises a sum of absolute errors. The estimates of remaining conditional quantile functions are obtained by minimising an asymmetrically weighted sum of absolute errors, where weights are the function of the quantile of interest. This makes QR a robust technique even in presence of outliers. Taken together, the ensemble of estimated conditional quantile functions of $(Y|X)$ offers a much more

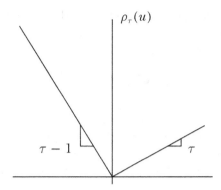

Figure 7.3:   Quantile regression $\rho$ function

complete view of the effect of covariates on the location, scale and shape of
the distribution of the response variable.

For parameter estimation in QR, quantiles as proposed by Koenker and
Bassett Jr. (1978) can be defined through an optimisation problem. To solve
an OLS regression problem, a sample mean is defined as the solution of the
problem of minimising the sum of squared residuals, in the same way the
median quantile (0.5%) in QR is defined through the problem of minimising
the sum of absolute residuals. The symmetrical piecewise linear absolute
value function assures the same number of observations above and below
the median of the distribution.

The other quantile values can be obtained by minimising a sum of asym-
metrically weighted absolute residuals (giving different weights to positive
and negative residuals). Solving

$$\min \xi \varepsilon R \sum \rho_\tau(y_i - \xi), \tag{7.4}$$

where $\rho_\tau(\bullet)$ is the tilted absolute value function as shown in Figure 7.3,
which gives the $\tau$th sample quantile with its solution. Taking the directional
derivatives of the objective function with respect to $\xi$ (from left to right)
shows that this problem yields the sample quantile as its solution.

After defining the unconditional quantiles as an optimisation problem,
it is easy to define conditional quantiles similarly. Taking the least squares
regression model as a base to proceed, for a random sample, $y_1, y_2, \ldots, y_n$,
we solve

$$\min_{\mu \varepsilon R} \sum_{i=1}^{n} (y_i - \mu)^2, \tag{7.5}$$

which gives the sample mean, an estimate of the unconditional population mean, $E(Y)$. Replacing the scalar $\mu$ by a parametric function $\mu(x, \beta)$ and then solving

$$\min_{\mu \varepsilon R^p} \sum_{i=1}^{n} (y_i - \mu(x_i, \beta))^2 \qquad (7.6)$$

gives an estimate of the conditional expectation function $E(Y|x)$.

Proceeding the same way for QR, to obtain an estimate of the conditional median function, the scalar $\xi$ in the first equation is replaced by the parametric function $\xi(x_t, \beta)$ and $\tau$ is set to $1/2$. The estimates of the other conditional quantile functions are obtained by replacing absolute values by $\rho_\tau(\bullet)$ and solving

$$\min_{\mu \varepsilon R^p} \sum \rho_\tau(y_i - \xi(x_i, \beta)). \qquad (7.7)$$

The resulting minimisation problem, when $\xi(x, \beta)$ is formulated as a linear function of parameters, and can be solved very efficiently by linear programming methods. Further insight into this robust regression technique can be obtained from Koenker (2005) or a text book introduction to QR as can be found in Alexander (2008).

### 7.3.1   Estimating QR

The *quantreg* package in R provides functions for QR. The function `rq` in the *quantreg* package calculates linear QR. Like `lm`, `rq` also takes a `formula` object as input which defines the linear QR model. The function `rq` has the following arguments

```
library(quantreg)
args(rq)

# function (formula, tau = 0.5, data, subset, weights, na.action,
#     method = "br", model = TRUE, contrasts = NULL, ...)
# NULL
```

Here, *formula* is same as in `lm` with the response or dependent variable on the left of ~ operator and the independent variables on the right. More than one independent variables are separated by + operator. The second argument *tau* specifies the quantile(s) to be estimated, it is a number strictly between 0 and 1. The data used for the regression is specified using *data* argument and if only a subset of the data is used in the fitting process, a *subset* argument is specified. See `help(rq)` for the details on the rest of the arguments. There is also a vignette for the Quantreg package (run `vignette("rq", package = quantreg)`) which demonstrates various functions in the package.

The following example estimates the same regression as previously estimated with linear regression (Equation (7.3)) but here we use QR to estimate the lower 5% quantile.

```
qreg1 = rq(formula = GE ~ DJI, tau = 0.05, data = ch7_data1)
qreg1

# Call:
# rq(formula = GE ~ DJI, tau = 0.05, data = ch7_data1)
#
# Coefficients:
# (Intercept)         DJI
#   -1.870964     1.345727
#
# Degrees of freedom: 3522 total; 3520 residual
```

Here, `qreg1` is an rq object which can be used with extractor functions as in the case of `lm` to get more information on the model. Similar to `lm`, `summary` provides more information for the QR model.

```
summary(qreg1)

#
# Call: rq(formula = GE ~ DJI, tau = 0.05, data = ch7_data1)
#
# tau: [1] 0.05
#
# Coefficients:
#              Value      Std. Error  t value
# (Intercept)  -1.87096   0.08465     -22.10273
# DJI           1.34573   0.06750      19.93545
#              Pr(>|t|)
# (Intercept)   0.00000
# DJI           0.00000
```

The QR results above show that the market return has a different effect on the stock return for the lower 5% quantile of the stock returns compared to the OLS regression. The `summary` function for QR (for the objects of class rq) facilitates more options for standard error calculations. The default method to calculate standard errors for an object of class rq is the rank method which produces confidence intervals for the estimated parameters

by inverting a rank test (Koenker, 1994). The other options available are
*iid, nid, ker* and *boot*. See `help(summary.rq)` for more details.

It is possible to calculate QR for more than one quantile using the
function `rq`. Let us calculate the same regression for five different quantiles
ranging from the lower 5% to the higher 95% quantile.

```
qreg2 = rq(formula = GE ~ DJI, tau = c(0.05, 0.25, 0.5,
    0.75, 0.95), data = ch7_data1)
summary(qreg2)

#
# Call: rq(formula = GE ~ DJI, tau = c(0.05, 0.25, 0.5, 0.75, 0.95),
#     data = ch7_data1)
#
# tau: [1] 0.05
#
# Coefficients:
#               Value      Std. Error  t value
# (Intercept)   -1.87096   0.08465     -22.10273
# DJI            1.34573   0.06750      19.93545
#               Pr(>|t|)
# (Intercept)    0.00000
# DJI            0.00000
#
# Call: rq(formula = GE ~ DJI, tau = c(0.05, 0.25, 0.5, 0.75, 0.95),
#     data = ch7_data1)
#
# tau: [1] 0.25
#
# Coefficients:
#               Value      Std. Error  t value
# (Intercept)   -0.59120   0.01890     -31.27738
# DJI            1.22905   0.01513      81.21676
#               Pr(>|t|)
# (Intercept)    0.00000
# DJI            0.00000
#
# Call: rq(formula = GE ~ DJI, tau = c(0.05, 0.25, 0.5, 0.75, 0.95),
#     data = ch7_data1)
#
# tau: [1] 0.5
#
# Coefficients:
```

```
#               Value   Std. Error  t value   Pr(>|t|)
# (Intercept)  -0.05346  0.01746    -3.06156  0.00222
# DJI           1.23050  0.01415    86.94785  0.00000
#
# Call: rq(formula = GE ~ DJI, tau = c(0.05, 0.25, 0.5, 0.75, 0.95),
#     data = ch7_data1)
#
# tau: [1] 0.75
#
# Coefficients:
#               Value   Std. Error  t value   Pr(>|t|)
# (Intercept)   0.53347  0.02094    25.47006  0.00000
# DJI           1.26014  0.01703    73.98023  0.00000
#
# Call: rq(formula = GE ~ DJI, tau = c(0.05, 0.25, 0.5, 0.75, 0.95),
#     data = ch7_data1)
#
# tau: [1] 0.95
#
# Coefficients:
#               Value   Std. Error  t value   Pr(>|t|)
# (Intercept)   1.87191  0.09464    19.77870  0.00000
# DJI           1.24831  0.07596    16.43350  0.00000
```

The summary above shows the effect of the market return on the stock returns for different quantiles of the stock returns. For more than one quantile in the QR object, a plot function can be used to plot the QR coefficients.

```
# figure-7.4
plot(qreg2)
```

These plots show that the market effect varies across the quantile of the stock return distribution. In other words, GE returns have a different relationship with DJI returns for lower and higher GE returns. The **summary** object can also be used to plot these graphs where it also plots the error bounds.

```
# figure-7.5
plot(summary(qreg2))
```

We shall now discuss multiple OLS regression and multiple QR with a case study in the next section.

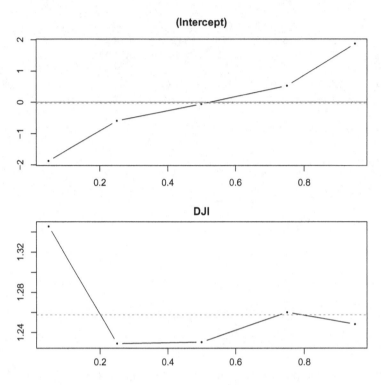

Figure 7.4:   Quantile regression coefficient plot

## 7.4   Example: Fama–French Factor Model and Multiple Regression

### 7.4.1   Introduction

The Capital Asset Pricing Model (CAPM), the Fama–French three factor model and other related Asset Pricing models are based on a linear relationship between dependent and independent variables in their specification. As we saw earlier in the chapter, these linear relationship are mostly quantified by OLS which quantifies the effect of the independent variable (risk factors in the case of asset pricing models) around the mean of the distribution.

The CAPM developed independently by Treynor (1961, 1962), Sharpe (1964), Lintner (1965) and Mossin (1966) bifurcate the risk into two components; systematic and unsystematic risk. Beta, a measure of systematic risk is defined as the dependence of asset returns on the market return (when market return is the independent factor; Equation (7.3)). These

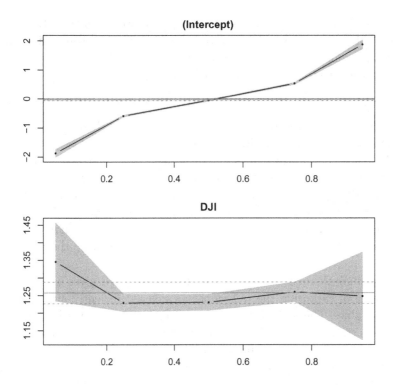

Figure 7.5: Quantile regression coefficient plot (with error bounds)

factor models propose a linear relationship between factors and asset returns, which fails to model the tails of the distribution; linear regression works around the mean or average of the distribution with an assumption of normality in the data.

Fama and French (1992, 1993) extended the basic CAPM to include size and book-to-market effects as explanatory factors in explaining the cross-section of stock returns. Small minus Big (SMB) gives the size premium which is the additional return received by investors from investing in companies having a low market capitalisation. High minus Low (HML), gives the value premium which is the return provided to investors for investing in companies having high book-to-market values.

SMB is a factor measuring "size risk", which comes from the view that small companies (companies with low market capitalisation) are expected to be relatively more sensitive to various risk factors, which is a result of their undiversified nature and their inability to absorb negative financial events. HML, on the other hand, is a factor which proposes an association of higher risk with "value" stocks (high B/M values) as compared to "growth" stocks (low B/M values). This is intuitively justified as firms or companies ought to attain a minimum size in order to enter an Initial Public Offering (IPO).

The three factor Fama–French model is written as:

$$r_A - r_F = +\beta_A(r_M - r_F) + s_A SMB + h_A HML + \alpha + e, \qquad (7.8)$$

where $s_A$ and $h_A$ capture the security's sensitivity to these two additional factors. This relationship, first emphasised by Fama and French (1992, 1993) has been confirmed in subsequent work by Fama and French and many other researchers to be quite effective across a wide range of markets and time periods. Studies of the Fama French model on international asset markets include Maroney and Protopapadakis (2002), Drew (2003), Michou, Mouselli and Stark (2007), among others. The common denominator in most of the studies is the use of OLS for evaluating the regression model.

Modelling the behaviour of factor models using QR gives us the added advantage of capturing the tail values as well as efficiently analysing the median values. The coefficients obtained from lower quantiles (5% or lower) represent the lower tail risk in the return distribution of every stock, which is of interest when it comes to efficient asset selection. Barnes and Hughes (2002) applied QR to study CAPM in their work on cross-sections of stock market returns. Chan and Lakonishok (1992) applied QR to robust measurement of size and book to market effects. Allen *et al.* (2011), apply QR to test the Fama–French factor model in the DJIA-30 stocks which focuses on the applicability of better estimates of factor based risk factors across quantiles. In this case study, we evaluate the Fama–French factor model using both OLS and QR, hence demonstrating multiple linear regression using R.

The rest of the case study is designed as follows: the data used for the case study is presented in Section 7.4.2. Section 7.4.3 evaluates the Fama–French factor model using OLS followed by QR in Section 7.4.4.

### 7.4.2 Data

The case study requires data with stock returns and returns for the three Fama–French factors. As Kenneth French provides the three factors of the model for the US market on his website,[2] these original factors are used in

---

[2] http://mba.tuck.dartmouth.edu/pages/faculty/ken.french/data_library.html.

the study of the factor model. We use the stock returns for GE traded in the DJIA stock market given in the datafile *ch7_data1.csv* from year 2007 to 2013. The case study will analyse the effect of Fama–French on GE returns using both OLS and QR.

### 7.4.2.1   *Data preprocessing*

The three factors daily data is downloaded as a text file from the Kenneth French website. This data library is updated quite frequently and provides daily factors since 01/07/1926. As we only need data from the years 2007 to 2013 and the data obtained from the web page is not in the same format as our other data file, we have to preprocess the data. The following code snippets will preprocess three factor data and stock return data and then combine it in one single file `data_cs7.csv` which will be used for the analysis. Let us start with the factor data[3] in the file *F − F_Research_Data_Factors_daily.txt*.

```
# use read.table for text file

ff_data = read.table("F-F_Research_Data_Factors_daily.txt",
    skip = 3, header = TRUE, row.names = NULL)
head(ff_data)

#   row.names Mkt.RF   SMB   HML    RF
# 1  19260701   0.10 -0.24 -0.31 0.009
# 2  19260702   0.45 -0.39 -0.20 0.009
# 3  19260706   0.17  0.26 -0.38 0.009
# 4  19260707   0.08 -0.59  0.18 0.009
# 5  19260708   0.22 -0.35  0.21 0.009
# 6  19260709  -0.72  0.41  0.68 0.009
```

Here, additional arguments 'skip' and 'row.names' are used to skip the first three rows as they contain information about the data and to avoid importing dates as row names. As there is no name assigned to the first column R assumes that it refers to row names and assigns row.names to it. Let us change this column name to "Date" using the function `colnames`.

```
# name the first column
colnames(ff_data)[1] = "Date"
head(ff_data)
```

---

[3]Note if downloading data directly from the Kenneth French website, it has to be first unzipped to get the text file.

```
#       Date Mkt.RF    SMB   HML     RF
# 1 19260701    0.10 -0.24 -0.31 0.009
# 2 19260702    0.45 -0.39 -0.20 0.009
# 3 19260706    0.17  0.26 -0.38 0.009
# 4 19260707    0.08 -0.59  0.18 0.009
# 5 19260708    0.22 -0.35  0.21 0.009
# 6 19260709   -0.72  0.41  0.68 0.009
```

The dates in *ff_data* are in a format which is not directly recognised by R to convert it into a *date* class. The following code extracts the dates from the 'Date' column using the `strptime` function before converting them to dates.

```
# convert dates in R date format
ff_data$Date = as.Date(strptime(ff_data$Date, format = "%Y%m%d"))
head(ff_data)
```

```
#          Date Mkt.RF    SMB   HML     RF
# 1 1926-07-01    0.10 -0.24 -0.31 0.009
# 2 1926-07-02    0.45 -0.39 -0.20 0.009
# 3 1926-07-06    0.17  0.26 -0.38 0.009
# 4 1926-07-07    0.08 -0.59  0.18 0.009
# 5 1926-07-08    0.22 -0.35  0.21 0.009
# 6 1926-07-09   -0.72  0.41  0.68 0.009
```

Now this data appears similar to the stock return data. Still we have to extract a subset from year 2007 to 2013 from the factor data. The same subset has to be extracted from the stock return data. We can extract this subset using conditional subsetting.

```
# create conditional subset
ff_data0713 = ff_data[ff_data$Date >= as.Date("2007-01-01") &
    ff_data$Date <= as.Date("2013-12-31"), ]
# check the subset
head(ff_data0713)
```

```
#              Date Mkt.RF    SMB   HML     RF
# 21372 2007-01-03  -0.04  0.08 -0.11 0.022
# 21373 2007-01-04   0.17  0.24 -0.65 0.022
# 21374 2007-01-05  -0.73 -0.87 -0.31 0.022
# 21375 2007-01-08   0.24 -0.07  0.04 0.022
# 21376 2007-01-09   0.00  0.26 -0.16 0.022
# 21377 2007-01-10   0.23 -0.08 -0.24 0.022
```

```
tail(ff_data0713)
```

```
#            Date Mkt.RF    SMB    HML     RF
# 23129 2013-12-24   0.34   0.10   0.14  0.000
# 23130 2013-12-26   0.44  -0.31  -0.36  0.000
# 23131 2013-12-27  -0.05  -0.05   0.30  0.000
# 23132 2013-12-30   0.00   0.03  -0.31  0.000
# 23133 2013-12-31   0.44  -0.20   0.09  0.000
# NA           <NA>    NA   <NA>   <NA>   <NA>

# remove NAs
ff_data0713 = na.omit(ff_data0713)
```

The code for conditional subsetting first converts the character dates ("2007-01-01" and "2013-12-31") to class *date* before comparing it with the Date column in *ff_data*. This is a necessary step as you can only compare variables of the same data type (or which can be internally converted to the same data type). We will now repeat the same conditional formatting for the stock return data.

```
ch7_data0713 = ch7_data1[ch7_data1$Date >= as.Date("2007-01-01") &
    ch7_data1$Date <= as.Date("2013-12-31"), ]
head(ch7_data0713)
```

```
#          Date        DJI         AXP         MMM
# 1759 2007-01-03  0.09062585  -0.51227081   0.4225629
# 1760 2007-01-04  0.04968904  -0.73162947  -0.3969021
# 1761 2007-01-05 -0.66482818  -1.32719294  -0.6822450
# 1762 2007-01-08  0.20546711   0.94260923   0.2193408
# 1763 2007-01-09 -0.05555533  -0.63865763   0.1159271
# 1764 2007-01-10  0.20596335  -0.06746501   0.2186074
#            ATT          BA         CAT        CISCO
# 1759 -2.2631800   0.3707661  -0.2775739   1.45298597
# 1760 -1.2959145   0.4029104  -0.2619517   2.59847330
# 1761 -1.5775963  -0.4253420  -1.2869341   0.03513086
# 1762 -0.4426745  -0.2358359   0.1161729   0.56042178
# 1763  0.3837643  -1.0625171   0.5458619  -0.56042178
# 1764  0.2648229   1.4328671  -0.4961148   0.73491144
#             DD         XOM          GE
# 1759  0.67519438  -3.3438169   2.02188319
# 1760 -0.69572615  -1.8934026  -0.58108985
# 1761 -1.34368947   0.7125270  -0.50458214
# 1762  0.04161465  -0.8088330  -0.02662761
# 1763  0.64282233  -0.7738052   0.00000000
# 1764 -0.24834450  -1.5376316   0.02662761
```

```
tail(ch7_data0713)
```

```
#          Date         DJI        AXP        MMM
# 3515 2013-12-23   0.451904846 0.8414878 0.05849664
# 3516 2013-12-24   0.385518618 0.4293792 0.13879253
# 3517 2013-12-26   0.745067844 0.3489226 0.94449990
# 3518 2013-12-27  -0.008920366 0.2132556 0.76358245
# 3519 2013-12-30   0.156930787 0.4474781 0.05022061
# 3520 2013-12-31   0.437533477 1.2644357 0.59355843
#              ATT          BA        CAT       CISCO
# 3515   1.13061068  -0.1977516   1.1515584 2.0609629
# 3516   0.74670077   0.3147534   1.0504879 0.5547864
# 3517   0.59906041   1.0469016   0.2636495 0.5058645
# 3518   0.05686665  -0.9957563  -0.3076587 1.0041161
# 3519   0.05683433  -0.7184255   0.0000000 1.0390877
# 3520  -0.11370098   0.4184875  -0.0660502 0.8057340
#              DD          XOM         GE
# 3515 0.3032966  -0.1724226 0.1460921
# 3516 1.7224097   0.7181541 0.7635013
# 3517 0.6558425   1.6790320 0.7936550
# 3518 0.0000000   0.6027388 0.0000000
# 3519 0.6206381  -1.1891925 0.2153626
# 3520 0.4937520   0.8833366 0.5007164
```

This gives us two datasets with the same timeline. Although not necessary for the regression, we will create a single data object for the analysis as follows

```
# first check if the dates in ff_data0713 and
# ch7_data0713 are same using setdiff
setdiff(ff_data0713$Date, ch7_data0713$Date)

# numeric(0)

# With no difference in dates we combine the two
# datasets by columns
data_cs7 = cbind(ff_data0713, ch7_data0713[11])
head(data_cs7)

#            Date Mkt.RF   SMB   HML    RF
# 21372 2007-01-03  -0.04  0.08 -0.11 0.022
# 21373 2007-01-04   0.17  0.24 -0.65 0.022
# 21374 2007-01-05  -0.73 -0.87 -0.31 0.022
# 21375 2007-01-08   0.24 -0.07  0.04 0.022
# 21376 2007-01-09   0.00  0.26 -0.16 0.022
# 21377 2007-01-10   0.23 -0.08 -0.24 0.022
#              GE
# 21372   2.02188319
```

```
# 21373  -0.58108985
# 21374  -0.50458214
# 21375  -0.02662761
# 21376   0.00000000
# 21377   0.02662761

# save the data for further analysis
write.csv(data_cs7, file = "data_cs7.csv", row.names = FALSE)
```

We will now use this dataset for evaluating OLS and QR coefficients.

### 7.4.3 OLS regression analysis of the Fama–French three factor model

We use the OLS regression to analyse the effect of the Fama–French three factor model in a multiple regression setting. We will extend our simple linear regression model with GE to include the three additional factors. As OLS assumes a normal distribution between the independent and dependent variables, the estimated coefficients quantify the relationship between the dependent and independent variables around the mean of the distribution.

```
# import the data
data_cs7.1 = read.csv("data_cs7.csv")
# create another column with GE-RF
data_cs7.1$GE.RF = data_cs7.1$GE - data_cs7.1$RF
ff_lreg = lm(GE.RF ~ Mkt.RF + SMB + HML, data = data_cs7.1)
summary(ff_lreg)

#
# Call:
# lm(formula = GE.RF ~ Mkt.RF + SMB + HML, data = data_cs7.1)
#
# Residuals:
#      Min       1Q   Median       3Q      Max
# -12.9804  -0.5133  -0.0190   0.5272  12.8772
#
# Coefficients:
#              Estimate Std. Error t value Pr(>|t|)
# (Intercept) -0.05093    0.03383  -1.505    0.132
# Mkt.RF       1.01501    0.02632  38.559   <2e-16
# SMB         -0.07648    0.05708  -1.340    0.180
# HML          0.69397    0.05912  11.739   <2e-16
#
# (Intercept)
```

```
# Mkt.RF       ***
# SMB
# HML          ***
# ---
# Signif. codes:
# 0 '***' 0.001 '**' 0.01 '*' 0.05 '.' 0.1 ' ' 1
#
# Residual standard error: 1.419 on 1758 degrees of freedom
# Multiple R-squared:  0.6031,  Adjusted R-squared:  0.6024
# F-statistic: 890.4 on 3 and 1758 DF,  p-value: < 2.2e-16
```

A plot function can be used to plot the four regression plots similar to a simple regression.

```
par(mfrow = c(2, 2))
plot(ff_lreg)    #figure-7.6
```

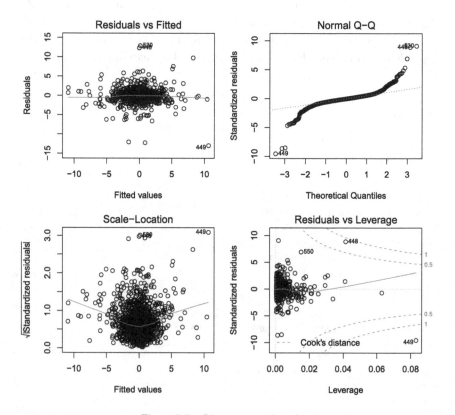

Figure 7.6:  Linear regression plots

There are packages in R which provide functions to export the summary output of a regression model in a LATEX, HTML or ASCII files. These are very useful functions to export the results in a formatted table which can then be directly imported in to a LATEX or Word document. *Stargazer* and *texreg* are two such packages, a list of more packages can be found in the *ReproducibleResearch* task view in R. The following code uses the `stargazer` function to print the OLS results in ASCII format. The same output can also be exported to a LATEX file which can be later used in a LATEX document. Table 7.2 shows the table generated by `stargazer` function in LATEX format.[4]

```
library(stargazer)
stargazer(ff_lreg, summary = TRUE, title = "OLS Results",
    type = "text", no.space = TRUE)

#
# OLS Results
# =================================================
#                         Dependent variable:
#                        ----------------------------
#                                  GE.RF
# -------------------------------------------------
# Mkt.RF                          1.015***
#                                 (0.026)
# SMB                             -0.076
#                                 (0.057)
# HML                             0.694***
#                                 (0.059)
# Constant                        -0.051
#                                 (0.034)
# -------------------------------------------------
# Observations                     1,762
# R2                               0.603
# Adjusted R2                      0.602
# Residual Std. Error      1.419 (df = 1758)
# F Statistic          890.376*** (df = 3; 1758)
# =================================================
# Note:                  *p<0.1; **p<0.05; ***p<0.01
```

---

[4]The default format for stargazer function is LATEX, an additional 'out' argument with the file name and path has to be given to export the tex formatted table.

Table 7.2:  OLS results

| | Dependent variable |
|---|---|
| | Stock return |
| Mkt.RF | 1.015*** |
| | (0.026) |
| SMB | −0.076 |
| | (0.057) |
| HML | 0.694*** |
| | (0.059) |
| Constant | −0.051 |
| | (0.034) |
| Observations | 1,762 |
| $R^2$ | 0.603 |
| Adjusted $R^2$ | 0.602 |
| Residual Std. Error | 1.419 (df = 1758) |
| F Statistic | 890.376*** (df = 3; 1758) |

Note: *$p < 0.1$; **$p < 0.05$; ***$p < 0.01$

The results in Table 7.2 show that GE stock returns are significantly dependent on the Market returns and the HML factor. SMB factor does not have a significant effect on GE returns around the mean of the distribution. We shall now check these results using QR.

### 7.4.4    Quantile analysis of the Fama–French three factor model

The analysis of the Fama–French three factor model across the distribution using QR is performed as the second part of our analysis. The approach here is to examine the effect of the three Fama–French factors of size and value premium on GE returns. OLS and QR based factor values are used to evaluate if these two factors are statistically significant and, if so, whether they vary across quantiles. This part of the analysis quantifies the relationship between Fama–French three factors and GE stock returns across five quantile (5%, 25%, 50%, 75%, 95%) levels covering the lower and upper quantiles.

OLS models the relationship between the dependent and independent variables around the mean of the distribution and it assumes normal distribution between the variables. If the variables do not have normal distribution, then it is highly likely that OLS cannot provide a solution for the whole distribution in the regression setting. Quantile–Quantile plot is an easy way to visualise the distributions. The following generates Q–Q plots for GE returns and three Fama–French factors. The plots demonstrate that none of the variables have normal distributions. We can also evaluate the distribution using descriptive statistics (Chapter 5) and using the test for normality.

```
# generate Q-Q Plots (figure-7.7)
par(mfrow = c(2, 2))
# GE.RF
qqnorm(data_cs7.1$GE.RF, main = "GE")
qqline(data_cs7.1$GE.RF, col = 2)
# Mkt.RF
qqnorm(data_cs7.1$Mkt.RF, main = "Mkt.RF")
qqline(data_cs7.1$Mkt.RF, col = 2)
# SMB
qqnorm(data_cs7.1$SMB, main = "SMB")
qqline(data_cs7.1$SMB, col = 2)
# HML
qqnorm(data_cs7.1$HML, main = "HML")
qqline(data_cs7.1$HML, col = 2)
```

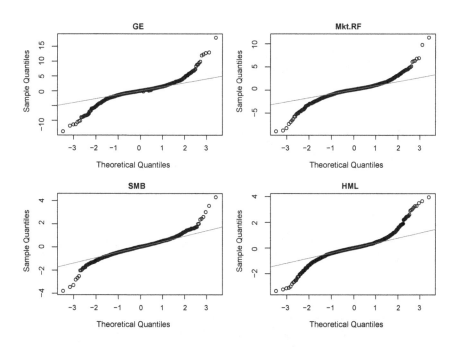

Figure 7.7: Q–Q plots

As the return distributions do not follow normality, QR can provide more insights into the relationship between the dependent and the independent variables. The following code is used to calculate QR for the five quantile levels.

```
# load the package
library(quantreg)
# create a vector of quantiles
tau = c(0.05, 0.25, 0.5, 0.75, 0.95)
ff_qreg = rq(GE.RF ~ Mkt.RF + SMB + HML, tau = tau, data = data_cs7.1)
ff_qreg

# Call:
# rq(formula = GE.RF ~ Mkt.RF + SMB + HML, tau = tau,
data = data_cs7.1)
#
# Coefficients:
#               tau= 0.05   tau= 0.25   tau= 0.50
# (Intercept) -1.7806250  -0.5536252  -0.05469323
# Mkt.RF       1.0460026   1.0735679   1.08404676
# SMB         -0.1974679  -0.1678772  -0.23712294
# HML          0.7803288   0.5216191   0.42422185
#               tau= 0.75   tau= 0.95
# (Intercept)  0.4635983   1.7043778
# Mkt.RF       1.0824108   1.0350481
# SMB         -0.2855506  -0.2147389
# HML          0.4684618   0.5030699
#
# Degrees of freedom: 1762 total; 1758 residual
```

More information is provided by invoking summary on the QR object.

```
sum.ff_qreg = summary(ff_qreg)
sum.ff_qreg

#
# Call: rq(formula = GE.RF ~ Mkt.RF + SMB + HML, tau = tau,
  data = data_cs7.1)
#
# tau: [1] 0.05
#
# Coefficients:
#               Value     Std. Error  t value
# (Intercept)  -1.78063   0.10763    -16.54391
# Mkt.RF        1.04600   0.07913     13.21940
```

```
# SMB          -0.19747   0.13194   -1.49667
# HML           0.78033   0.16745    4.65996
#              Pr(>|t|)
# (Intercept)   0.00000
# Mkt.RF        0.00000
# SMB           0.13466
# HML           0.00000
#
# Call: rq(formula = GE.RF ~ Mkt.RF + SMB + HML, tau = tau,
  data = data_cs7.1)
#
# tau: [1] 0.25
#
# Coefficients:
#              Value     Std. Error  t value
# (Intercept)  -0.55363  0.02611    -21.20407
# Mkt.RF        1.07357  0.01626     66.03240
# SMB          -0.16788  0.04281     -3.92118
# HML           0.52162  0.04029     12.94796
#              Pr(>|t|)
# (Intercept)   0.00000
# Mkt.RF        0.00000
# SMB           0.00009
# HML           0.00000
#
# Call: rq(formula = GE.RF ~ Mkt.RF + SMB + HML, tau = tau,
  data = data_cs7.1)
#
# tau: [1] 0.5
#
# Coefficients:
#              Value     Std. Error  t value    Pr(>|t|)
# (Intercept)  -0.05469  0.02207     -2.47791   0.01331
# Mkt.RF        1.08405  0.01759     61.62823   0.00000
# SMB          -0.23712  0.03726     -6.36378   0.00000
# HML           0.42422  0.03600     11.78383   0.00000
#
# Call: rq(formula = GE.RF ~ Mkt.RF + SMB + HML, tau = tau,
  data = data_cs7.1)
#
# tau: [1] 0.75
#
# Coefficients:
#              Value     Std. Error  t value    Pr(>|t|)
# (Intercept)   0.46360  0.02808     16.50849   0.00000
```

```
# Mkt.RF        1.08241  0.01928   56.14138  0.00000
# SMB          -0.28555  0.04142   -6.89451  0.00000
# HML           0.46846  0.04577   10.23504  0.00000
#
# Call: rq(formula = GE.RF ~ Mkt.RF + SMB + HML, tau = tau,
  data = data_cs7.1)
#
# tau: [1] 0.95
#
# Coefficients:
#              Value    Std. Error  t value  Pr(>|t|)
# (Intercept)  1.70438  0.12254     13.90908  0.00000
# Mkt.RF       1.03505  0.09093     11.38240  0.00000
# SMB         -0.21474  0.19347     -1.10996  0.26717
# HML          0.50307  0.20922      2.40454  0.01630
```

*Quantreg* provides a `latex` function to export this summary object to
a LaTeX table. Table 7.3 is generated using the following function. Note
the `latex` function will create a *table.tex* file which can be imported in
the LaTeX documents. Table 7.3 shows the regression coefficients with their
standard errors.

```
latex(sum.ff_qreg, file = "table3")
```

Table 7.3:   QR results

| Covariates | 0.05 | 0.25 | 0.50 | 0.75 | 0.95 |
|---|---|---|---|---|---|
| (Intercept) | −1.781 | −0.554 | −0.055 | 0.464 | 1.704 |
|  | (0.108) | (0.026) | (0.022) | (0.028) | (0.123) |
| Mkt.RF | 1.046 | 1.074 | 1.084 | 1.082 | 1.035 |
|  | (0.079) | (0.016) | (0.018) | (0.019) | (0.091) |
| SMB | −0.197 | −0.168 | −0.237 | −0.286 | −0.215 |
|  | (0.132) | (0.043) | (0.037) | (0.041) | (0.193) |
| HML | 0.780 | 0.522 | 0.424 | 0.468 | 0.503 |
|  | (0.167) | (0.040) | (0.036) | (0.046) | (0.209) |

The results in Table 7.3 show that the Fama–French factors have varied
effect across the return distribution of GE returns. It is interesting to note
that SMB has significant effect for 0.25%, 0.5% and 0.75% when using QR
as compared to not being significant in OLS. We can also visualise these
different effects by plotting the QR summary object.

```
# figure-7.8
plot(sum.ff_qreg)
```

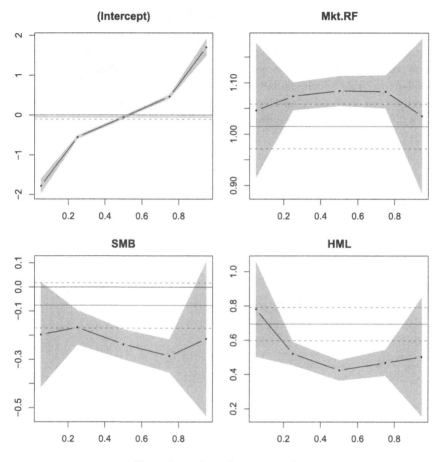

Figure 7.8: Quantile estimate plots

It can be of interest for a research question to check if the effect across quantiles are statistically different. Quantreg provides an **anova** function which can be used to check for this significant difference across quantiles. We leave this as an exercise for the reader.

## 7.5 Summary

In this chapter, we began our discussion on Regression Analysis using R. The chapter introduced linear regression and two different methods to calculate linear regression, viz., OLS and QR. The chapter demonstrated the use of R to evaluate OLS regression and QR in a simple and multiple regression setting. The case study in the chapter evaluated the Fama–French factor model using OLS and QR. The major results from the case study show that the factor effects can vary across the distribution of the dependent variable which can be modelled more efficiently using QR. We will continue our discussion on Regression Analysis in the next chapter where we will discuss Panel Regression.

Chapter 8

# Regression Analysis-II

## 8.1 Introduction

In the last chapter, we began our discussion on Linear Regression Analysis and covered Ordinary Least Square (OLS) regression and Quantile Regression. The examples discussed till now have used either cross-sectional or time series data with continuous variables, but there are cases in economics and finance where the data can be in a panel format, where individuals are observed at several points in time or cross-sectional with a binary (a factor variable with two levels) response variable. This chapter will focus on two regression techniques which are for panel data and data with two level factor variables, viz., Panel Regression and Logistic Regression. We will introduce panel data and the most widely used the Panel Regression models in the plm package followed by a brief introduction to Logistic Regression. This chapter will also discuss an example using panel regression models.

## 8.2 Panel Data Linear Regression

The last two decades have seen a considerable rise in interest in panel data econometrics. The growing popularity of panel data studies in economics and finance can be accounted for by the ease of collecting and maintaining panel data and the advantages which panel data offers over simple time series or cross-sectional data. For example, the use of panel data can improve the accuracy of parameter estimates as it provides more information, more variability, less collinearity among variables with more degrees of freedom. See Baltagi (2005), Hsiao (2001) and Matyas and Sevestre (1996) for a discussion of the major advantages of panel data estimation.

Panel data or longitudinal data is a data structure which contains individuals/variables (e.g. persons, firms, countries, cities, etc.) observed at several points in time (days, months, years, quarters, etc.). The dataset GDP_1.RData introduced in Chapter 6 is an example of panel data where each country's GDP is recorded over several years in time. A typical panel data in economics can be the national economic statistics data published by the government, for example the Australian Bureau of Statistics in Australia publishes economic indicators for various time frequencies like monthly, quarterly, yearly.

```
# Panel data
load("GDP_1.RData")
# data snapshot
GDP_1[c(1:5, 25:29, 241:245), ]

#      Year  Country      GDP
# 1    1990 Australia 18247.3946
# 2    1991 Australia 18837.1893
# 3    1992 Australia 18599.0012
# 4    1993 Australia 17658.0794
# 5    1994 Australia 18080.6975
# 25   1990    China   314.4310
# 26   1991    China   329.7491
# 27   1992    China   362.8081
# 28   1993    China   373.8003
# 29   1994    China   469.2128
# 241  1990    World  4220.6460
# 242  1991    World  4357.3096
# 243  1992    World  4591.0928
# 244  1993    World  4604.2533
# 245  1994    World  4882.0794
```

The GDP data here has a balanced panel structure, where all the variables have values for all points in time.

Here, we will discuss the two basic panel regression models viz., the *Fixed Effects Model* and the *Random Effects Model* for balanced panel data. In basic econometric terms, fixed and random effect estimators models account for cross-sectional variations in the intercept. A standard *fixed effects model* can be written as

$$y_{it} = X_{it}\beta + c_i + \varepsilon_{it}, \qquad (8.1)$$

where $y_{it}$ represents the dependent variable across $i$ entities for time $t$. $X_{it}$ is a K-dimensional row vector of time-varying explanatory variables minus the constant, $\beta$ is a vector of parameters, $c_i$ gives the individual specific effect and $\varepsilon_{it}$ is the idiosyncratic error term. In general, the analysis is done to investigate $\beta$ and not individual $c_i$. The individual specific effect in the fixed effect model is correlated with the explanatory variables (independent variables) whereas in the *random effects model* this individual specific effect is uncorrelated with the explanatory variable $X_{it}$. We will not provide any further econometric or estimation details for these models but focus on the application using R. For an extensive discussion, see econometrics textbooks including Baltagi (2005), Wooldridge (2010), Greene (2008) and Stock and Watson (2012). The package *plm* (Croissant and Millo, 2008) provides methods for calculating these models, which will be used in illustrative code. We will use the very popular Grunfeld panel dataset. Grunfeld (1958) available in the *plm* package for demonstration which are based on similar examples in Croissant and Millo (2008) and Kleiber and Zeileis (2008). We will later use these two models in an example exercise where we will explore the relationship between economic growth and unemployment using panel regression.

### 8.2.1 Fixed and random effects using the *plm* package

Panel data models in the *plm* package can be used to estimate fixed and/or random effects of entity or time or both. The model argument in plm is set to within for fixed effects model and random for a random effects model. The current version of the *plm* package is capable of working with data structures with individual (identifier variable for country, person, etc.) and time in the first two columns without any data preprocessing. The data can be converted to the required panel format using pdata.frame function, which transforms a regular data frame object into a panel data structure. index is the main argument in the pdata.frame function which specifies the panel structure, i.e. columns with individual and time variables.

```
# Grunfeld Data representation as per pdata.frame function
library(plm)
data(Grunfeld)   #load data
head(Grunfeld)   #data snapshot

#   firm year   inv  value capital
# 1    1 1935 317.6 3078.5     2.8
# 2    1 1936 391.8 4661.7    52.6
# 3    1 1937 410.6 5387.1   156.9
# 4    1 1938 257.7 2792.2   209.2
# 5    1 1939 330.8 4313.2   203.4
# 6    1 1940 461.2 4643.9   207.2

pdata1 = pdata.frame(Grunfeld, index = c("firm", "year"))
head(pdata1)
```

```
#          firm year   inv   value capital
# 1-1935      1 1935 317.6 3078.5     2.8
# 1-1936      1 1936 391.8 4661.7    52.6
# 1-1937      1 1937 410.6 5387.1   156.9
# 1-1938      1 1938 257.7 2792.2   209.2
# 1-1939      1 1939 330.8 4313.2   203.4
# 1-1940      1 1940 461.2 4643.9   207.2
```

As seen in the example above, pdata.frame creates a column with row-
names formed by combining index values which then defines the panel structure. In most cases, this data transformation can be done internally by plm
function as per the index argument. The panel data structure is similar
to the so-called long format whereas in finance, we typically have data in
wide format. Wide data can be transformed to long format using the melt
function in the *reshape2* package as shown in Chapter 6.

The plm function has four major arguments, viz., formula, effect,
model and data. Here, the panel data regression model is specified using
a formula similar to simple linear regression using lm, data specifies the
dataset to use, model specify the regression method (fixed effect, random
effect, etc.) to use and effect specifies if the model has individual-specific
effect, time effects or both. Although we have discussed only individual
specific effects in fixed effects and random effects model in fact all these
models can be estimated using plm.

#### 8.2.1.1  Fixed effect estimation

We can use the *plm* package to replicate the following investment equation
as considered by Grunfeld (1958).

$$I_{it} = \alpha + \beta_1 F_{it} + \beta_2 C_{it} + \varepsilon_{it}. \tag{8.2}$$

The model in Equation (8.2) is a one-way panel regression model which at-
tempts to quantify the dependence of real gross investment $(I_{it})$ on the real
value of the company $(F_{it})$ and real value of its capital stock $(C_{it})$. Grunfeld
(1958) studied 10 large manufacturing firms from the United States over
20 years (1935–1954). A fixed effect estimation can be obtained with the
following code

```
# using plm with 'within' estimator for fixed effects
fe1 = plm(inv ~ value + capital, data = pdata1, model = "within")
# the output can be summarised with summary
summary(fe1)
```

```
# Oneway (individual) effect Within Model
#
# Call:
# plm(formula = inv ~ value + capital, data = pdata1,
model = "within")
#
# Balanced Panel: n=10, T=20, N=200
#
# Residuals :
#     Min.  1st Qu.  Median  3rd Qu.     Max.
# -184.000  -17.600   0.563   19.200  251.000
#
# Coefficients :
#          Estimate Std. Error t-value  Pr(>|t|)
# value   0.110124   0.011857  9.2879 < 2.2e-16 ***
# capital 0.310065   0.017355 17.8666 < 2.2e-16 ***
# ---
# Signif. codes:
# 0 '***' 0.001 '**' 0.01 '*' 0.05 '.' 0.1 ' ' 1
#
# Total Sum of Squares:     2244400
# Residual Sum of Squares: 523480
# R-Squared:        0.76676
# Adj. R-Squared: 0.72075
# F-statistic: 309.014 on 2 and 188 DF, p-value: < 2.22e-16
```

The summary output for the `fe1` fitted model object gives details about the fitted object and the data including the data structure, estimated coefficient along with significance tests for the estimated coefficients. The individual fixed effects can be obtained using the function `fixef`, a summary method is also available as shown next

```
# individual fixed effects
fixef(fe1)

#          1          2          3          4          5
#  -70.296717 101.905814 -235.571841  -27.809295 -114.616813
#          6          7          8          9         10
#  -23.161295  -66.553474  -57.545657  -87.222272   -6.567844

# summary
summary(fixef(fe1))

#     Estimate Std. Error t-value  Pr(>|t|)
# 1   -70.2967    49.7080 -1.4142   0.15730
```

```
# 2     101.9058      24.9383   4.0863 4.383e-05 ***
# 3    -235.5718      24.4316  -9.6421 < 2.2e-16 ***
# 4     -27.8093      14.0778  -1.9754   0.04822 *
# 5    -114.6168      14.1654  -8.0913 6.661e-16 ***
# 6     -23.1613      12.6687  -1.8282   0.06752 .
# 7     -66.5535      12.8430  -5.1821 2.194e-07 ***
# 8     -57.5457      13.9931  -4.1124 3.915e-05 ***
# 9     -87.2223      12.8919  -6.7657 1.327e-11 ***
# 10     -6.5678      11.8269  -0.5553   0.57867
# ---
# Signif. codes:
# 0 '***' 0.001 '**' 0.01 '*' 0.05 '.' 0.1 ' ' 1
```

### 8.2.1.2    *Random effect estimation*

A random effect model of Equation (8.2) can be estimated by setting the
`model` argument to "`random`". There are five different methods available
for estimation of the variance component (Baltagi (2005) provides further details on these estimation methods) which can be selected using the
`random.method` argument. The following output is obtained using the default Swamy–Arora (Swamy and Arora, 1972) random method which shows
significant regression coefficients as with the fixed effects model.

```
# random effect model
re1 = plm(inv ~ value + capital, data = pdata1, model = "random")
# summary
summary(re1)

# Oneway (individual) effect Random Effect Model
#    (Swamy-Arora's transformation)
#
# Call:
# plm(formula = inv ~ value + capital, data = pdata1,
model = "random")
#
# Balanced Panel: n=10, T=20, N=200
#
# Effects:
#                    var std.dev share
# idiosyncratic 2784.46   52.77 0.282
# individual    7089.80   84.20 0.718
# theta:  0.8612
#
# Residuals :
```

```
#    Min. 1st Qu.  Median 3rd Qu.    Max.
# -178.00  -19.70    4.69   19.50  253.00
#
# Coefficients :
#              Estimate Std. Error t-value Pr(>|t|)
# (Intercept) -57.834415  28.898935 -2.0013  0.04674 *
# value         0.109781   0.010493 10.4627  < 2e-16 ***
# capital       0.308113   0.017180 17.9339  < 2e-16 ***
# ---
# Signif. codes:
# 0 '***' 0.001 '**' 0.01 '*' 0.05 '.' 0.1 ' ' 1
#
# Total Sum of Squares:    2381400
# Residual Sum of Squares: 548900
# R-Squared:       0.7695
# Adj. R-Squared: 0.75796
# F-statistic: 328.837 on 2 and 197 DF, p-value: < 2.22e-16
```

### 8.2.1.3  *Panel or OLS*

In simple terms, the fixed effects model is calculated using dummy variables (for each unobserved variable) in the OLS regression estimation. This leads to a natural test to verify if a fixed effect model is actually any better than the simple OLS. The function **pFtest** in the *plm* package can be used to test a fitted fixed effect model against a fitted OLS model to check which regression is a better choice. An OLS model is estimated using the "**pooling**" model in **plm** function as illustrated below:

```
# Simple OLS (without the intercept) using pooling
ols1 = plm(inv ~ value + capital - 1, data = pdata1, model =
"pooling")
# summary of results
summary(ols1)

# Oneway (individual) effect Pooling Model
#
# Call:
# plm(formula = inv ~ value + capital - 1, data = pdata1,
model = "pooling")
#
# Balanced Panel: n=10, T=20, N=200
#
# Residuals :
```

```
#     Min. 1st Qu.  Median    Mean 3rd Qu.    Max.
# -270.00  -51.30  -23.70  -21.00   -4.51  477.00
#
# Coefficients :
#           Estimate Std. Error t-value  Pr(>|t|)
# value   0.1076384  0.0058256 18.4769 < 2.2e-16 ***
# capital 0.1832062  0.0242750  7.5471 1.587e-12 ***
# ---
# Signif. codes:
# 0 '***' 0.001 '**' 0.01 '*' 0.05 '.' 0.1 ' ' 1
#
# Total Sum of Squares:    9359900
# Residual Sum of Squares: 1935600
# R-Squared:       0.8113
# Adj. R-Squared: 0.80319
# F-statistic: 379.734 on 2 and 198 DF, p-value: < 2.22e-16
```

The above OLS model can now be tested against the fixed effect model to check for the best fit. In the following, the *p*-value <0.05 from the test indicates that the fixed effect model should be used.

```
# Testing for the better model, null: OLS is a better
pFtest(fe1, ols1)

#
#   F test for individual effects
#
# data:  inv ~ value + capital
# F = 50.714, df1 = 10, df2 = 188, p-value < 2.2e-16
# alternative hypothesis: significant effects
```

Similar to the fixed effect and OLS comparison one can also check if the random effects are needed using one of the available Lagrange multiplier tests (Breusch and Pagan (1980) test here) test in **plmtest** function as illustrated below

```
# plmtest using the Breuch-Pagan method
plmtest(ols1, type = c("bp"))

#
#   Lagrange Multiplier Test - (Breusch-Pagan)
#
# data:  inv ~ value + capital - 1
# chisq = 727.84, df = 1, p-value < 2.2e-16
# alternative hypothesis: significant effects
```

A $p$-value $<0.05$ in the above test indicates that the Random Effect model is required. Therefore, we should check for fixed and random effects.

### 8.2.1.4   Fixed effect or random effect

As seen in previous examples, both fixed effect and random effect models on the Grunfeld data resulted in statistically significant coefficients. These results warrant a method to decide which model to use with a particular problem. The Hausman test (Hausman, 1978) is the standard approach to test for model specification which can be computed using the `phtest` function in the *plm* package. The following tests the model specification for the fixed effect and random effect models for the Grunfeld data.

```
# phtest using the fitted models in fe1 and re1
phtest(fe1, re1)

#
#   Hausman Test
#
# data:  inv ~ value + capital
# chisq = 2.3304, df = 2, p-value = 0.3119
# alternative hypothesis: one model is inconsistent
```

A $p$-value $<0.05$ suggests that the fixed effect model is appropriate so in this case the random effect model should be used.

There are various other tests/diagnostics available which can be used to test for individual or time effects, serial correlation, cross-sectional dependence, etc. We will not discuss these further but leave them for the advanced learners.

## 8.3   Logistic Regression

The two regression models, OLS and Panel Regression discussed till now have focussed on continuous numerical response variables. There are many research problems, such as credit scoring in finance (e.g. Altman and Sabato (2007); Hauser and Booth (2011); Ohlson (1980); Zaghdoudi (2013), among others), gender or level of income based studies in economics (e.g. Agnello *et al.* (2015); Alonso-Rodríguez (2001); Bazen *et al.* (1994); Sanders and Scanlon (2000), among others), etc., however we are interested in regression modelling but with categorical or factor variables with two levels (a dichotomous variable). For example, a gender based study with response variable as *Male/Female* or a general study with a series of *yes/no* responses.

Logistic Regression which belongs to the class of generalised linear models (glms) can be used to model data with a dichotomous response variable. The major difference between logistic regression and simple linear regression with a continuous response variable is that logistic regression models the conditional probability of the response variable rather than its value. A logit link function, defined as $\text{logit}\, p = \log[p/(1-p)]$, is used to transform the output of a linear regression to be suitable for probabilities. A linear model for these transformed probabilities can be setup as

$$\text{logit}\, p = \beta_0 + \beta_1 x_1 + \beta_2 x_2 + \cdots + \beta_k x_x. \tag{8.3}$$

We will not go further into the mathematical details of the model but rather keep the discussion to computation of logistic regressions (see Faraway (2005); Hilbe (2009); Sheather (2009), among others for further details). R provides the function `glm` for modelling generalised linear models including logistic regression models. We use the Australian Credit Approval data available at `https://archive.ics.uci.edu/ml/datasets/Statlog+%28Australian+Credit+Approval%29`. The dataset is available in the `aus_credit.RData` file.

```
# load data
load("aus_credit.RData")
# data snapshot
head(aus_credit)
```

```
#    A1     A2      A3 A4 A5 A6     A7 A8 A9 A10 A11 A12 A13  A14
# 1  1 22.08 11.460  2  4  4 1.585  0  0   0   1   2 100 1213
# 2  0 22.67  7.000  2  8  4 0.165  0  0   0   0   2 160    1
# 3  0 29.58  1.750  1  4  4 1.250  0  0   0   1   2 280    1
# 4  0 21.67 11.500  1  5  3 0.000  1  1  11   1   2   0    1
# 5  1 20.17  8.170  2  6  4 1.960  1  1  14   0   2  60  159
# 6  0 15.83  0.585  2  8  8 1.500  1  1   2   0   2 100    1
#    A15
# 1    0
# 2    0
# 3    0
# 4    1
# 5    1
# 6    1
```

As the labels in the dataset have been changed to symbols for confidentiality, we will refer them by their symbols where "A1" is the dichotomous response variable (1 = application accepted, 0 = application rejected) and "A2" to "A15" are predictor variables. Although the dataset has a mixed set of numerical (six) and categorical (eight) attributes, will use only the numerical attributes (continuous) as the independent (predictor) variables. According to the data description, A2, A3, A7, A10, A13 and A14 are continuous which gives us total seven variables in the subsample.

```
# take a subsample with all continuous variables
aus_credit_sub = aus_credit[, c(1, 2, 3, 7, 10, 13, 14)]
```

We can now use the `glm` function to predict A1 using the other predictor variables. `glm` is similar to the `lm` function which we used to calculate OLS, both these functions take the model as model formulas and have extractor functions like `summary`, `plot`, etc. We need to specify the glm model which needs to be computed using the `family` argument with `family = binomial("logit")` for logistic regression (see `help(glm)` for more details) as illustrated below:

```
m_logit = glm(A1 ~ A2 + A3 + A7 + A10 + A13 + A14, data
= aus_credit_sub, family = binomial("logit"))
summary(m_logit)

#
# Call:
# glm(formula = A1 ~ A2 + A3 + A7 + A10 + A13 + A14,
family = binomial("logit"),
#     data = aus_credit_sub)
#
# Deviance Residuals:
#     Min      1Q   Median      3Q      Max
# -2.2322  -1.4182   0.8258   0.9107   1.3423
#
# Coefficients:
#               Estimate Std. Error z value Pr(>|z|)
# (Intercept)  5.084e-01  2.663e-01   1.909  0.05624 .
# A2           1.372e-03  7.512e-03   0.183  0.85508
# A3          -1.947e-02  1.794e-02  -1.085  0.27781
# A7           8.853e-02  3.233e-02   2.738  0.00617 **
# A10         -1.334e-02  1.815e-02  -0.735  0.46245
# A13          7.610e-04  5.403e-04   1.409  0.15897
# A14          1.020e-07  1.598e-05   0.006  0.99491
# ---
# Signif. codes:
# 0 '***' 0.001 '**' 0.01 '*' 0.05 '.' 0.1 ' ' 1
```

```
#
# (Dispersion parameter for binomial family taken to be 1)
#
#     Null deviance: 866.88   on 689   degrees of freedom
# Residual deviance: 854.47   on 683   degrees of freedom
# AIC: 868.47
#
# Number of Fisher Scoring iterations: 4
```

The coefficient section from the model summary indicates that A7 is the only statistically significant factor with $p$-value $< 0.05$ which indicates that the probability of credit card application acceptance increases with an increase in A7. Ruppert (2011) provides a rather comprehensive take on credit card application example using the CreditCard data in the *AER* package which includes methods to find a better model using stepAIC model in the *MASS* package.

## 8.4  Example: Economic Growth and Unemployment — A Panel Analysis

Economic growth and unemployment are two of the important economic indicators for any economy in the world. Economic policies around the globe are targeted towards increasing economic growth and reducing unemployment. First suggested by Okun in 1962 (Okun, 1962), it is widely accepted that there is an inverse relationship between economic growth and unemployment. Özel, Sezgin and Topkaya (2013), Huang and Yeh (2013), Ball, Jalles and Loungani (2015), among others are a few recent examples which support the relationship though with varied strength.

In this brief example, we analyse the relationship between Unemployment and GDP growth in a sample of seven countries viz., Australia, New Zealand, Japan, Singapore, China, the UK and the USA using panel data regression.

We will now discuss the data and methodology followed by pre-data processing and model estimation using the panel regression model.

### 8.4.1  Data and methodology

We analyse the relationship of the unemployment rate defined as percentage of total labour force with the GDP Growth rate. We use yearly data from 1991 to 2013 for our seven sample countries. The Unemployment data and

GDP rate are obtained from World Bank's World Development Indicator database.[1] The following simple linear panel regression model is tested to analyse the relationship.

$$U_{it} = \alpha + \beta_1 G_{it} + \varepsilon_{it}, \tag{8.4}$$

where $U_{it}$ is the unemployment rate of a country and $G_{it}$ is its GDP growth. It is important to note that although here the analysis is done in a simple one factor model, this analysis can include several other independent variables like *Productivity, Interest Rates, Inflation, etc.*

### 8.4.2  Data preprocessing

The data used in this example is though freely available and is in easy to use CSV or Excel formats but is not in long format (panel structure). The data in the csv file Unemp_GDP.csv is obtained after filtering the data file obtained from the World Bank dataset for the *GDP growth (annual %)* and *Unemployment, total (% of total labour force)* (*modelled ILO estimate*) for year 1991–2013. These indicator names are changed to GDP_G and UNEMP for brevity. The data in the file has the following structure

```
# load the data file
d1_ex1 = read.csv("Unemp_GDP.csv", header = TRUE, check.names = FALSE)
head(d1_ex1)
```

```
#   Country Indicator  1991    1992    1993    1994   1995   1996
# 1    AUS    GDP_G   -0.426  0.404   4.020   4.040  3.88   3.95
# 2    AUS    UNEMP    9.600 10.800  10.900  9.700  8.50   8.50
# 3    CHN    GDP_G    9.180 14.200  14.000 13.100 10.90  10.00
# 4    CHN    UNEMP    4.900  4.400   4.300  4.300  4.50   4.60
# 5    JPN    GDP_G    3.320  0.819   0.171  0.867  1.94   2.61
# 6    JPN    UNEMP    2.100  2.200   2.500  2.900  3.20   3.40
#     1997   1998   1999  2000   2001 2002   2003   2004   2005   2006
# 1   3.94   4.43   5.000 3.87   1.930 3.86   3.08   4.16   3.22   2.99
# 2   8.50   7.70   6.900 6.30   6.800 6.40   5.90   5.40   5.00   4.80
# 3   9.30   7.83   7.620 8.43   8.300 9.08  10.00  10.10  11.30  12.70
# 4   4.60   4.70   4.700 4.50   4.500 4.40   4.30   4.30   4.10   4.00
# 5   1.60  -2.00  -0.199 2.26   0.355 0.29   1.69   2.36   1.30   1.69
# 6   3.40   4.10   4.700 4.80   5.000 5.40   5.20   4.70   4.40   4.10
#     2007   2008   2009  2010   2011 2012 2013
# 1   3.76   3.70   1.73  1.96   2.320 3.73 2.51
```

[1] Available at http://data.worldbank.org/data-catalog/world-development-ind-icators

```
# 2  4.40   4.20   5.60   5.20   5.100 5.20 5.70
# 3 14.20   9.63   9.21  10.40   9.300 7.65 7.67
# 4  3.80   4.40   4.40   4.20   4.300 4.50 4.60
# 5  2.19  -1.04  -5.53   4.65  -0.453 1.75 1.61
# 6  3.90   4.00   5.00   5.00   4.500 4.30 4.00
```

We have used an additional argument, check.names in the read.csv function as the column names in the dataset includes years in numbers and they can be misinterpreted when read as factors. This additional argument forces R to read them as it is. The dataset as shown above has a somewhat mixed structure where the Country and Indicator fields are in a long format but the time field (Year) is in wide format. The panel structure required for the analysis should have the years in one column, countries in other column and the three factors in three separate columns. We can transform this data to required format by first converting the data to long format with years as a time variable and countries as individual variables. This transformation can be achieved using the melt function from the *reshape* package as illustrated below

```
# convert separate time columns to one Year variable column
library(reshape2)
d2_ex1 = melt(data = d1_ex1, id.vars = c("Indicator", "Country"),
    measure.vars = c(3:25), variable.name = "Year")
# data snapshot
head(d2_ex1)

#   Indicator Country Year   value
# 1     GDP_G     AUS 1991  -0.426
# 2     UNEMP     AUS 1991   9.600
# 3     GDP_G     CHN 1991   9.180
# 4     UNEMP     CHN 1991   4.900
# 5     GDP_G     JPN 1991   3.320
# 6     UNEMP     JPN 1991   2.100
```

The above transformation results in time and country values in one column but it still has the Indicators (two factors for the analysis) in one column which should be in two different columns. The "Indicator" column has the two variables in long format which can be converted to wide format (separated in two columns) using the **dcast** function (from the *data.table* package) as shown below

```
# coverting long to wide
data_panel = dcast(d2_ex1, Year + Country ~ Indicator,
fun.aggregate = NULL)
# data snapshot
head(data_panel)

#   Year Country  GDP_G UNEMP
# 1 1991     AUS -0.426   9.6
# 2 1991     CHN  9.180   4.9
# 3 1991     JPN  3.320   2.1
# 4 1991     NZL -1.610  10.6
# 5 1991     SGP  6.690   3.3
# 6 1991      UK -1.240   8.5
```

As shown above, the structure of the wide format data is provided in the form of a casting formula. The arguments on the left of the formula refer to the ID variables and the arguments on the right refer to the measured variables. We can now convert the data to a panel data frame using **pdata.frame** from the *plm* package and save it in Rdata format.

```
# convert to panel data frame
data_panel = pdata.frame(data_panel, index = c("Country", "Year"))
# save data to RData format
## save(data_panel, file = "Ex_Ch8.RData")
head(data_panel)  # a plm generated panel data frame structure

#            Year Country  GDP_G UNEMP
# AUS-1991 1991     AUS -0.426   9.6
# AUS-1992 1992     AUS  0.404  10.8
# AUS-1993 1993     AUS  4.020  10.9
# AUS-1994 1994     AUS  4.040   9.7
# AUS-1995 1995     AUS  3.880   8.5
# AUS-1996 1996     AUS  3.950   8.5
```

### 8.4.3  Linear panel regression analysis

We can start the analysis with some data visualisation. The panel data obtained from data preprocessing can easily be used with the **ggplot** function in the *ggplot2* package as discussed in Chapter 6. The following illustration generates a bar and line plot with GDP growth represented by a bar chart and Unemployment rate as a line plot. The plots are grouped by country using faced_grid().

```
# figure-8.1
library(ggplot2)
# define the base aesthetics
p1 = ggplot(data_panel, aes(Year, GDP_G, group = Country))

p1 + geom_bar(stat = "identity", aes(fill = "GDP"), colour = "black")
+ scale_fill_manual(values = c("grey")) + geom_path(data = data_panel,
    aes(x = Year, y = UNEMP, colour = "Unemployment"), size = 0.5) +
    scale_colour_manual(values = c("blue")) + facet_grid(Country ~
    .) + ylab("GDP/Unemployment") + theme(legend.title =
    element_blank(),legend.position = "top", legend.box =
    "horizontal")
```

Figure 8.1 shows the GDP growth rate and Unemployment for the seven sample countries. It can be seen that China has had a positive growth rate during the sample period followed by Australia, the rest of the countries have experienced a negative growth rate during 2008–2009 which can be accounted to the Global Financial Crisis. The unemployment figures have been decreasing for Australia but have started showing an increasing trend in the most recent years. Surprisingly Chinese unemployment data looks fairly stable. A slight to severe peak in the unemployment rate during the GFC is a common feature in all seven countries.

The analysis conducts panel data regression for three models, simple pooled linear regression, fixed effects and random effects. The analysis is conducted only for individual effects for the sake of brevity.[2] We will now discuss the results from the regression analysis.

---

[2]Time and mixed effects along with diagnostic tests are left as an exercise.

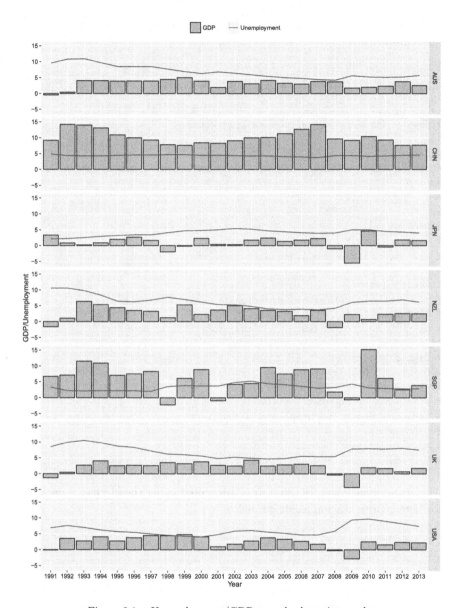

Figure 8.1:   Unemployment/GDP growth plot suing ggplot

The pooled regression model (OLS regression) can be estimated as illustrated below

```
# pooled regression using plm
m_pooling = plm(UNEMP ~ GDP_G, data = data_panel, model = "pooling")
summary(m_pooling)

# Oneway (individual) effect Pooling Model
#
# Call:
# plm(formula = UNEMP ~ GDP_G, data = data_panel, model = "pooling")
#
# Balanced Panel: n=7, T=23, N=161
#
# Residuals :
#    Min. 1st Qu.  Median 3rd Qu.    Max.
#  -3.840  -1.210  -0.116   0.792   5.460
#
# Coefficients :
#             Estimate Std. Error t-value  Pr(>|t|)
# (Intercept)  6.196678   0.220525 28.0997 < 2.2e-16 ***
# GDP_G       -0.188148   0.040404 -4.6567 6.743e-06 ***
# ---
# Signif. codes:
# 0 '***' 0.001 '**' 0.01 '*' 0.05 '.' 0.1 ' ' 1
#
# Total Sum of Squares:    666.14
# Residual Sum of Squares: 586.2
# R-Squared:        0.12001
# Adj. R-Squared: 0.11852
# F-statistic: 21.6847 on 1 and 159 DF, p-value: 6.7425e-06
```

The summary results can also be presented using the *stargazer* package for better presentation as shown below

```
library(stargazer)
stargazer(m_pooling, title = "OLS Results")
```

The results in Table 8.1 show that the GDP growth rate has a significant negative effect on unemployment but this model does not account for any panel effects. The following illustrates calculation of the fixed effects and random effects models using the plm function.

Table 8.1: OLS results

| | Dependent variable |
|---|---|
| | UNEMP |
| GDP_G | −0.188*** |
| | (0.040) |
| Constant | 6.197*** |
| | (0.221) |
| Observations | 161 |
| $R^2$ | 0.120 |
| Adjusted $R^2$ | 0.119 |
| F Statistic | 21.685*** (df = 1; 159) |

Note: $^*p < 0.1$; $^{**}p < 0.05$; $^{***}p < 0.01$

```
# fixed effect or 'within' model
m_within = plm(UNEMP ~ GDP_G, data = data_panel, model = "within")
m_random = plm(UNEMP ~ GDP_G, data = data_panel, model = "random")
```

Table 8.2 summarises the results from both fixed effects and random effects models. These results indicate that both these models display a significant negative effect on unemployment.

Table 8.2: Fixed/random effects result

| | Fixed effects (within) | Random effects (random) |
|---|---|---|
| GDP_G | −0.130** | −0.136*** |
| | (0.051) | (0.049) |
| Constant | | 5.990*** |
| | | (0.581) |
| Observations | 161 | 161 |
| $R^2$ | 0.041 | 0.047 |
| Adjusted $R^2$ | 0.039 | 0.046 |
| F Statistic | 6.521** (df = 1; 153) | 7.765*** (df = 1; 159) |

Note: $^*p < 0.1$; $^{**}p < 0.05$; $^{***}p < 0.01$

The results in Tables 8.1 and 8.2 give a similar picture, i.e. a negative impact of growth rate on unemployment in the sample dataset. Although the results are intuitive, the analysis does not clearly point out which model to select. This warrants some diagnostics to check if the panel regression estimation is required or if OLS is a sufficient model. We use the **pFtest** to test for fixed effects, **plmtest** to check for random effects and **phtest** to check for fixed vs random effects. As shown below, the **pFtest** suggests that the fixed effect model is a better choice as compared to OLS

```
# pFtest for fixed effects
pFtest(m_within, m_pooling)

#
#   F test for individual effects
#
# data:  UNEMP ~ GDP_G
# F = 18.673, df1 = 6, df2 = 153, p-value = 3.137e-16
# alternative hypothesis: significant effects
```

The results from **plmtest** suggest that the random effects model is also appropriate.

```
# plmtest (Breuch-Pagan Test)for random effects
plmtest(m_pooling, type = c("bp"))

#
#   Lagrange Multiplier Test - (Breusch-Pagan)
#
# data:  UNEMP ~ GDP_G
# chisq = 271.07, df = 1, p-value < 2.2e-16
# alternative hypothesis: significant effects
```

Fr establish that the model has panel effects and simple OLS may result in inferior analysis. Finally, the Hausman Test suggests that random effects model is the preferred model.

```
# Hausman test for fixed vs random model
phtest(m_within, m_random)

#
#   Hausman Test
#
# data:  UNEMP ~ GDP_G
# chisq = 0.22481, df = 1, p-value = 0.6354
# alternative hypothesis: one model is inconsistent
```

Table 8.3:   Combined results

|  | OLS | Fixed effects | Random effects |
|---|---|---|---|
| GDP_G | −0.188*** | −0.130** | −0.136*** |
|  | (0.040) | (0.051) | (0.049) |
| Constant | 6.197*** |  | 5.990*** |
|  | (0.221) |  | (0.581) |
| Observations | 161 | 161 | 161 |
| $R^2$ | 0.120 | 0.041 | 0.047 |
| Adjusted $R^2$ | 0.119 | 0.039 | 0.046 |
| F Statistic | 21.685*** (df = 1; 159) | 6.521** (df = 1; 153) | 7.765*** (df = 1; 159) |

*Note*: $^*p < 0.1$; $^{**}p < 0.05$; $^{***}p < 0.01$

Table 8.3 summarises the results from all three models with unanimous negative dependence of Unemployment on GDP Growth. The most appropriate random effects model indicates that GDP growth negatively effects the level of unemployment such that for every 1% increase in GDP growth across time and between countries the unemployment level reduces by 0.136%.

## 8.5   Summary

In this chapter, we concluded our discussion about Regression Analysis using R. The chapter discussed two specialised cases of regression modelling, Logistic Regression using `glm` and Panel Regression using `plm`. The chapter demonstrated how to get started with these regression techniques and the use of them in modelling economics and finance problems. The chapter also included an example with a step-by-step guide on using Panel Regression analysis in applied economics research. We will now shift focus in the next chapter from regression analysis to time series econometrics and discuss a few of the most widely used methods in applied econometrics.

Chapter 9

# Time Series Analysis

## 9.1 Introduction

Time series analysis consists of statistical methods for analysing datasets with observations recorded over time, i.e. time series data, for example stock price data recorded daily for a period of $n$ years. Time series methods can be used for modelling statistical properties and characteristics of time series data which may be used for forecasting future values. These models are widely popular and implemented in econometric analysis, forecasting and many other business and scientific fields, e.g. volatility forecasting in finance, weather forecasting, etc.

In this chapter, we will discuss classic time series econometric analysis in the context of financial risk and return time series modelling and forecasting. We will start our discussion with a brief overview of some of the major properties of time series data in the next section followed by a discussion of a few of the most widely used time series econometric models, viz., $ARMA(p,q)$; based on autoregression, moving average and $ARCH/GARCH$ models for stochastic volatility. We will discuss these models with an application based focus using various R packages rather than going into extensive mathematical details. For extensive discussion, see Tsay (2010), Taylor (2007), Alexander (2008), Gujarati (2012), Shumway and Stoffer (2013), Cowpertwait and Metcalfe (2009), amongst others.

## 9.2 Time Series-Some Properties

### 9.2.1 Stochastic process

A univariate time series $(Y_t)$ is a series of observations recorded over discrete time and the continuous state of the same variable. For example, the daily index levels of the ASX All Ordinaries stock exchange (AORD) given in *data_asx.RData* file. Figure 9.1 plots this 10 year (January 2005

to December 2014) daily time series dataset after converting it to an `xts`
object as illustrated below:

```
# load xts package
library(xts)
# load data
load("data_asx.RData")
d1 = xts(data_asx$Close, order.by = data_asx$Date)
# figure-9.1
plot(d1, main = "ASX All Ordinaries Closing Prices")
```

Figure 9.1:   ASX all ordinaries closing prices

In a time series model, the observed data is usually considered as a
sample from an infinite *stochastic process* (as a sequence of random variables) as it is not possible to observe the entire population of the time series
data.

### 9.2.2   Stationarity

Stationarity is one of the important concepts which forms the foundation
of statistical inference in time series analysis. In simple terms, a time series
$(Y_t, t \in T)$ is stationary if all its statistical properties (mean, variance,

covariance, etc.) do not change over time shifts. A strict form of stationarity requires that all the statistical properties or the joint distribution of $(Y_{t_1}, \ldots, Y_{t_k})$ are invariant over a time shift which is rather too restrictive for time series modelling algorithms. In particular, time series analysis models are based on the concept of *weak stationarity* which is when the first two moments (mean and variance) and covariance (also correlation) are invariant over time shifts. In the rest of the chapter, stationarity will refer to weak stationarity unless otherwise stated.

Figure 9.2 plots the daily logarithmic returns from 2013 to 2014 for AORD data as given in *asx_ret.RData* file using the code below:

```
load("asx_ret.RData")
asx_ret2 = asx_ret["2012/2014"]
# figure-9.2
plot(asx_ret2, main = "AORD Log Returns")
```

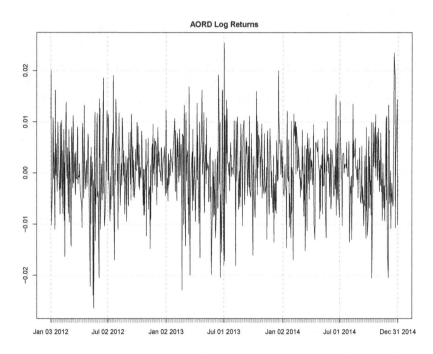

Figure 9.2:   AORD log returns

As illustrated in Figure 9.2, the daily log returns of AORD index are around 0 and lie roughly in $[-0.2, 0.2]$ over the time period of two years which will result in similar statistical properties (mean, standard deviation, etc.) even if the data is divided into subsamples. When we compare Figures 9.1 and 9.2 with prices and returns respectively, it can be concluded that log returns exhibit weak stationarity properties as compared to price data, which is mostly true in financial time series analysis. Although the first difference $(Y_t - Y_{t-1})$ or log transformation of the first difference of most financial time series is stationary, there are statistical tests known as Unit Root Tests which can be used to test stationarity in a time series.

A linear time series stochastic process has a unit root and is nonstationary if 1 is the root of the time series process. The stochastic process as given in Equation (9.1) is a nonstationary random walk if $a_1 = 1$. This process is stationary if $|a_1| < 1$ and nonstationary for $a_1 = 1$ which is used as the basis in so-called unit root tests.

$$y_t = a_1 y_{t-1} + \varepsilon_t. \tag{9.1}$$

The Augmented Dickey–Fuller (ADF) test (Said and Dickey, 1984) and Kwiatkowski–Phillips–Schmidt–Shin (KPSS) (Kwiatkowski et al., 1992) are two of the popular unit root tests widely used to test for stationary time series. The null hypothesis in the ADF test is that there is a unit root whereas the null hypothesis for the KPSS test is no unit root (stationarity). The tseries package has adf.test and kpss.test functions which can be used for ADF and KPSS tests as illustrated below:

```
# ADF test for ASX Returns
library(tseries)
adf.test(asx_ret)

#
#    Augmented Dickey-Fuller Test
#
# data:  asx_ret
# Dickey-Fuller = -13.537, Lag order = 13, p-value
# = 0.01
# alternative hypothesis: stationary

# KPSS test for ASX Returns
kpss.test(asx_ret)

#
#    KPSS Test for Level Stationarity
#
# data:  asx_ret
# KPSS Level = 0.1013, Truncation lag parameter =
```

```
# 11, p-value = 0.1
```

Both ADF and KPSS tests in the above example suggest that the ASX log return series is stationary.

### 9.2.3 Autocorrelation function (ACF)

For a time series $Y_t$, the ACF is defined as the correlation between $y_t$ and $y_{t-h}$ for $h = 1, 2, 3$, etc. As one of the conditions of *weak stationarity* suggests that the covariance (and correlation) should be time invariant, this implies that the theoretical value of an autocorrelation for a given lag is the same for the whole stationary time series. The ACF for $l$-lag sample autocorrelation of a stationary time series can be defined as

$$\rho_l = \frac{Cov(y_t, y_{t-l})}{Var(y_t)}. \tag{9.2}$$

ACF is used to create an ACF plot to draw sample autocorrelations for various lags in a time series which is used to visually capture the linear dynamics of the data. The correlations from the ACF are plotted within statistical bounds to test for the zero autocorrelation coefficient. The `ACF` function in the package *tseries* can be used to create the ACF plot as illustrated in the following R code.

```
library(tseries)
# acf for the price series (figure-9.3a)
acf(data_asx$Close, main = "ACF (ASX Prices)")
# acf for the price series (figure-9.3b)
acf(asx_ret, main = "ACF (ASX returns)")
```

Figure 9.3 shows two ACF plots for the ASX prices and returns respectively, as shown in the figure the ASX price ACF shows a very slow decay in the level of autocorrelation which is usually considered as a sign of non-stationarity in financial time series. On the other hand, the second ACF plot for ASX returns in Figure 9.3 shows a rapid decay to zero characterising the return series as *weak stationary*.

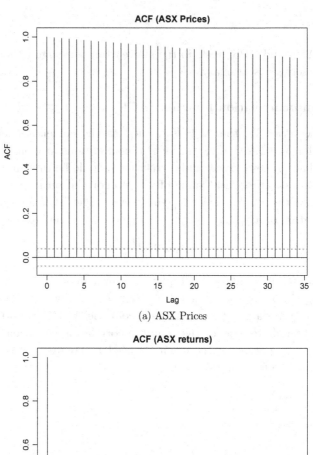

(a) ASX Prices

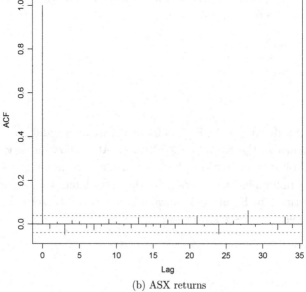

(b) ASX returns

Figure 9.3:   ACF plot of (a) ASX prices and (b) returns

The Ljung–Box test (Ljung and Box, 1978) or simply Box test can be used to test if several autocorrelations of $y_t$ are zero. The Box.test function from the *stats* package provides the test statistics as shown below

```
# Ljung-Box test on price series for 20 lags
Box.test(data_asx$Close, lag = 20, type = "Ljung")

#
#    Box-Ljung test
#
# data:  data_asx$Close
# X-squared = 47962, df = 20, p-value < 2.2e-16

# Ljung-Box test on return series for 20 lags
Box.test(asx_ret, lag = 20, type = "Ljung")

#
#    Box-Ljung test
#
# data:  asx_ret
# X-squared = 20.73, df = 20, p-value = 0.4132
```

With the null hypothesis of no significant autocorrelation, the results above show that the price series exhibits serial autocorrelation as compared to the stationary return series.

### 9.2.4 White noise

A time series $Y_t$ is called a white noise $\{Y_t\}$ if each element in the time series is an independent and identically distributed (*i.i.d.*) mean-zero variable. White noise is a stationary process with zero ACFs, i.e. it has uncorrelated elements. A white noise process is used to model unpredictable innovations or shocks (or noise in engineering terms) in time series models. For example, a Gaussian white noise process is sequence of *i.i.d* normal random variables. We can generate a plot of Gaussian white noise process using normal random variable generator function (rnorm). Figure 9.4 is generated using the following:

```
# generate 200 random normal values
y = rnorm(200)
# figure-9.4
plot(y, type = "l", main = "Gaussian White Noise Process")
abline(h = 0, col = "blue")  #draw horizontal line
```

### 9.3 Autoregressive Moving Average Model (ARMA)

In the analysis of time series data, ARMA models or as generalisation ARMA$(p, q)$ (Box, Jenkins and Reinsel, 1994) models are a class of

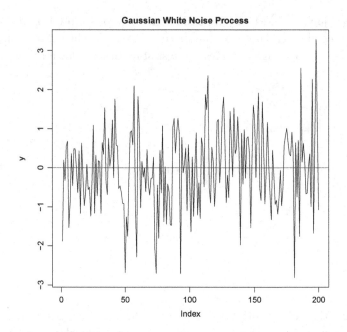

Figure 9.4:   Gaussian white noise process

univariate time series models which model linear dependence in time series observations. ARMA($p, q$) models a stationary time series by combining two small classes of time series models, autoregressive process (AR) and a moving average (MA) process resulting in a parsimonious two polynomial model with autoregression and moving average. For a time series $Y_t$, an ARMA($p, q$) model statistically describes the time series and provides a mathematical model for predicting future values with a $p$ order AR($p$) component and $q$ order MA($q$) component.

A time series $y_t$ can be represented as an ARMA($p, q$) model if there exist $a_1, \ldots, a_p, b_1, \ldots, b_q$ such that

$$y_t = \sum_{j=1}^{p} a_j y_{t-j} + \sum_{j=1}^{q} b_j \varepsilon_{t-j} + \varepsilon_t, \qquad (9.3)$$

where $\varepsilon_t$ is white noise (or $i.i.d.$).

ARMA($p, q$) model given in Equation (9.2) has two components, $\sum_{j=1}^{p} a_j y_{t-j} + \varepsilon_t$ gives the AR($p$) process and $\sum_{j=1}^{q} b_j \varepsilon_{t-j}$ gives the MA($q$) process.

Out of the two components of the ARMA($p, q$) model, finite MA($q$) is always weakly stationary as it has linear combination of a white noise sequence. AR($p$) component on the other hand is not always stationary, for example an AR(1) model (with $a_1 = 1$) as shown in Equation (9.1) is a *random walk* model which is nonstationary.

Although not discussed here, Autoregressive Integrated Moving Average (ARIMA$(p, d, q)$) models are a further generalisation of ARMA$(p, q)$ models which includes a differencing parameter ($d$). The difference parameter is used to finitely difference a nonstationary time series to fit it to an ARMA$(p, q)$ model. This allows ARIMA$(p, d, q)$ models suitable for both stationary and nonstationary time series.

### 9.3.1 Fitting an ARMA model

There are various packages in R which can be used to fit an ARMA model among them *fArma, tseries* and *forecast* are three packages which provide useful functions to model ARMA. We will use a time series of monthly logarithmic changes of 90-day Australian bank bills from 2010 to 2014 given in the file **bbrate.RData** to demonstrate estimation of an ARMA$(p, q)$ process. Figure 9.5 shows the time series plot of the data.

```
load("bbrate.RData")
# note the data is already in xts time series format
# figure-9.5
plot(bbrate, main = "90 Day Bank Bills")
```

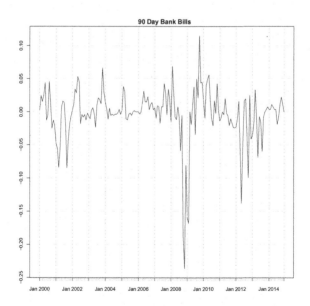

Figure 9.5: Monthly log returns for 90-day bank bills

The first step in modelling a time series is to check for stationarity. ADF test statistics calculated using the **adf.test** a function shows stationarity in the time series (*p-value* <0.05).

```
# ADF Test
adf.test(bbrate)

#
#    Augmented Dickey-Fuller Test
#
# data:  bbrate
# Dickey-Fuller = -4.2673, Lag order = 5, p-value
# = 0.01
# alternative hypothesis: stationary
```

After establishing stationarity in the time series, the next step is to identify the order $(p,q)$ of the ARMA model. An ACF can be used to identify the order of the MA $q$ term and although not discussed here as Partial Autocorrelation Function (PACF), which is the conditional correlation between $Y_t$ and $Y_{t+k}$ given $Y_{t+1}, \ldots, Y_{t+k-1}$ (see Ramsey *et al.*, 1974; Box *et al.*, 1994, etc.) can be used to identify the AR $p$ term. The Extended Autocorrelation Function (EACF) (Tsay and Tiao, 1984) is useful in simultaneously identifying both $p$ and $q$ orders of the model. A less sophisticated and easier way is to check the best fit model using the information criterion such as AIC or BIC. We can fit several models with a combination of orders using a loop to fetch the model with lowest AIC which gives the best fit. A simple R code with two **for** loops and **arma** function from the *tseries* package can be used as illustrated below

```
# to find the best fit model set the best order to
# default
best_order <- c(0, 0)
# set best AIC to Inf to accept any value
best_aic <- Inf
# check till p=5 and q=5
for (i in 0:5) {
    for (j in 0:5) {
        # fit the model
        fit = arma(bbrate, order = c(i, j))
        # extract AIC from the summary method
        fit_aic = summary(fit)$aic
        # compare the AIC with previous AIC
        if (fit_aic < best_aic) {
```

```
        best_aic = fit_aic
        best_order = c(i, j)
      }
    }
}
print(c(best_order, best_aic))

# [1]    3.0000    3.0000 -702.3858
```

The best order for the bank bill time series is $p = 3$, $q = 3$ as identified by the above routine using the AIC. The *forecast* package in R also provides the function auto.arima to iteratively select the best order using AIC/BIC. The specified order can now be used to fit the ARMA(3,3) process to the bank bill time series. We use the armaFit function from the *fArma* package to illustrate as it provides better functionality for graphs and forecasting.

```
load("bbrate.RData")
library(fArma)
fit1 = armaFit(~arma(3, 3), data = bbrate, description = "ARMA(3,3)")
```

A summary can be generated using the summary method to get the model fit statistics along with diagnostic plots of the residuals as shown below.

```
par(mfrow = c(2, 2))
# figure-9.6
summary(fit1)

#
# Title:
#  ARIMA Modelling
#
# Call:
#  armaFit(formula = ~arma(3, 3), data = bbrate,
description = "ARMA(3,3)")
#
# Model:
#  ARIMA(3,0,3) with method: CSS-ML
#
# Coefficient(s):
#       ar1       ar2       ar3       ma1       ma2
#  1.217640  0.241725 -0.510619 -0.696145 -0.702485
#       ma3 intercept
#  0.455923 -0.003982
```

```
#
# Residuals:
#       Min        1Q     Median       3Q       Max
# -0.173299 -0.010025  0.003461  0.014940  0.097073
#
# Moments:
# Skewness Kurtosis
#   -1.175     5.368
#
# Coefficient(s):
#              Estimate  Std. Error  t value Pr(>|t|)
# ar1          1.217640    0.187632    6.490 8.61e-11 ***
# ar2          0.241725    0.301880    0.801 0.423286
# ar3         -0.510619    0.135231   -3.776 0.000159 ***
# ma1         -0.696145    0.180789   -3.851 0.000118 ***
# ma2         -0.702485    0.168547   -4.168 3.07e-05 ***
# ma3          0.455923    0.096712    4.714 2.43e-06 ***
# intercept  -0.003982    0.002905   -1.371 0.170442
# ---
# Signif. codes:
# 0 '***' 0.001 '**' 0.01 '*' 0.05 '.' 0.1 ' ' 1
#
# sigma^2 estimated as: 0.001064
# log likelihood:       360.25
# AIC Criterion:       -704.49


#
# Description:
#   ARMA(3,3)
```

The coefficients generated above show that all but the AR(2) terms are significant. The diagnostic plots in Figure 9.6 also show that the residuals do not show any autocorrelation and are *i.i.d.* or white noise.

The **predict** function can be used to forecast future values which also generates a plot of the forecasted values as illustrated next.

```
# 6 Step ahead (6 month) forecast(figure-9.7)
p1 = predict(fit1, n.ahead = 6)
```

```
# extract predicted values
p1$pred

# Time Series:
# Start = 181
# End = 186
# Frequency = 1
# [1]   0.0042084375   0.0033580766   0.0019675086
# [4]   0.0008544488  -0.0004027827  -0.0014926430
```

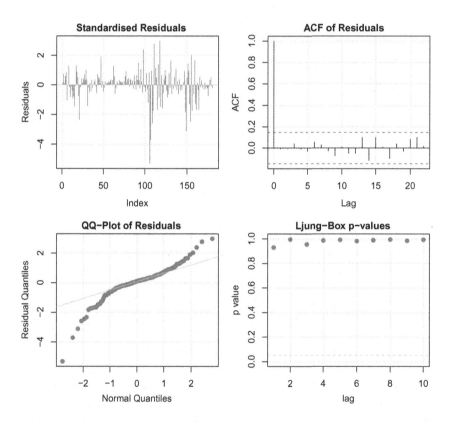

Figure 9.6:   Diagnostic plots for the ARMA(3,3) fit

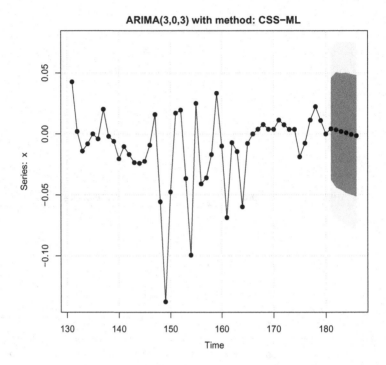

Figure 9.7:   Forecast plot

## 9.4    Volatility Modelling using Generalised Autoregressive Conditional Heteroskedasticity (GARCH)

Asset risk modelling and forecasting is one of the most important areas in empirical finance where volatility is considered the most common measure of financial risk. The $ARMA(p,q)$ model discussed in the previous section assumes a constant volatility and hence are not useful to model and forecast varying volatility in a time series. In this section, we will discuss the GARCH models (Bollerslev, 1986; Engle, 2001; Engle, 1982), the most popular time series models used for forecasting conditional volatility. These models are conditional heteroskedastic as they take into account the conditional variance in a time series. GARCH models are one of the most widely used models for forecasting financial risk measures like Value at Risk (VaR) and Conditional Value at Risk (CVaR) in financial risk modelling and management.

The GARCH models are a generalised version of ARCH models. A standard $ARCH(p)$ process with $p$ lag terms designed to capture volatility clustering can be written as follows

$$\sigma_t^2 = \omega + \sum_{i=1}^{p} \alpha_i Y_{t-i}^2, \tag{9.4}$$

where the return on day $t$, is $Y_t = \sigma_t Z_t$ and $Z_t \sim i.i.d(0,1)$, i.e. the innovation in returns are driven by random shocks. The ARCH(1) model for financial volatility is similar to ARMA(1,0) model for returns. The GARCH($p$,$q$) model include lagged volatility in an ARCH($p$) model to incorporate the impact of historical returns which can be written as follows

$$\sigma_t^2 = \omega + \sum_{i=1}^{p} \alpha_i Y_{t-i}^2 + \sum_{j=1}^{q} \beta_j \sigma_{t-j}^2. \tag{9.5}$$

GARCH(1,1), which employs only one lag per order, is the most common version used in empirical research and analysis. We will now discuss GARCH(1,1) estimation using the *rugarch* package, one of the most versatile and powerful time series volatility modelling packages in R.

### 9.4.1 Fitting a GARCH(1,1) model using the *rugarch* package

There are few specialised R packages available to model conditional volatility in time series like *fGarch, tseries, rugarch, rmgarch* (for multivariate time series), etc. One of the most versatile and capable of them is the *rugarch* package. Here, we use previously introduced *asx_ret.RData* dataset to demonstrate modelling GARCH using the functions and methods available in the rugarch package. Here, we will mainly focus on the functions required for model estimation and extracting different results. We will further demonstrate the functions used for forecasting in an example later in the next section.

Fitting a GARCH model using the *rugarch* package requires setting the model specification using the `ugarchspec` function. The `ugarchspec` function has various arguments as shown below

```
function (variance.model = list(model = "sGARCH", garchOrder = c(1,
1), submodel = NULL, external.regressors = NULL, variance.targeting
= FALSE), mean.model = list(armaOrder = c(1, 1), include.mean =
TRUE, archm = FALSE, archpow = 1, arfima = FALSE,
external.regressors = NULL, archex = FALSE), distribution.model =
"norm", start.pars = list(), fixed.pars = list(), ...)
NULL
```

We can view these arguments in the console using the following code

```
# arguments for the model specification using ugarchspec
library(rugarch)
args(ugarchspec)
```

The `variance.model` argument specifies the GARCH model to use and its order in a list format. There are various GARCH variants possible in *rugarch* package (see `help(ugarchspec)` or the package vignette (Ghalanos, 2014)), setting `model = "sGARCH"` specifies the simple GARCH model. A GARCH(1,1) model with a constant mean equation (`mean.model = list(armaOrder = c(0,0))`) can be specified as follows:

```
garch_spec = ugarchspec(variance.model = list(model = "sGARCH",
    garchOrder = c(1, 1)), mean.model = list(armaOrder = c(0,
    0)))
```

The above specification stored in `garch_spec` can now be used to fit the GARCH(1,1) model to our data. The following code fits the GARCH(1,1) model to a subset of two years ASX log returns using the `ugarchfit` function and shows the results.

```
fit_garch = ugarchfit(spec = garch_spec, data = asx_ret2)
# show the estimates and other diagnostic tests3
fit_garch

#
# *---------------------------------*
# *          GARCH Model Fit        *
# *---------------------------------*
#
# Conditional Variance Dynamics
# -----------------------------------
# GARCH Model     : sGARCH(1,1)
# Mean Model      : ARFIMA(0,0,0)
# Distribution    : norm
#
# Optimal Parameters
# -----------------------------------
#           Estimate  Std. Error   t value  Pr(>|t|)
# mu        0.000471    0.000248    1.8948  0.058124
# omega     0.000005    0.000000   21.5164  0.000000
# alpha1    0.086025    0.010346    8.3152  0.000000
# beta1     0.814940    0.018220   44.7285  0.000000
```

```
#
# Robust Standard Errors:
#         Estimate  Std. Error  t value Pr(>|t|)
# mu       0.000471  0.000267   1.7657 0.077448
# omega    0.000005  0.000000  19.7184 0.000000
# alpha1   0.086025  0.005748  14.9662 0.000000
# beta1    0.814940  0.017718  45.9954 0.000000
#
# LogLikelihood : 2682.993
#
# Information Criteria
# ------------------------------------
#
# Akaike       -7.0593
# Bayes        -7.0349
# Shibata      -7.0593
# Hannan-Quinn -7.0499
#
# Weighted Ljung-Box Test on Standardised Residuals
# ------------------------------------
#                          statistic p-value
# Lag[1]                     0.0685  0.7935
# Lag[2*(p+q)+(p+q)-1][2]    0.2040  0.8518
# Lag[4*(p+q)+(p+q)-1][5]    0.9437  0.8723
# d.o.f=0
# HO : No serial correlation
#
# Weighted Ljung-Box Test on Standardised Squared Residuals
# ------------------------------------
#                          statistic p-value
# Lag[1]                     0.001212 0.9722
# Lag[2*(p+q)+(p+q)-1][5]    0.836430 0.8955
# Lag[4*(p+q)+(p+q)-1][9]    2.930123 0.7705
# d.o.f=2
#
# Weighted ARCH LM Tests
# ------------------------------------
#               Statistic Shape Scale P-Value
# ARCH Lag[3]     0.8909  0.500 2.000  0.3452
# ARCH Lag[5]     1.0380  1.440 1.667  0.7217
# ARCH Lag[7]     2.7533  2.315 1.543  0.5613
#
# Nyblom stability test
# ------------------------------------
# Joint Statistic:  30.0574
```

```
# Individual Statistics:
# mu     0.1865
# omega  3.7533
# alpha1 0.1150
# beta1  0.1107
#
# Asymptotic Critical Values (10% 5% 1%)
# Joint Statistic:        1.07 1.24 1.6
# Individual Statistic:   0.35 0.47 0.75
#
# Sign Bias Test
# -------------------------------------
#                      t-value    prob sig
# Sign Bias            2.0532 0.0404   **
# Negative Sign Bias   0.7760 0.4380
# Positive Sign Bias   0.5439 0.5867
# Joint Effect         5.2495 0.1544
#
#
# Adjusted Pearson Goodness-of-Fit Test:
# -------------------------------------
#   group statistic p-value(g-1)
# 1    20    26.22        0.1242
# 2    30    33.77        0.2479
# 3    40    44.74        0.2434
# 4    50    57.27        0.1951
#
#
# Elapsed time : 0.232013
```

Selected fitted statistics can be obtained using the various methods available to the `ugarchfit` object class. For example, the fitted coefficients can be obtained using the `coef` method. See `help(uGARCHfit)` for a full list of available methods. The `plot` method is also available to the `ugarchfit` object which can be used to selectively produce different types of plots as illustrated below:

```
# generate plots using the which argument 1. ACF of
# standardised residuals (figure-9.8a)
plot(fit_garch, which = 10)
# 2. Conditional SD (vs |returns|)(figure-9.8b)
plot(fit_garch, which = 3)
```

A list of available plots is produced when `plot` is used with argument `which = "ask"`.

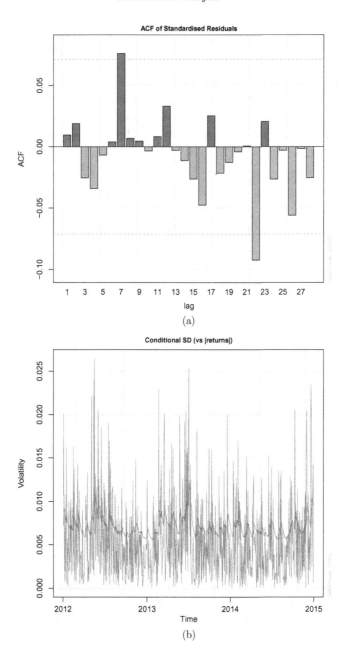

(a)

(b)

Figure 9.8: Two informative plots for GARCH(1,1)

The GARCH(1,1) fit demonstration here assumed that (1,1) is a suitable order for the model. We can also evaluate various order combination using the information criterion (AIC or BIC) for the best order $(p,q)$ as done previously in the case of ARMA$(p,q)$ models.

ugarchforecast function from the *rugarch* package can be used for prediction. ugarchforecast takes the fitted object and can forecast n-step ahead where 'n' or forecast horizon is specified by **n.ahead** argument as shown below:

```
# 10 step ahead forecast using fit_garch object
fore1 = ugarchforecast(fit_garch, n.ahead = 10)
# print series and volatility forecasts
show(fore1)

#
# *------------------------------------*
# *       GARCH Model Forecast         *
# *------------------------------------*
# Model: sGARCH
# Horizon: 10
# Roll Steps: 0
# Out of Sample: 0
#
# 0-roll forecast [T0=2014-12-31]:
#          Series     Sigma
# T+1   0.0004707  0.009003
# T+2   0.0004707  0.008840
# T+3   0.0004707  0.008690
# T+4   0.0004707  0.008552
# T+5   0.0004707  0.008427
# T+6   0.0004707  0.008312
# T+7   0.0004707  0.008207
# T+8   0.0004707  0.008111
# T+9   0.0004707  0.008024
# T+10  0.0004707  0.007945
```

The above forecasts are based on previous data but with the model fitted on the whole dataset, as often required we can keep an out of sample dataset to check the forecasts. This requires fitting the garch model with the out of sample period specified using the **out.sample** argument in **ugarchfit** function. The fitted object can then be used to do rolling $n$-step ahead forecasts using the **n.roll** argument in **ugarchforecast** function. The following code illustrates

```
# fit the model with 10 out of sample observations
fit_garch2 = ugarchfit(spec = garch_spec, data = asx_ret2,
    out.sample = 10)
# 1-step out of sample rolling forecast
fore2 = ugarchforecast(fit_garch2, n.ahead = 1, n.roll = 9)
# forecasted series
show(fitted(fore2))

#       2014-12-15   2014-12-16   2014-12-17
# T+1 0.0004264727 0.0004264727 0.0004264727
#       2014-12-18   2014-12-19   2014-12-22
# T+1 0.0004264727 0.0004264727 0.0004264727
#       2014-12-23   2014-12-24   2014-12-29
# T+1 0.0004264727 0.0004264727 0.0004264727
#       2014-12-30
# T+1 0.0004264727

# forecasted sigma
show(sigma(fore2))

#       2014-12-15 2014-12-16   2014-12-17   2014-12-18
# T+1 0.007242564 0.00719975 0.006884619 0.007118258
#       2014-12-19 2014-12-22 2014-12-23   2014-12-24
# T+1  0.0095565 0.01039665 0.01015224 0.009423424
#       2014-12-29 2014-12-30
# T+1 0.00966622 0.009493509
```

We can also plot these forecasts using the available **plot** method, which depending on the type of forecasts can generate four plots for unconditional and rolling predicted series and volatility.[1]

```
par(mfrow = c(2, 1))
# figure-9.9 2:Time Series Prediction (rolling)
plot(fore2, which = 2)
# 4:Sigma Prediction (rolling)
plot(fore2, which = 4)
```

---

[1] run plot(fore2) to see all the four options.

*R in Finance and Economics*

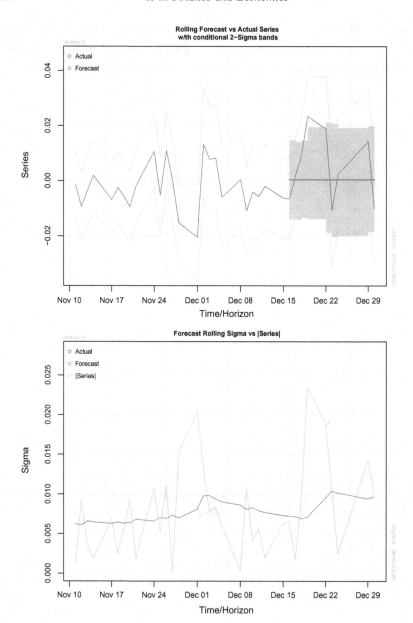

Figure 9.9:   Forecast plots

## 9.5 Example: Modelling and Forecasting Daily VaR using GARCH

VaR is the most widely used market risk measure in financial risk management and it is also used by practitioners such as portfolio managers to account for future market risk. VaR can be defined as loss in market value of an asset over a given time period that is exceeded with a probability $\theta$. For a time series of returns $r_t$, $VaR_t$ would be such that

$$P[r_t < -VaR_t[I_{t-1}] = \theta, \qquad (9.6)$$

where $I_{t-1}$ represents the information set at time $t - 1$.

Despite the appealing simplicity of VaR in its offering of a simple summary of the downside risk of an asset portfolio, there is no single way to calculate it (see Manganelli and Engle (2001) for an overview on VaR methods in finance). A very common approach to estimating VaR assumes normality in the return distribution which makes the VaR calculations as simple as calculating the lower extreme quantile of the return distribution of a portfolio or an asset with a given confidence level. Figure 9.10 shows the 1% VaR for randomly generated normal data.

Although it is fairly simple to calculate VaR with a normal distribution, financial returns mostly have characteristics such as skewness, excess kurtosis and heteroskedasticity which does not conform to a normal distribution. The GARCH family of models are capable of being used to model time-varying volatility with various underlying distributions which can be used to model and forecast VaR (see Engle (2001) for an example) for different time horizons.

In this example, we will use a GARCH(1,1) with normal and student-t distribution to model and forecast daily VaR for the ASX All Ordinaries log returns. We will now discuss the data with some descriptive statistics followed by model estimation and forecasting using the *rugarch* package.

### 9.5.1 Data and methodology

We use a sample of the ASX All Ordinaries daily log returns from year 2012 to 2014 from the previously introduced *asx_ret.RData* dataset for forecasting daily value at risk using a GARCH(1,1) model. The following code extracts the data sample and generates some descriptive statistics for our data sample.

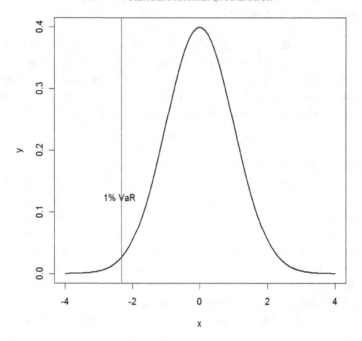

Figure 9.10:   1% VaR normal distribution

```
ex_data = asx_ret["2012/2014"]
# load PerformanceAnalytics package
library(PerformanceAnalytics)
ex_desc = table.Stats(ex_data)
show(ex_desc)


#                        ASX_R
# Observations      759.0000
# NAs                 0.0000
# Minimum            -0.0264
# Quartile 1         -0.0038
# Median              0.0006
# Arithmetic Mean     0.0004
# Geometric Mean      0.0003
# Quartile 3          0.0049
# Maximum             0.0254
# SE Mean             0.0003
# LCL Mean (0.95)    -0.0002
# UCL Mean (0.95)     0.0009
```

```
# Variance      0.0001
# Stdev         0.0072
# Skewness     -0.2290
# Kurtosis      0.7988
```

The descriptive statistics as generated above indicates that our data is not symmetric with a low value of Skewness and Kurtosis. We use the Shapiro–Wilk test for normal distribution using the `shapiro.test` function which confirms that the data sample is not normally distributed.

```
# Shapiro-Wilk Test

# notice the use of coredata function to extract just
# the returns
shapiro.test(coredata(ex_data))

#
#   Shapiro-Wilk normality test
#
# data:   coredata(ex_data)
# W = 0.99088, p-value = 0.0001219
```

A further graphical check is done via a quantile–quantile plot generated using the `chart.QQPlot` function from the *PerformanceAnalytics* package as shown below:

```
# chart.QQPlot function from PerformanceAnalytics
# package figure-9.11
chart.QQPlot(ex_data)
```

The model in the example is calibrated with a rolling window of 500 days (approximately two years) for model estimation with model re-estimation after every five days (a trading week) to forecast one day ahead 1% and 5% VaR. A rolling window forecast is preferred as it enables the model to capture a variance that changes over time. The model will be used to forecast VaR for 100 days which will then be tested for VaR violations against the daily returns using Unconditional (Kupiec) and Conditional (Christoffersen) Coverage tests (see Christoffersen (1998) and Christoffersen, Hahn and Inoue (2001)).

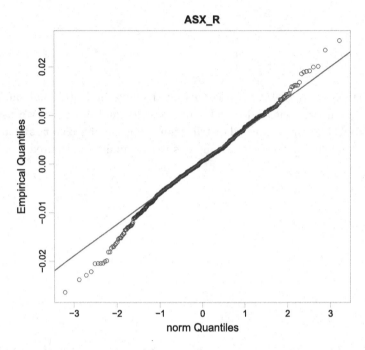

Figure 9.11:   Q–Q plot

## 9.5.2   VaR forecasts

Although the data sample for the example is not normally distributed, we use two GARCH(1,1) specifications with normal and student-t distributions for demonstration purposes. We can define the specifications in a similar way as done previously for GARCH(1,1). The following illustrates

```
# spec1 with normal distribution
spec1 = ugarchspec(variance.model = list(model = "sGARCH",
    garchOrder = c(1, 1)), mean.model = list(armaOrder = c(0,
    0)))
# spec2 with student-t distribution
spec2 = ugarchspec(variance.model = list(model = "sGARCH",
    garchOrder = c(1, 1)), mean.model = list(armaOrder = c(0,
    0)), distribution.model = "std")
```

The *rugarch* package has a very useful `ugarchroll` function for estimating moving window models and forecasting VaR. The `ugarchroll` function provides a method for creating rolling forecasts from GARCH models and has various arguments to specify the forecast length (`forecast.length`), window size (`window.size`), model refitting frequency (`refit.every`), a rolling or recursive estimation window (`refit.window`), etc.

```
args(ugarchroll)

# function (spec, data, n.ahead = 1, forecast.length = 500,
n.start = NULL,
#      refit.every = 25, refit.window = c("recursive", "moving"),
#      window.size = NULL, solver = "hybrid", fit.control = list(),
#      solver.control = list(), calculate.VaR = TRUE,
      VaR.alpha = c(0.01,
#           0.05), cluster = NULL, keep.coef = TRUE, ...)
# NULL
```

As we are modelling both 1% and 5% VaR, we will keep `calculate.VaR = TRUE` and `VaR.alpha = c(0.01, 0.05)`, which are also the default options. For the estimation we set `forecast.length = 100`, `refit.every = 5` and `window.size = 500` which sets the rolling window size for 100 forecasts and 5 day refitting frequency. The following R code fits both GARCH(1,1) models with normal and student-t distributions in a rolling window.

```
# GARCH(1,1) with normal distribution
var.n = ugarchroll(spec1, data = ex_data, n.ahead = 1,
forecast.length = 100,
    refit.every = 5, window.size = 500, refit.window = "rolling",
    calculate.VaR = TRUE, VaR.alpha = c(0.01, 0.05))
# GARCH(1,1) with student-t distribution
var.t = ugarchroll(spec2, data = ex_data, n.ahead = 1,
forecast.length = 100,
    refit.every = 5, window.size = 500, refit.window = "rolling",
    calculate.VaR = TRUE, VaR.alpha = c(0.01, 0.05))
```

var.n and var.t objects can now be used with plot methods and generate reports for the backtests. We can plot the 1% and 5% VaR forecasts against the actual returns as given in Figure 9.12 using the following routine.

```
# note the plot method provides four plots with option-4
# for the VaR forecasts figure-9.12 1% Normal GARCH VaR
plot(var.n, which = 4, VaR.alpha = 0.01)
# 1% Student-t GARCH VaR
plot(var.t, which = 4, VaR.alpha = 0.01)
# 5% Normal GARCH VaR
plot(var.n, which = 4, VaR.alpha = 0.05)
```

```
# 5% Student-t GARCH VaR
plot(var.t, which = 4, VaR.alpha = 0.05)
```

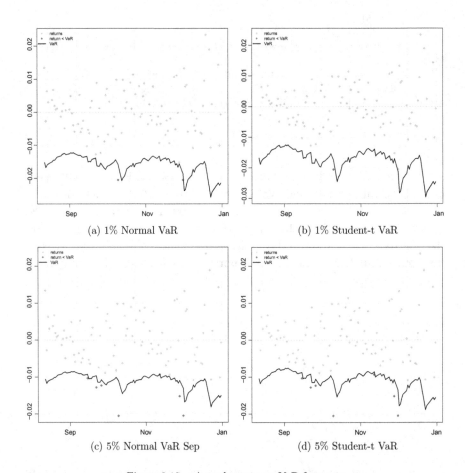

(a) 1% Normal VaR                    (b) 1% Student-t VaR

(c) 5% Normal VaR Sep                (d) 5% Student-t VaR

Figure 9.12:   Actual return vs VaR forecasts

Figure 9.12 shows that there are very few exceedances (return<VaR) for both 1% and 5% VaR forecasts. Finally, we can generate the backtesting results using the **report** method as shown below for 1% VaR forecasts using both normal and student-t distributions. Figures 9.12 (a) and 9.12(b) and the backtesting results show that 1% VaR forecasts using a student-t GARCH(1,1) model has only one violation as compared to two from a normal GARCH(1,1).

```
# backtest results 1% student-t-GARCH(1,1)
report(var.t, VaR.alpha = 0.01)

# VaR Backtest Report
# ===========================================
# Model:   sGARCH-std
# Backtest Length:  100
# Data:
#
# ===========================================
# alpha:   1%
# Expected Exceed:  1
# Actual VaR Exceed:  1
# Actual %:   1%
#
# Unconditional Coverage (Kupiec)
# Null-Hypothesis:  Correct Exceedances
# LR.uc Statistic:  0
# LR.uc Critical:   3.841
# LR.uc p-value:  1
# Reject Null:  NO
#
# Conditional Coverage (Christoffersen)
# Null-Hypothesis:  Correct Exceedances and
# Independence of Failures
# LR.cc Statistic:  NaN
# LR.cc Critic al:  5.991
# LR.cc p-value:   NaN
# Reject Null:    NA

# backtest results 1% normal-GARCH(1,1)
report(var.n, VaR.alpha = 0.01)

# VaR Backtest Report
# ===========================================
# Model:   sGARCH-norm
# Backtest Length:  100
# Data:
#
# ===========================================
# alpha:   1%
# Expected Exceed:  1
# Actual VaR Exceed:  2
# Actual %:   2%
#
# Unconditional Coverage (Kupiec)
```

```
# Null-Hypothesis:   Correct Exceedances
# LR.uc Statistic:   0.783
# LR.uc Critical:    3.841
# LR.uc p-value:     0.376
# Reject Null:       NO
#
# Conditional Coverage (Christoffersen)
# Null-Hypothesis:   Correct Exceedances and
# Independence of Failures
# LR.cc Statistic:   NaN
# LR.cc Critical:    5.991
# LR.cc p-value:     NaN
# Reject Null:       NA
```

As shown in the results above, both Kupiec and Chistoffersen test fail to reject the null hypothesis of correct exceedances for 1% VaR forecasts using a student-t-GARCH(1,1) and a normal-GARCH(1,1) model. The backtesting results for other VaR forecasts are left as an exercise which can be easily generated by changing the value of VaR.alpha and the fitted object.[2]

## 9.6   Summary

In this chapter, we introduced time series analysis using various R packages. We focussed on two major class of time series econometrics models to model stochastic processes, viz., ARMA$(p,q)$ models for modelling financial returns or prices and conditional heteroskedastic GARCH$(p,q)$ models for returns and stochastic volatility. We also discussed VaR forecasting using a GARCH(1,1) model via an empirical example while demonstrating functions from the *rugarch* package. We will now shift our focus from time series models to Extreme Value Theory in the next chapter.

---

[2]The conditional coverage test (Christoffersen) can fail in case of 1% VaR due to very low VaR exceedances.

Chapter 10

# Extreme Value Theory Modelling

## 10.1 Introduction

A common assumption in quantitative financial risk modelling is the distributional assumption of normality as describing the asset's return series, which makes modelling easy but proves to be inefficient if the data exhibit extreme tails. When dealing with extreme financial events to quantify extreme market risk, Extreme Value Theory (EVT) proves a natural statistical modelling technique of interest. EVT provides well established statistical models for univariate and multivariate tail distributions which are useful for forecasting financial risk or modelling the tail dependence of risky assets.

In this chapter, we will discuss two types of statistical methods using EVT which are widely used in univariate and multivariate problems with heavy tailed distributions in finance. We will first provide an introduction to EVT and related statistical methods used to model extreme events like severe shocks in the stock market and associated risk as well as extremal dependence in financial assets. We will demonstrate these two modelling tools with some empirical examples on financial risk modelling and dependence analysis.

## 10.2 EVT and Financial Risk Modelling

With growing turbulence in the financial markets worldwide, evaluating the probability of extreme events like the GFC, has become an important issue in financial risk management. Quantification of the extreme losses in a financial market is important in current market conditions. EVT provides a solid theoretical base on which statistical models describing extreme scenarios can be formed. The distinguishing feature of EVT is the capacity to quantify the stochastic behaviour of a process at unusually large or small levels. Specifically, EVT usually requires estimation of the probability of events that are more extreme than any other that has been previously observed.

EVT is a well-known technique in many fields of applied sciences including engineering and insurance (McNeil, 1999; Reiss and Thomas, 2007; Giesecke and Goldberg, 2005). There are various other studies which analyse the extremes in financial markets due to currency crises, stock market turmoil and credit defaults. The behaviour of financial series tail distributions has, amongst others, been discussed in Mancini and Trojani (2011), Onour (2010), Gilli *et al.* (2006), Neftci (2000), McNeil (1998), Diebold, Schuermann and Stroughair (1998) discuss the potential of EVT in risk management. This section reviews EVT and extreme data modelling with a focus on the financial risk measurements of Value at Risk (VaR), ES and Tail Dependence. Our discussion of EVT in this chapter is adopted from Embrechts, Klüppelberg and Mikosch (1997), Coles (2001), McNeil, Frey and Embrechts (2005), McNeil and Frey (2000), Gilli *et al.* (2006), Franke, Härdle and Hafner (2008) and Singh, Allen and Powell (2013).

There are two broad categories of EVT. The first is known as the Block Maxima (Minima) Method (BMM) approach which is based on extreme value distributions of the Gumbel, Fréchet or Weibull distributions which are generalised as the GEV distribution, and the second based on the Generalized Pareto Distribution (GPD) known as the peak over threshold (POT) approach. BMM models are the most traditional of the two and the BMM approach fits a block of maxima or minima (extreme events) in a data series of independent and identically distributed observations (*iid*) to GEV using Maximum Likelihood Estimation (MLE). POT is considered more efficient in modelling limited data (Gilli *et al.*, 2006; McNeil, Frey and Embrechts, 2005) as it fits the excesses over a given threshold in a dataset to GPD and is hence not as dependent on large datasets as BMM. In this section, we will discuss how to implement the POT method to calculate VaR and Expected Shortfall (ES) for financial returns followed by tail dependence using EVT in the next section. There are various R packages available for EVT analysis like *fExtremes, evd, evir, extRemes, ismev, POT*, etc., which can be used to model extreme value data. We will use few of these packages in demonstrative examples.

### 10.2.1 GPD and POT methods

The POT method uses all the data which exceeds a particular threshold level whereas in BMM only the maximum from a block length is retained for distribution estimation.

**Definition 1 (GPD).** The distribution function for GPD is given by

$$G_{\xi,\sigma}(y) = \begin{cases} \left(1 + \frac{\xi}{\sigma}y\right)^{-1/\xi} & \text{if } \xi \neq 0, \\ 1 - e^{-y/\sigma} & \text{if } \xi = 0, \end{cases} \tag{10.1}$$

where $\sigma > 0$, and $y \geq 0$ when $\xi \geq 0$ and $0 \leq y \leq -\sigma/\xi$ when $\xi < 0$. Here, $\xi$ is the shape parameter and $\sigma$ is the scale parameter for GPD.

```
library(fExtremes)
x = seq(0.1, 10, length = 1000)
# figure-10.1
plot(x, dgpd(x, xi = -1/4), col = "blue", type = "l", xlab = "x",
    ylab = "dpareto(x)", main = "Pareto Probability Density")
lines(x, dgpd(x, xi = 0), col = "green")
lines(x, dgpd(x, xi = 1/4), col = "red")
legend("topright", title = expression(xi), c("-0.25", "0", "0.25"),
    fill = c("blue", "green", "red"))
```

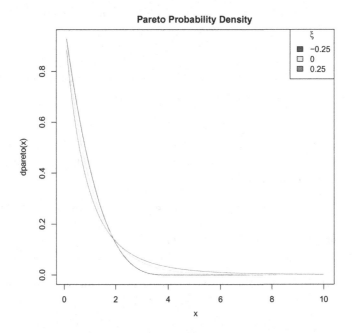

Figure 10.1: Density plots for GPD

Figure 10.1 gives the density plots for different values of $\xi$, the shape parameter in GPD.

**Definition 2 (Excess Distribution).** For a random variable $X$ with df $F$, the excess distribution over a threshold $u$ is given by

$$F_u(y) = P(X - u \leq y | X > u) = \frac{F(y + u) - F(u)}{1 - F(u)} = \frac{F(x) - F(u)}{1 - F(u)}, \quad (10.2)$$

for $0 < y < x_F - u$ where $x_F \leq \infty$ is the right endpoint of $F$ and $y = x - u$. $F_u$ is the conditional excess distribution function.

**Definition 3 (Mean Excess Function).** For a random variable $X$, the mean excess function is given by

$$e(u) = E(X - u | X > u). \quad (10.3)$$

The mean excess function $e(u)$ gives the mean of $F_u$ (excess df for the distribution of the excess above a threshold $u$) as a function of $u$.

#### 10.2.1.1 *Sample mean excess plot*

The mean excess function is used to plot the *mean excess plot* (also known as mean residual life plot) for threshold selection. For a positive-valued extreme data (loss data) $X_1, \ldots, X_n$, the estimator $e(u)$ is given by

$$e_n(v) = \frac{\sum_{i=1}^{n}(X_i - v)I_{\{X_i > v\}}}{\sum_{i=1}^{n} I_{\{X_i > v\}}}, \quad (10.4)$$

where $u \leq v < \infty$ and $I_{\{X_i > v\}}$ are the values exceeding threshold $v$. This function is explored by mean excess plot

$$\{(X_{i,n}, e_n(X_{i,n})) : 2 \leq i \leq n\},$$

$X_{i,n}$ is the $i$th order statistic. The plot shows linearity in a region where above the threshold $v$ the data supports the GPD model. In ideal situations, the linearity can be interpreted as

- Upward linear trend indicates a positive shape parameter $(\xi)$ for the GPD.
- Horizontal linear trend indicates a GPD with $\xi \approx 0$.
- Linear downward trend can be interpreted as GPD with negative $\xi$.

The `meplot` function from the package *fExtremes* can be used to plot the mean excess plot. The code below uses `meplot` function to plot the mean excess function (Figure 10.2) for ASX All Ordinaries and Dow Jones Industrial Average return data from 1985 to 2015 given in *data_chapter10.RData* as illustrated below.

```
# figure-10.2
library(fExtremes)
# load data
load("data_chapter10.RData")
mePlot(-data.ch10$ASX) # figure-10.2(a)
mePlot(-data.ch10$DJI) # figure-10.2(b)
```

Figure 10.2 gives a mean excess plot for the ASX-All Ords and DJIA daily percentage log return data. It can be seen that we can safely assume a threshold $u = 0.014$ (95% of $-$returns) for ASX All Ords (Figure 10.2(a)) as the plot shows an upward linear trend at $u$ and hence a positive $\xi$.

Figure 10.3 gives the plot of excesses above the lower 5% (95% of $-r_t$) quantile of the ASX-All Ordinaries, it plots the time series of returns above $u$ for the left tail using the R code below

```
library(xts)
u = quantile(data.ch10$ASX, 0.05)  #threshold
asx_ex = data.ch10[data.ch10$ASX <= u, c(1, 2)]  #generate excesses
# convert excesses into xts object
asx_ex_ts = xts(asx_ex[, 2], order.by = as.Date(asx_ex[, 1]))
# figure-10.3
plot(-asx_ex_ts, type = "h", main = "ASX All Ords", xlab = "Date",
    ylab = "Returns")
```

### 10.2.1.2  *Estimation of GPD*

For a sample of data $X_1, \ldots, X_n$ from $F$, there is some $N_u$ which exceeds the threshold $u$, the sample is relabelled as $\tilde{X}_1, \ldots, \tilde{X}_{N_u}$. $Y_j = \tilde{X}_j - u$ is calculated for every $\tilde{X}_j$, the parameters of a GPD model are estimated by fitting this distribution to the $N_u$ excess losses. The most widely used method for fitting a distribution to GPD is MLE which is also easy to implement.

Functions like **gpdFit** from the *fExtremes* package, **gpd** from the *evir* package among others can be used to fit a POT model to the GPD distribution. The following code fits the POT model to the left tail of ASX

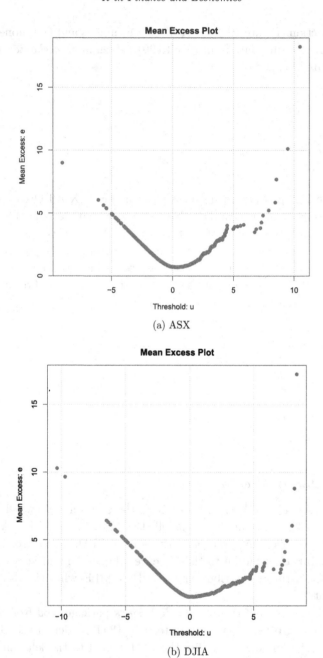

(a) ASX

(b) DJIA

Figure 10.2:   Mean excess plots for positive left tail of ASX and DJI returns

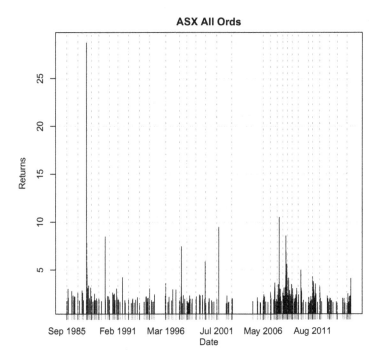

Figure 10.3: Excess plot-ASX All Ords

return data using the `gpdFit` function followed by some diagnostic plots of the fit

```
x1 = -data.ch10$ASX
# fit POT with 95% quantile threshold
fit1 = gpdFit(x1, u = quantile(x1, 0.95))
# fitted values
fit1

#
# Title:
#   GPD Parameter Estimation
#
# Call:
#   gpdFit(x = x1, u = quantile(x1, 0.95))
#
# Estimation Method:
#   gpd mle
#
```

```
# Estimated Parameters:
#         xi         beta
# 0.3443284 0.6116385
#
# Description
#    Mon Mar 07 10:57:15 2016 by user: Abhaykus

# plot all four diagnostic plots (figure-10.4)
par1 = par()
par(mfrow = c(2, 2))
summary(fit1)

#
# Title:
#   GPD Parameter Estimation
#
# Call:
# gpdFit(x = x1, u = quantile(x1, 0.95))
#
# Estimation Type:
#    gpd mle
#
# Estimated Parameters:
#         xi         beta
# 0.3443284 0.6116385
#
# Standard Deviations:
#          xi         beta
# 0.06634706 0.05067083
#
# Log-Likelihood Value:
#    305.2837
#
# Type of Convergence:
#    0
#
# Description
#    Mon Mar 07 10:57:15 2016 by user: Abhaykus

par(par1)
```

Figure 10.4 shows that the over threshold data fits quite well to the GPD.

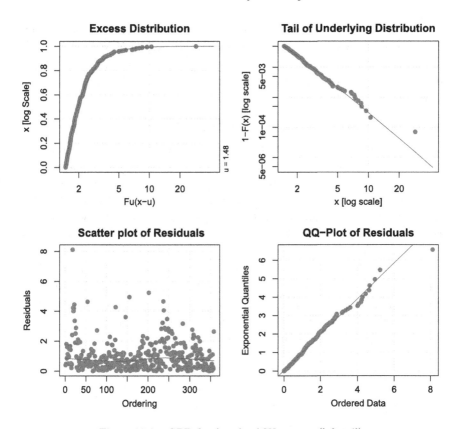

Figure 10.4:   GPD fit plots for ASX returns (left tail)

### 10.2.1.3   *VaR and expected shortfall*

VaR as discussed in the last chapter in simple terms is a lower extreme quantile of the return distribution of a portfolio or an asset calculated with a given confidence level. In distribution terms, for a distribution $F$, VaR can be defined as its $p$th quantile given by

$$VaR_p(V_p) = F^{-1}(1 - p),\qquad(10.5)$$

where $F^{-1}$ is the inverse of the distribution function also called the quantile function. Hence, VaR is easy to calculate once a distribution for the return series can be defined.

VaR is the $q$th quantile of the distribution over a time horizon $t$, which is a well-accepted measure of risk in financial management. VaR suffers from the disadvantage of taking no account of losses beyond a certain quantile in the distribution. ES (also known as Conditional Value at Risk or the tail conditional expectation) is defined as the expectation of returns given that it exceeds VaR, and overcomes this disadvantage of VaR. ES is also considered as being a coherent measure of risk as it satisfies the conditions of monotonicity, sub-additivity, homogeneity, and translational invariance (Artzner *et al.*, 1999).

$$Expected\,Shortfall\,(ES_p) = E(X|X > V_p).  \quad (10.6)$$

ES is a critical measure of losses beyond VaR which is of importance in financial risk management with increasing volatility in the financial markets. EVT can be used to quantify both VaR and ES measure of risk after fitting the extremes to extreme distributions. In the POT method, GPD is fitted to the excess distribution (value above threshold a $u$) by MLE and the confidence interval estimates are calculated by profile likelihood and then the unconditional or static estimates for VaR and ES are calculated.

The following example illustrates how to use the function in the *fExtremes* package to calculate VaR and ES for the left tail of the ASX All Ord returns using the POT method. We first fit the GPD to the last 5000 ASX returns using a threshold level of the 10% quantile level (90% for $-r_t$) followed by 5% and 1% point estimates for VaR and ES.

```
# Extract last 5000 returns
x2 = -tail(data.ch10$ASX, 5000)
# Fit GPD to the data
fit2 = gpdFit(x2, u = quantile(x2, 0.9))
# VaR and ES Estimates using the tailRisk function
tailRisk(fit2, prob = c(0.95, 0.99))

#   Prob      VaR       ES
# 1 0.95 1.508933 2.385005
# 2 0.99 2.838216 4.052035
```

The *fExtremes* package also provides functions to plot the VaR and ES estimates on the tail of the fitted distribution and generates interval estimates simultaneously. The following code creates a tail plot using the fit2 object from above and adds 1% VaR and ES estimates to it.

```
# Generate the tail plot and store it in an object
t1 = gpdTailPlot(fit2)  #figure-10.5
```

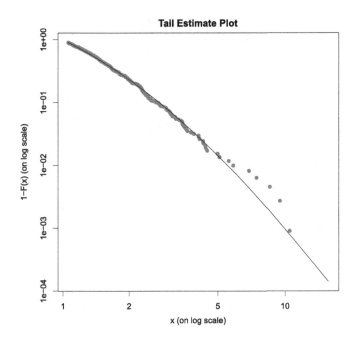

Figure 10.5: Tail plot

```
# Add VaR and ES estimates to the plot while generating the
# interval estimates
gpdQPlot(t1)   #VaR (figure-10.6)


# Lower CI Estimate Upper CI
# 2.657342 2.838216 3.059101

gpdSfallPlot(t1)   #ES (figure-10.7)


# Lower CI Estimate Upper CI
# 3.637300 4.052035 4.713026
```

The VaR and ES modelling using the POT method in the example above is considered as a *static* model due to the assumption of stationarity in the raw data. EVT can also be used in a *dynamic* model, where the conditional distribution of $F$ is taken into account and the volatility of returns is captured. The dynamic model as proposed by McNeil and Frey (2000) and also implemented by Singh, Allen and Powell (2013) uses an ARCH/GARCH type process along with the POT to model VaR and ES which reacts to market fluctuations and hence captures current risk. We will discuss the method in an example at the end of the chapter.

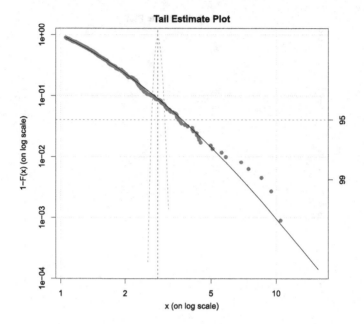

Figure 10.6:   VaR plot

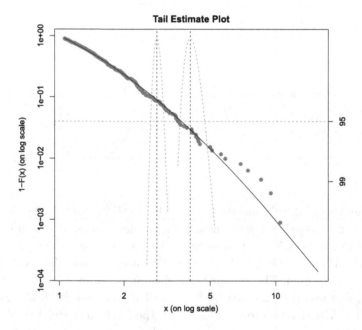

Figure 10.7:   VaR and ES plot

## 10.3    EVT and Tail Dependence

As discussed in the previous section, univariate EVT provides methods to quantify the tails of return distributions and hence is useful in the calculation of important risk measures such as VaR and Expected Shortfall (or CVaR) which can be more efficient than more traditional time series methods for risk forecasting. The multivariate EVT is relatively recent and is useful in the quantification of extreme tail dependence in various financial markets like stock or bond markets. There are various studies which have used multivariate EVT to study dependence in various financial markets. For example, among others, Stărică (1999) studied dependence in extremes of the European Union currencies, Marsh and Wagner (2004) implemented EVT based methods to evaluate extremal dependence between stock returns and trading volume, Hilal, Poon and Tawn (2011) use the methods of Heffernan and Tawn (2004) to model extremal dependence between financial time series and demonstrate how it can be effectively used in hedging.

The dependence relationships in a multivariate setting can be classified into four types: independence, perfect dependence, asymptotic dependence and asymptotic independence. The extreme values in a asymptotically dependent setting occur simultaneously whereas they occur at different times in an asymptotic independent structure. EVT provides parametric models for the quantification of multivariate dependence most of which assume asymptotic dependence structures for modelling extreme tail dependence like most of the dependence models. Heffernan (2000), Coles, Heffernan and Tawn (1999) and Poon, Rockinger and Tawn (2003, 2004) developed two measures $\chi$ and $\bar{\chi}$ as a measure of extremal dependence particularly helpful in quantifying the asymptotic dependence between two sets of random data variables. $\chi$ quantifies the asymptotic extreme dependence if it exists which is measured by $\bar{\chi}$ with the advantage of having a nonparametric estimation method. Where there is no asymptotic dependence, $\bar{\chi}$ provides the measure of tail dependence.

### 10.3.1    Measures of tail dependence

According to *Sklar's Theorem* (Sklar, 1959) each joint distribution can be decomposed into its marginal distributions and its dependence structure (also called Copula $C$). If the marginal aspects of a joint distribution are

removed by some transformation of data, the remaining differences between
the distributions are then purely due to dependence (Embrechts, McNeil
and Straumann, 2002). With bivariate returns $(X, Y)$, the marginal aspects
of the joint distribution can be removed by transforming them to standard
Fréchet marginals $(S, T)$ as follows:

$$S = -\frac{1}{\log F_X(X)} \quad \text{and} \quad T = -\frac{1}{\log F_Y(Y)}, \quad (10.7)$$

where $F_X$ and $F_Y$ are marginal distribution functions for $X$ and $Y$,
respectively. In practical applications, $F_X$ and $F_Y$ are empirical distribution functions of separate variables. We can use the following R code
to first transform the ASX and DJIA returns to uniform marginals using
rank transformation followed by transforming them to standard Fréchet
marginals.

```
# Create a subset of last 5000 returns
data.bevt = cbind(-tail(data.ch10[, c(2, 3)], 5000))
# simple bivariate return plot
plot(data.bevt)  #figure-10.8
```

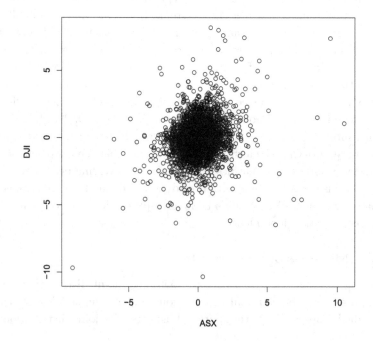

Figure 10.8:   Bivariate return plot-ASX/DJI

```
# Uniform Marginals-rank transformation
ula = apply(data.bevt, 2, rank)/(nrow(data.bevt) + 1)
# rank transformed variables
plot(ula, col = "dark blue")   #figure-10.9
```

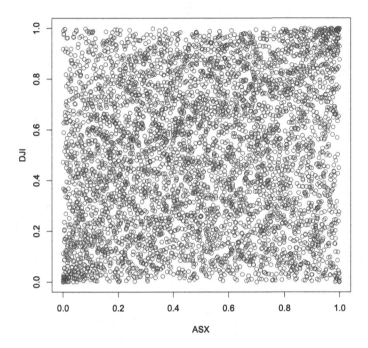

Figure 10.9:   Rank transformed returns

```
# Frechet Marginals
fla = -1/log(ula)
```

This transformation does not affect the dependence measures as it does not affect the dependence structure (Copula $C$ ) of the bivariate joint distribution. The Fréchet transformation is used as risk asset returns tend to exhibit fat tails (Loretan and Phillips, 1994). Here, $P(S > s) = P(T > s)$ $\sim s^{-1}$ as $s \to \infty$ and $S$ and $T$ have the same dependence structure as $(X, Y)$.

#### 10.3.1.1   *Asymptotic dependence — the conventional approach*

The transformed variables $S$ and $T$ are now on a common scale and possess the same dependence structure as $X$ and $Y$. If there is an extreme threshold

$s$ ($s$ can also be a quantile $q$) then the events $S > s$ and $T > s$ are equally extreme for both variables. The first nonparametric measure of dependence $\chi$ (Coles, Heffernan and Tawn, 1999; Poon, Rockinger and Tawn, 2003, 2004) is given by:

$$\chi = \lim_{s \to \infty} P(T > s | S > s)$$

$$= \lim_{s \to \infty} \frac{P(T > s, S > s)}{P(S > s)} \tag{10.8}$$

and $0 \le \chi \le 1$.

Here, $\chi$ can be used to investigate the dependence between $S$ and $T$. If $\chi > 0$, $S$ and $T$ are asymptotically dependent, and perfect dependence occurs if $\chi = 1$. If $\chi = 0$, $S$ and $T$ are asymptotically independent.

### 10.3.1.2  Asymptotic independence — an alternative measure of dependence

The conventional measure of dependence ($\chi$) does not provide a measure of dependence in case of $\chi = 0$, i.e. when variables are asymptotically independent and hence a second measure $\bar{\chi}$ was developed by Ledford and Tawn (1996) and Ledford *et al.* (1998). This measure ($\bar{\chi}$) can be used to measure dependence for asymptotically independent variables. As per Coles, Heffernan and Tawn (1999), $\bar{\chi}$ is defined as

$$\bar{\chi} = \lim_{s \to \infty} \frac{2 \log P(S > s)}{\log P(S > s, T > s)} - 1, \tag{10.9}$$

where $-1 < \bar{\chi} \le 1$. The measure $\bar{\chi}$ is a measure of the rate of $P(T > s | S > s) \to 0$.

The variables $S$ and $T$ have perfect dependence for $\bar{\chi} = 1$ and independence for $\bar{\chi} = 0$. The two cases where $\bar{\chi} > 0$ and $\bar{\chi} < 0$ indicate positive and negative association, respectively. It is also worth noting that for the bivariate Gaussian dependence structure $\bar{\chi} = \rho$, where $\rho$ is the Pearson correlation coefficient Heffernan (2000).

With these two dependence measures $(\chi, \bar{\chi})$, all the information needed to characterise the degree and type of extremal dependence can be obtained. In practice, first the bivariate distribution is tested for $\bar{\chi} = 1$, before quantifying the bivariate asymptotic dependence using the estimate $\chi$. If variables are not asymptotically dependent, i.e. $\bar{\chi} \ne 1$, the degree of dependence is given by the value of $\bar{\chi}$. In case of asymptotic dependence ($\bar{\chi} = 1$), the degree of dependence is quantified by the value of $\chi$.

The *extRemes*, *evd*, *POT* and *texmex* packages provide functions for bivariate $\chi$ and $\bar{\chi}$ estimation. We will now calculate the left tail dependence between ASX and DJIA demonstrating how to use the chiplot, taildep and chifunction from the *evd*, *extRemes* and *texmex* package, respectively.

```
# use data.bevt created in the last example create chi and
# chibar plots for various quantile thresholds ranging from
# 1% to 99%
library(evd)
chiplot(data.bevt, qlim = c(0.01, 0.99))  #(Figure-10.10)
```

Figure 10.10 shows plots of $\chi$ and $\bar{\chi}$ tail dependence measures. As evident in the plots, we can reject asymptotic dependence, i.e. $\bar{\chi} \neq 1$ and hence we can use only $\bar{\chi}$ to measure the degree of dependence. This process of selecting the required dependence measure is made simple by the chi function from *texmex* package which also has an accompanying plot method. The plot method to the chi functions greys out the $\chi$ plot if only $\bar{\chi}$ bar plot is required as shown in the following code

```
library(texmex)
# calculate chi measures
chi1 = chi(data.bevt, qlim = c(0.01, 0.99))
# plot using the plot.chi method
plot(chi1)  #figure-10.11
```

We can now calculate $\bar{\chi}$ measure for the required quantile threshold using the taildep function from the extRemes package. The following example calculates the left tail dependence between ASX and DJIA for the 90% and 95% quantile.

```
library(extRemes)
# 95% threshold
taildep(x = data.bevt$ASX, y = data.bevt$DJI, u = 0.95,
type = "chibar")

#     chibar
# 0.2658906

# 99% threshold
taildep(x = data.bevt$ASX, y = data.bevt$DJI, u = 0.99,
type = "chibar")

#     chibar
# 0.4820469
```

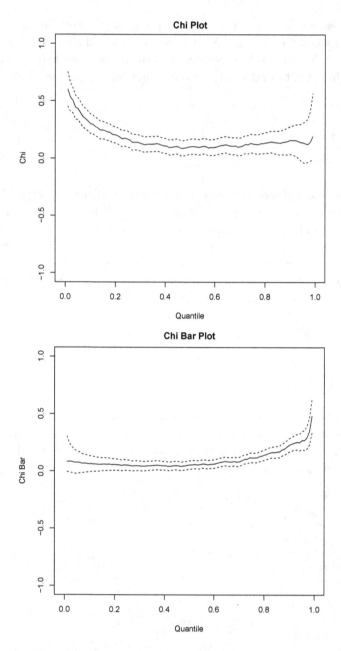

Figure 10.10:   EVT dependence measure chi and chi-bar

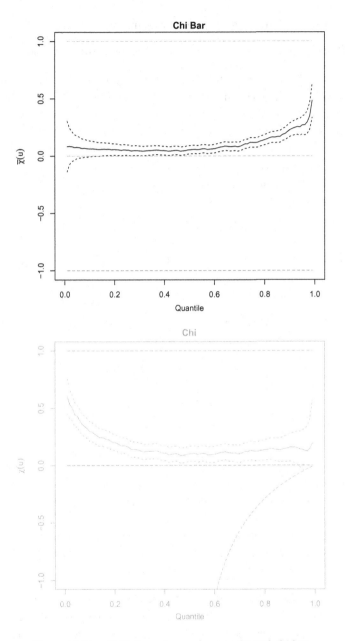

Figure 10.11: EVT dependence measure chi and chi-bar

## 10.3.2    Estimating $\chi$ and $\bar{\chi}$: nonparametric method

The following four assumptions are required to estimate $\chi$ and $\bar{\chi}$:

(i) the distribution $(S, T)$ has a joint tail behaviour that is bivariate regularly varying, satisfying the conditions of Ledford *et al.* (1998);

(ii) the sample characteristics of the empirical joint distribution, above some selected threshold, reflect the limiting behaviour;

(iii) the series has sufficient independence over time for the sample characteristics to converge to the population characteristics $\bar{\chi}$ and $\chi$;

(iv) the marginal variables can be transformed to identically distributed Fréchet variables.

The first three are same as those required to model the univariate EVT tail methods.

To estimate $\bar{\chi}$ and $\chi$, Ledford and Tawn (1996, 1998) established that under weak conditions,

$$P(S > s, T > s) \sim \mathcal{L}(s)s^{-1/\eta} \quad \text{as} \quad s \to \infty, \qquad (10.10)$$

where $0 < \eta \leq 1$ is a constant called the *coefficient of tail dependence* and $\mathcal{L}(s)$ is a slowly varying function. It follows that

$$\bar{\chi} = 2\eta - 1 \qquad (10.11)$$

and

$$\chi = \begin{cases} c & \text{if } \bar{\chi} = 1 \text{ and } \mathcal{L}(s) \to c > 0, \quad \text{as } s \to \infty, \\ 0 & \text{if } \bar{\chi} = 1 \text{ and } \mathcal{L}(s) \to 0, \quad \text{as } s \to \infty, \\ 0 & \text{if } \bar{\chi} < 1. \end{cases} \qquad (10.12)$$

If $\bar{\chi} = 1$ as $\eta = 1$, then $\chi = \lim_{s \to \infty} \mathcal{L}(s) = c$ which is the case of asymptotic dependence. If $0 < \eta < 1$ or if $\eta = 1$ and $\lim_{s \to \infty} \mathcal{L}(s) = 0$ (boundary case), then $\chi = 0$ and the variables are asymptotically independent with dependence given by $\bar{\chi} = 2\eta - 1$.

From the *coefficient of tail dependence* $(\eta)$, three kind of asymptotic independence can be identified in a class of asymptotically independent variables based on the sign of $\bar{\chi} = 2\eta - 1$ (Heffernan, 2000):

(i) Positive Association $(1/2 < \eta < 1$ or $\eta = 1$ and $\mathcal{L}(s) \to 0$ as $s \to \infty)$; in this case there is more frequent occurrence of observations for which both $X$ and $Y$ exceed a threshold $s$ than exact independence.

(ii) Negative Association $(0 < \eta < 1/2)$; in this case there is less frequent occurrence of observations for which both $X$ and $Y$ exceed a threshold $s$ than exact independence.

(iii) Finally, when $\eta = 1/2$, extremes of $X$ and $Y$ are near independent and they attain perfect independence in case $\mathcal{L}(s) = 1$.

It is evident from discussion of $\eta$ above that the degree of dependence between large values (extremes) of $X$ and $Y$ is determined by $\eta$ and $\mathcal{L}$, an increasing value of $\eta$ indicates a stronger association and for a given $\eta$ the relative strength of dependence is given by $\mathcal{L}$.

Therefore, estimation of $\eta$ and $\lim_{s \to \infty} \mathcal{L}(s)$ are required for estimating $\chi$ and $\bar{\chi}$. There is a possibility of the boundary case leading to asymptotic independence when $\eta = 1$ and $\mathcal{L}(s) \to 0$ as $s \to \infty$. It is not possible to identify this boundary case from the data as the slowly varying function $(\mathcal{L}(s))$ cannot take a value other than constant, and this makes the misspecification of the dependence structure unlikely to be important. This allows focus on the inference for $\eta$ and $\lim_{s \to \infty} \mathcal{L}(s)$, with the assumption of the slowly varying function being constant over a high threshold, i.e. $\mathcal{L}(s) = d$ for $s > u$.

If $Z = \min(S, T)$, following univariate EVT

$$
\begin{aligned}
P(Z > z) &= P\{\min(S, T) > z\} \\
&= P(S > z, T > z) \\
&= \mathcal{L}(z) z^{-1/\eta} \\
&= d z^{-1/\eta} \text{ for } z > u,
\end{aligned}
\tag{10.13}
$$

for a high threshold $u$. Here, $\eta$ is the tail index of the univariate $Z$ and an estimate of $\eta$ can be obtained by the Hill estimator (Coles, 2001; Embrechts *et al.*, 1997), restricted to interval $(0,1]$, and $d$ is the scale parameter. We can use the `tcplot` function from the *evd* package to plot $\eta$ within a specified quantile limit as shown in the following code

```
# Convert to univariate series Using previously generated
# Frechet Marginals
fla = apply(fla, 1, min)
thresh = quantile(fla, probs = c(0.025, 0.975))
# figure-10.12
t2 = tcplot(fla, thresh, nt = 30, pscale = TRUE, which = 2, vci =
FALSE,
    cilty = 2, type = "l", ylim = c(-0.2, 1.2),
    ylab = expression(eta))
```

This section of the chapter has discussed two dependence measures $(\chi, \bar{\chi})$ in multivariate EVT context. Multivariate EVT provides other parametric dependence models (see Beirlant *et al.* (2006)) as well which are

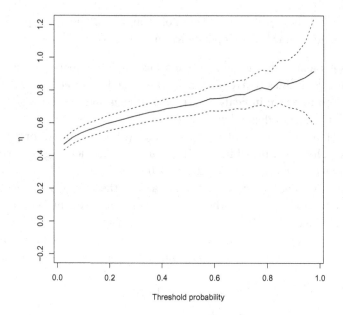

Figure 10.12:  Tail index plot

useful for various applications. We will not discuss these methods but will rather leave them as topic for further reading.

## 10.4    Example: EVT VaR — A Dynamic Approach

In VaR and ES calculations using POT when EVT is applied directly to raw return data assuming the distribution to be stationary or unconditional, the EVT model can be called a *static* model (McNeil and Frey, 2000). EVT can be used in a *dynamic* model, where the conditional distribution of $F$ is taken into account and the volatility of returns is captured. The dynamic model uses an ARCH/GARCH type process along with the POT to model VaR and ES which reacts to market fluctuations and hence captures current risk. We will now implement the dynamic method in this example.

McNeil and Frey (2000) proposed a *dynamic* VaR forecasting method using EVT. Their method makes use of GARCH to model current market volatility which is further fed into VaR estimates obtained from the POT model fitted to residuals of a GARCH model. By using GARCH models to forecast the estimates of conditional volatility, the model provides dynamic one day ahead forecasts for VaR and ES for the financial time series.

Let $R_t$ the return at time $t$ be defined by the following stochastic volatility (SV) model

$$R_t = \mu_t + \sigma_t Z_t, \qquad (10.14)$$

where $\mu_t$ is the expected return on day $t$ and $\sigma_t$ is the volatility and $Z_t$ gives the noise variable with a distribution $F_Z(z)$ (commonly assumed to be standard normal). It is assumed that $R_t$ is a stationary process.

In contrast to static risk modelling using EVT, which models the unconditional distribution $F_X(x)$ and gives loss for $k$ days in general, the dynamic approach models the conditional return distribution conditioned on the historical data to forecast the loss over the next $k \geq 1$ days. Using the GARCH(1,1) model, the one day ahead forecasts of VaR and ES are calculated as:

$$VaR_q = \mu_{t+1} + \sigma_{t+1} VaR(Z_q). \qquad (10.15)$$

With the assumption that $F_Z(z)$ is a known standard distribution, typically a normal distribution $Z_q$ can be easily calculated. The EVT approach (McNeil and Frey, 2000), instead of assuming $F_Z(z)$ to be normal applies the POT estimation procedure to this distribution of residuals.

For a return series at the close of day $t$ with time window of the last $n$ returns $(R_{t-n+1}, \ldots, R_t)$, the method is implemented in the following two steps:

(1) A GARCH(1,1) model is fitted to the historical data by pseudo maximum likelihood estimation (PML) also known as Quasi-maximum likelihood estimation. The GARCH (1,1) model in this step gives the residuals for step-2 and also 1 day ahead predictions of $\mu_{t+1}$ and $\sigma_{t+1}$.
(2) EVT (POT method) is applied to the residuals extracted from step-1 for a constant choice of threshold $u$ to estimate VaR$(Z)_q$ to calculate the risk measure.

The parameters of the GARCH model in step-1 can be estimated using the methods discussed in Chapter-9. The POT method in step-2 is fitted using MLE as discussed previously.

This method will be implemented to forecast one day ahead VaR for the ASX-All ordinaries and the S&P-500 indices and we will compare the results with a standard GARCH(1,1) based estimates later in the chapter in the empirical exercise. The results will be backtested by application of the binomial method based on the number of daily violations above VaR.

## 10.4.1　Data and methodology

We use the last 2500 ASX log return values from *data.ch10.RData* dataset.
The empirical exercise is conducted with a moving window of the last 1000
days log returns of ASX-All Ordinaries to forecast one day ahead 1% and
5% VaR estimates. The following code extracts the subset and generates a
quantile–quantile plot for the return series using the qqnorm function from
the *extRemes* package which also generates a confidence band.

```
# Subset of last 1500 returns
d.ex10 = tail(data.ch10[, c(1:2)], 2500)
# Q-Q Plot (figure-10.13)
qqnorm(d.ex10$ASX)
qqline(d.ex10$ASX)
```

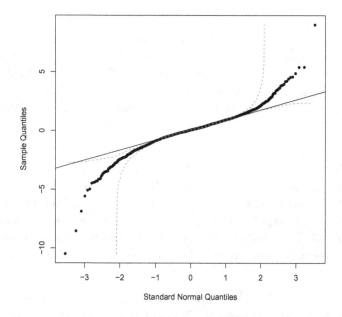

Figure 10.13:　Q–Q plot for ASX returns

Figure 10.13 shows that the sample return data shows deviation from
the normal distribution and should be suitable for our empirical example.

The method uses a two-step approach to predict the next day volatility
($\sigma$) and mean expected return ($\mu$) using a GARCH (1,1) model in the first
step and in the second step the residuals of the step-1 are fitted to GPD to
get quantile values for the final VaR calculations. A 90% quantile level is

chosen as the threshold, $u$ to fit the residuals from the GARCH(1,1) model to GPD.

### 10.4.2  VaR forecasts using dynamic EVT model

We use *fExtreme* and *fGarch* package to estimate the model for calculating 1% and 5% VaR for our data sample. With a total of 2500 returns and a moving window of 1000 returns, the analysis results in 1501 VaR forecasts for the left tail. We can estimate the model using the code below:

```
# load the required packages
library(fExtremes)
library(fGarch)


d1 = d.ex10
l1 = nrow(d1)  #Number of observations
win = 1000  #Windows size
# Create a matrix object to store VaR forecasts


VaR = matrix(0, nrow = l1 - win + 1, ncol = 2)
colnames(VaR) = c("VaR1", "VaR5")  #Name the columns for 1% and 5% VaR
# loop to cycle through the window
for (i in 1:(l1 - win + 1)) {
    # Initializing
    d2 = as.timeSeries(d1[i:(win + i - 1), 2])
    colnames(d2) = "ret"
    # GARCH(1,1) using garch Fit from fGarch
    fit.garch = garchFit(~garch(1, 1), data = d2, trace = FALSE)
    # Generate 1-step forecast
    pred = predict(fit.garch, 1)
    # Generate Residuals for POT method
    res = residuals(fit.garch)
    # Fit POT with 90% quantile (negative residuals for
    # left tail)
    fit.pot = gpdFit(-res, quantile(-res, 0.9))
    var1.pot = gpdRiskMeasures(fit.pot, prob = 0.99)  #1% VaR
    # Generate 1% Dynamic EVT VaR
    vard1 = pred$meanForecast + pred$standardDeviation *
        (var1.pot$q)
    VaR[i, 1] = vard1  #save 1% VaR
    var5.pot = gpdRiskMeasures(fit.pot, prob = 0.95)  #5% VaR
    # Generate 5% Dynamic EVT VaR
    vard5 = pred$meanForecast + pred$standardDeviation *
        (var5.pot$q)
    VaR[i, 2] = vard5  #save 5% VaR


}
```

These generated VaR forecasts can be visualised along with the actual returns using the following code

```
# first create a dataset with actual data and VaR forecasts
VaR2 = cbind(d1[1001:2500, ], VaR[1:1500, ])
# Convert it to timeseries
VaR2 = as.timeSeries(VaR2)
# plot in a single plot (figure-10.14)
plot(VaR2, plot.type = "single")
# Add legend
legend("topright", title = NULL, c("5% VaR", "1%VaR", "Return"),
    fill = c("green", "red", "black"), horiz = TRUE)
```

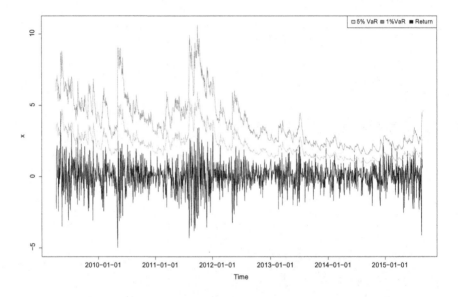

Figure 10.14:   Dynamic-EVT VaR forecasts

Figure 10.14 plots the actual returns against 1% and 5% Dynamic-EVT VaR forecasts. The plot shows only few VaR exceedances compared to actual return, which are mostly in the case of 5% VaR. The figure also shows how the Dynamic-EVT VaR adjusts itself to changing volatility. Although not implemented in this example, these generated VaR values can be tested for VaR violations against the actual returns as done previously in Chapter 9.

## 10.5   Summary

In this chapter we introduced EVT, in particular, the POT model from the EVT. We focused on the POT model and its implementation in quantifying extreme tail risk in financial data. We also discussed two bivariate measures $(\chi, \bar{\chi})$ for extreme tail dependence together and their implementation using various R packages. Finally we concluded this chapter with an example of Dynamic-EVT VaR forecasting which is capable of modelling VaR using EVT while reflecting changing volatility in a time series. In this chapter, we started our discussion on multivariate analysis beginning with bivariate EVT methods for tail dependence. We will now introduce multivariate modelling using Copula in the concluding chapter of this book.

Chapter 11

# Introduction to Multivariate Analysis using Copulas

## 11.1 Introduction

Multivariate analysis refers to methods and techniques used to model and analyse datasets with higher dimensions, i.e. more than one variable. The econometric analysis in Chapter 9 was performed on univariate data i.e. data with only one variable but there are various problems which require multivariate data with more than one variable e.g. Asset Dependence Modelling, Portfolio Selection and Risk Modelling. Dependence between random variables can be modelled using Copulas. A copula returns the joint probability of events as a function of the marginal probabilities of each event. This makes copulas attractive, as the univariate marginal behaviour of random variables can be modelled separately from their dependence.

Applications of copulas in financial risk measurement and aggregation can be seen in the papers of Bouyé et al. (2000), Embrechts, McNeil and Straumann (2002) and Embrechts, Lindskog and McNeil (2001). Palaro and Hotta (2006) used conditional copula to calculate VaR, Cherubini and Luciano (2001) estimated VaR using the Archimedean copula family and the historical empirical distribution in the estimation of marginal distributions. Other applications include modelling of conditional dependence by Jondeau and Rockinger (2001), copula in derivative pricing by Georges et al. (2001), implementation in risk of credit derivatives by Meneguzzo and Vecchiato (2004). Embrechts, McNeil and Straumann (2002) and Embrechts, Höing and Juri (2003) used copulas to model extreme value and risk limits. Patton (2006a, 2006b) extended unconditional copula theory to the conditional case and used it to model asymmetric dependence and on multivariate time series distributions of different lengths. More recently, Brechmann and Czado (2013), Allen et al. (2013) and Singh et al.

(2014) applied R-Vine multivariate copulas to study the financial risk and return dependence between financial markets and stocks.

In this chapter, we discuss multivariate Copula methods which are widely used in financial risk modelling and portfolio formation. We will first provide an introduction to Copula along with few types of copulas which are used to model dependence between variables in a multivariate setting with normal or non-normal distributions thus overcoming the limitation of the usual Correlation method and which are widely used in the financial portfolio selection and risk modelling. We will also provide a brief introduction to Vine Copulas, which provide even more flexible multivariate models which are formed using bivariate copulas. We discuss the types of copulas using an applied focus rather than going into extensive mathematical details. See, Bouyé *et al.* (2000), Joe (1997), Alexander (2008), Cheung (2009) and Franke, Härdle and Hafner (2015), among others for an extensive discussion on Copulas and, Dissmann (2010), Kurowicka (2011) and Aas *et al.* (2009) for further insights into Vine Copulas. We will demonstrate these tools with some empirical examples available in R packages like *Copula, fCopulae, CDVine* and *VineCopula*. We will also discuss an example to demonstrate the use of Copulas in calculating VaR for a multivariate portfolio at the end of the chapter.

## 11.2  Copula

Copulas are the statistical tool which can be used to model the underlying dependence structure of a multivariate distribution. According to the *Sklar's Theorem (Sklar, 1959)*, each joint distribution can be decomposed into its marginal distributions and a copula $C$ which gives the dependence structure. In simple terms, a copula is a joint distribution of the marginal distributions. Here, we define Copula with Sklar's theorem along with some important types of copula.

According to the most common definition (adapted from Franke *et al.* (2015)), a function $C : [0,1]^d \to [0,1]$ is a $d$-dimensional copula if it satisfies the following conditions for every $u = (u_1,\ldots,u_d)^\top \in [0,1]^d$ and $j \in \{1,\ldots,d\}$

(1)  if $u_j = 0$ then $C(u_1,\ldots,u_d) = 0$,
(2)  $C(1,\ldots,1,u_j,1,\ldots,1) = u_j$,
(3)  for every $v = (v_1,\ldots,v_d)^\top \in [0,1]^d, v_j \leq u_j$

$$V_C(u,v) \geq 0,$$

where $V_C(u, v)$ is given by

$$\sum_{i_1=1}^{2} \cdots \sum_{i_d=1}^{2} (-1)^{i_1 + \cdots + i_d} C(g_{1i_1}, \ldots, g_{di_d}).$$

According to (1) and (3), copulas are grounded functions and that all $d$-dimensional boxes with vertices in $[0, 1]^d$ have non-negative C-volume. Property second shows that the copulas have uniform marginal distributions.

### 11.2.1 Types of copula

Copula can be divided into two broad types, Elliptical Copulas e.g. Gaussian Copula and Student's t-copula and Archimedean Copulas, e.g. Gumbel copula and Clayton copula. Below we give a brief description of these copulas, complex mathematical details are left out for brevity.

#### 11.2.1.1 *Elliptical copulas*

Gaussian copula

The dependence structure of a multivariate normal distribution is represented by a Gaussian copula. The Gaussian copula is derived from the $n$-dimensional multivariate and univariate standard normal distributions. Correlation matrices act as parameters for Gaussian copula, and due to the wide use of correlation in finance Gaussian copula are frequently used for convenience. A density plot for a bivariate normal copula can be generated using functions available in the *copula* package. The *copula* package provides a useful set of functions which are helpful in quantifying various types of copulas. The following code uses the `normalCopula` function to simulate a bivariate Gaussian copula with correlation of 0.5 and plots its density using the `persp` function.

```
library(copula)
# Generate the copula with rho=0.5
normc = normalCopula(param = 0.5, dim = 2)
# plot the density using persp (figure-11.1)
persp(normc, dCopula, col = "dark grey", ticktype = "detailed")
```

Figure 11.1 gives the density plot for a bivariate Gaussian copula with a correlation of 0.5. As shown in the figure, the normal copula is a symmetric copula. They also suffer from very weak tail dependence and thus are not usually appropriate for modelling financial assets.

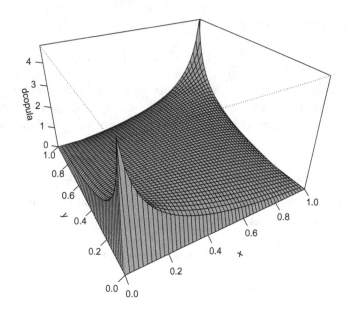

Figure 11.1:   The Gaussian copula density plot

Figure 11.2 gives the same bivariate Gaussian copula density plot but with the fitted normal copula on bivariate stock return data given in *data_ch11.RData* file. The Gaussian copula is fitted using the `fitCopula` function on ASX and DJIA returns converted to uniform marginals using the rank method as shown below:

```
# load data
load("data_ch11.RData")
# select ASX & DJIA
data1 = data_ch11[, c(1:2)]
# convert to uniform marginals using rank method
ula = apply(data1, 2, rank)/(nrow(data1) + 1)
fit1 = fitCopula(normc, ula, method = "ml")
summary(fit1)
# figure-11.2
persp(fit1@copula, dCopula, theta = 45, ticktype = "detailed",
    col = "steel blue")

# $method
# [1] "maximum likelihood"
#
# $loglik
```

```
# [1] 0.001636084
#
# $convergence
# [1] 0
#
# $coefficients
#          Estimate Std. Error    z value  Pr(>|z|)
# rho.1 0.002714956 0.04746139 0.05720347 0.9543831
#
# attr(,"class")
# [1] "summary.fitCopula"
```

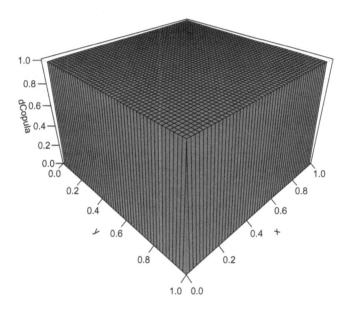

Figure 11.2: Gaussian copula density for return data

Although we have used the nonparametric rank method to convert return data to uniform marginals, one can also use parametric distributions
like the Student-t for marginals in empirical analysis.

### Student's-t Copula

The Student's-t copula models the dependence structure of multivariate
Student-t distributions. The parameters for the student's-t-copula are the
correlation matrix and degrees of freedom. Student's-t-copula also show

symmetrical dependence but have higher tail dependence than those in the Gaussian copula which makes it useful in financial risk modelling. We can fit the Student-t copula to the financial return data in the same way as we did with the Gaussian copula. The following example illustrates

```
# sample t copula
tcop = tCopula(-0.3, df = 4, dim = 2)
# density of tcop (figure-11.3)
persp(tcop, dCopula, col = "dark grey")
```

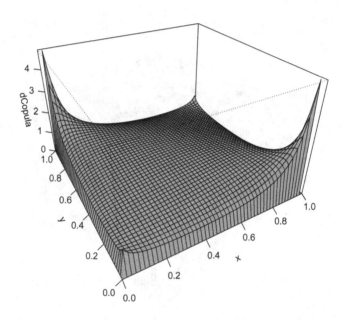

Figure 11.3:   Student-t copula density plot

```
# fit using fitCopula and sample tCopula.
fit2 = fitCopula(tCopula(-0.3, df = 20, dim = 2), ula, method = "ml")
summary(fit2)

# $method
# [1] "maximum likelihood"
#
# $loglik
# [1] 2.134595
#
# $convergence
# [1] 0
```

```
#
# $coefficients
#        Estimate Std. Error    z value    Pr(>|z|)
# rho.1 0.003262517 0.05097278 0.06400509 0.94896618
# df    9.007672644 4.82247213 1.86785375 0.06178246
#
# attr(,"class")
# [1] "summary.fitCopula"

# plot the fitted copula density (figure-11.4)
persp(fit2@copula, dCopula, theta = 45, ticktype = "detailed",
    col = "steel blue")
```

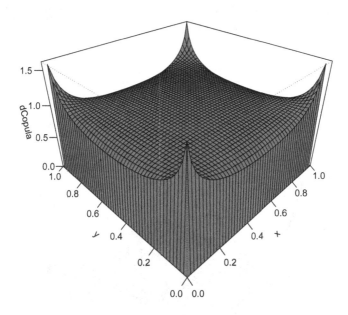

Figure 11.4:   Student-t copula density for return data

## 11.2.1.2   *Archimedean copulas*

Archimedean copulas are explicit copulas which are built on a generator function, with some restrictions. There can be various copulas in this family of copulas due to various generator functions available (see Nelsen (1999)). The Clayton and Gumbel are two archimedean copulas which are popular in financial risk modelling due to their ability to capture tail dependence.

The Clayton copula captures lower tail dependence whereas the Gumbel copula captures upper tail dependence.

Clayton copula

The Clayton copula (Clayton (1978)) has a generator function:

$$\phi(u) = \alpha^{-1}(u^{-\alpha} - 1), \quad \alpha \neq 0. \tag{11.1}$$

With variation in parameter $\alpha$, the Clayton copulas capture a range of dependence. The Clayton copula is particularly helpful in capturing lower tail dependence.

Figure 11.5 gives a density plot for bivariate Clayton copula with $\alpha = 1$, the asymmetric lower tail dependence is evident from the figure. The following code generates Figure 11.5.

```
# sample Clayton copula with alpha=1
claycop = claytonCopula(param = 1)
# plot the density (figure-11.5)
persp(claycop, dCopula, theta = 45, col = "dark grey")
```

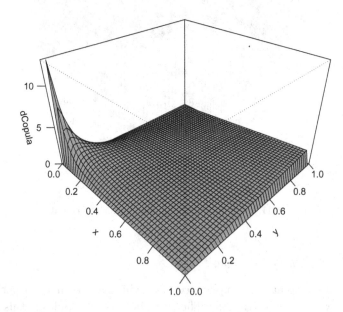

Figure 11.5:   Clayton copula density with lower tail dependence

We can fit the stock index return data to the Clayton copula and also plot the density as follows

```
# fit to Clayton copula
fit3 = fitCopula(claycop, ula)
summary(fit3)

# $method
# [1] "maximum pseudo-likelihood"
#
# $loglik
# [1] 0.002745893
#
# $convergence
# [1] 0
#
# $coefficients
#          Estimate Std. Error       z value  Pr(>|z|)
# param -0.003618001 0.04667518 -0.07751446 0.9382143
#
# attr(,"class")
# [1] "summary.fitCopula"

# plot the fitted copula density (figure-11.6)
persp(fit3@copula, dCopula, theta = 45, col = "steel blue")
```

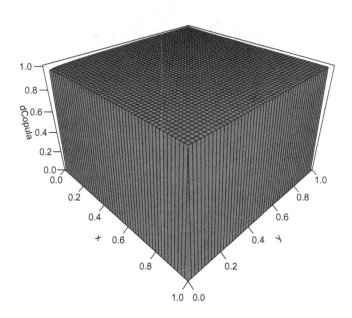

Figure 11.6:   Clayton copula density for the return data

## Gumbel Copula

The generating function for the Gumbel copula (Gumbel, 1960) is given by

$$\phi(u) = -(\ln u)^{\alpha}, \quad \alpha \geq 1. \tag{11.2}$$

For $\alpha > 1$, the Gumbel copula has positive upper tail dependence. Figure 11.7 gives the density plot for bivariate Gumbel copula with $\alpha = 2$, the upper tail dependence can be seen in the figure. The following code is used to generate Figure 11.7

```
# sample copula
gumcop = gumbelCopula(param = 2)
# plot the density (figure-11.7)
persp(gumcop, dCopula, theta = 45, col = "dark grey")
```

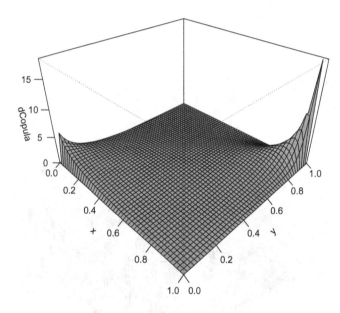

Figure 11.7:   Gumbel copula density with upper tail dependence

We can also check how well our stock index return data fits to the Gumbel copula as shown below:

```
# fit to gumbel copula
fit4 = fitCopula(gumcop, ula)
summary(fit4)
```

```
# $method
# [1] "maximum pseudo-likelihood"
#
# $loglik
# [1] 0.1709648
#
# $convergence
# [1] 0
#
# $coefficients
#         Estimate Std. Error  z value        Pr(>|z|)
# param 1.015519 0.02719695 37.33944 3.761932e-305
#
# attr(,"class")
# [1] "summary.fitCopula"

# plot the fitted copula density (figure-11.8)
persp(fit4@copula, dCopula, theta = 45, col = "steel blue")
```

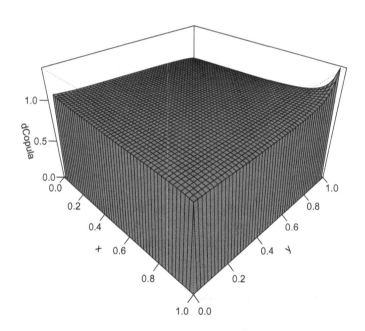

Figure 11.8: Gumbel copula density for the return data

The Frank copula (Frank, 1979) is another popular symmetric archimedean copula with no tail dependence.

## 11.2.2    Copula selection

We can see from the above examples of copulas that the best fit copula for the stock index return data is the Student-t copula according to the log-likelihood. R packages *VineCopula* and *CDVine* provide the function BiCopSelect which can be used to iteratively select the best fit copula based on the information criterion of AIC/BIC. The function provides options to fit various copulas with several types of dependence characteristics which can be tested, see help(BiCopSelect) for more details. We can check for the best fit copula for the stock index return data of ASX and DJIA using the AIC criterion as shown below:

```
# load package
library(VineCopula)
# use BiCopSelect to find the best fit copula out of 10
# copulas see help(BiCopSelect) for the list of copulas
cop1 = BiCopSelect(u1 = ula[, 1], u2 = ula[, 2], familyset = c(1:10),
    indeptest = FALSE, level = 0.05)
# best fit copula
cop1$family

# [1] 2

# copula parameters
cop1$par

# [1] 0.003262071

cop1$par2

# [1] 9.0094
```

We can see from the above example that the best fit copula is number "2" copula which is the Student-t copula in the list. We can verify now that the stock market return data shows the Student-t copula dependence structure.

## 11.3    Multivariate Vine Copulas

There are various types of bivariate copulas available (including the ones discussed in the previous section) which exhibit flexible and complex dependence patterns. With all different types of bivariate copulas, there is a limited choice of multivariate copulas which can model dependence structures which exhibit properties from more than one type of copulas. Joe (1996) proposed the so-called pair copula constructions (PCC) to overcome this issue as PCC facilitate multivariate copula construction using different types of copulas. PCC has been further explored and extended by Bedford and Cooke (2001, 2002) and Kurowicka and Cooke (2006).

PCC provides the building blocks for Vine Copula construction, which are flexible multivariate dependence models constructed using bivariate copulas. Aas *et al.* (2009) provided key insights into the special cases of canonical vine (C-Vine) and drawable vine (D-Vine) to deduce multivariate copulas based on PCC. C and D vines have a restrictive dependency structure on the data in high dimensions. Regular vines (R-Vines) are another class of hierarchical graphical model classifying PCC and are more flexible than C and D-Vine copulas in constructing the dependency structure of the data in high dimensions. Dissmann (2010) provides more details into R-Vines using graph theoretic algorithms.

The Vine Copula models have recently gained popularity in their use in financial risk modelling and research. Brechmann and Czado (2013), Allen *et al.* (2013) and Singh *et al.* (2014) recently applied R-Vine copulas to study the financial risk and return dependence between the stocks of the Euro Stoxx-50, the Dow Jones Industrial Average and stock markets from the ASEAN region, respectively. Brechmann, Czado and Paterlini (2014), Low *et al.* (2013), Schirmacher and Schirmacher (2008), Aas *et al.* (2009), Fischer *et al.* (2009), Aas and Berg (2009), Heinen *et al.* (2009) are some other illustrative applications of vine copulas.

Aas *et al.* (2009) provided the major statistical inference into C-Vine and D-Vine categories of vine copulas which belong to the more generalised R-Vine copulas. R-Vines can be depicted in a graphical theoretic model to determine which pairs are included in a pair-copula decomposition. An R-Vine is a special case for which all constraints are two-dimensional or conditional two-dimensional. Regular vines generalise trees, and are themselves specialisations of Cantor trees. Combined with copulas, regular vines have proven to be a flexible tool in high-dimensional dependence modelling.

We will not discuss any further mathematical details of Vine Copula but discuss the implementation using *CDVine* and *VineCopula* packages in R. In depth, details on vine copula modelling, estimation and inference are available in Aas *et al.* (2009), Dissmann (2010), Kurowicka (2011), Dissmann *et al.* (2013) and Brechmann (2010).

## 11.3.1  Estimating R-Vine copulas using R

*VineCopula* and *CDVine* are two major packages which can be used to model Vine Copulas in R. The *CDVine* package is particularly useful in calibrating C and D-Vine copulas whereas the *VineCopula* package is useful in modelling dependence using the R-Vine copula structure. We can fit a multivariate dataset of uniform marginals to Vine copula using the RVineStructureSelect function from the *VineCopula* package, see help(RVineStructureSelect) for various arguments to the function. In the following example, we use the *worldindices* dataset from *CDVine* package to fit C-Vine and R-Vine copula to the stock market data while selecting from first six (from 1 to 6) different types of copulas (see help(BiCopName) for copula family names and numbers).

```
library(CDVine)
library(VineCopula)
data(worldindices)
# fit C-Vine with type=1 argument
st_cvine = RVineStructureSelect(worldindices, familyset = c(1:6),
    type = 1, selectioncrit = "AIC", indeptest = FALSE,
    level = 0.05, progress = FALSE, rotations = FALSE)
# C-Vine Structure
st_cvine$Matrix

#       [,1] [,2] [,3] [,4] [,5] [,6]
# [1,]    3    0    0    0    0    0
# [2,]    4    1    0    0    0    0
# [3,]    1    4    4    0    0    0
# [4,]    6    6    6    2    0    0
# [5,]    2    2    2    6    5    0
# [6,]    5    5    5    5    6    6

# Copulas selected in the structure
st_cvine$family

#       [,1] [,2] [,3] [,4] [,5] [,6]
# [1,]    0    0    0    0    0    0
# [2,]    2    0    0    0    0    0
# [3,]    6    4    0    0    0    0
# [4,]    1    3    2    0    0    0
# [5,]    1    5    1    1    0    0
# [6,]    2    2    2    1    2    0

# Copula parameters
st_cvine$par  #first parameter
```

```
#            [,1]       [,2]        [,3]        [,4]
# [1,]  0.00000000  0.0000000  0.00000000  0.00000000
# [2,] -0.01136065  0.0000000  0.00000000  0.00000000
# [3,]  1.03877121  1.0953485  0.00000000  0.00000000
# [4,]  0.11214608  0.1406430  0.06174718  0.00000000
# [5,]  0.27566031 -0.4163130 -0.14835617 -0.03383658
# [6,]  0.21135125  0.7257671  0.96311972  0.31160843
#           [,5] [,6]
# [1,] 0.0000000    0
# [2,] 0.0000000    0
# [3,] 0.0000000    0
# [4,] 0.0000000    0
# [5,] 0.0000000    0
# [6,] 0.9388581    0

st_cvine$par2  #second parameter

#            [,1]      [,2]       [,3] [,4]      [,5] [,6]
# [1,]  0.000000 0.000000  0.000000    0  0.00000    0
# [2,]  8.985533 0.000000  0.000000    0  0.00000    0
# [3,]  0.000000 0.000000  0.000000    0  0.00000    0
# [4,]  0.000000 0.000000  9.029789    0  0.00000    0
# [5,]  0.000000 0.000000  0.000000    0  0.00000    0
# [6,] 11.839906 4.407638 14.054805    0 13.48021    0
```

The C-Vine copula structure selected above can be plotted using the `RVineTreePlot` function which uses a tree graph to plot the multiple dependence structures. The following code illustrates with first two plots of C-Vine structure.

```
# figure-11.9
pc1 = RVineTreePlot(x = st_cvine, tree = 1, edge.labels = c("family"),
      P = NULL, type = 1)
pc2 = RVineTreePlot(x = st_cvine, tree = 2, edge.labels = c("family"),
      P = NULL, type = 1)
```

We can also estimate an R-Vine structure using the above procedure. The following code illustrates by fitting an R-Vine structure and first two tree plots.

```
# fit R-Vine with type=0 argument
st_rvine = RVineStructureSelect(worldindices, familyset = c(1:6),
    type = 0, selectioncrit = "AIC", indeptest = FALSE,
    level = 0.05, progress = FALSE, rotations = FALSE)
# R-Vine Structure
```

```
st_rvine$Matrix

#       [,1] [,2] [,3] [,4] [,5] [,6]
# [1,]    3    0    0    0    0    0
# [2,]    6    2    0    0    0    0
# [3,]    1    6    1    0    0    0
# [4,]    4    1    6    4    0    0
# [5,]    5    4    5    6    5    0
# [6,]    2    5    4    5    6    6
```

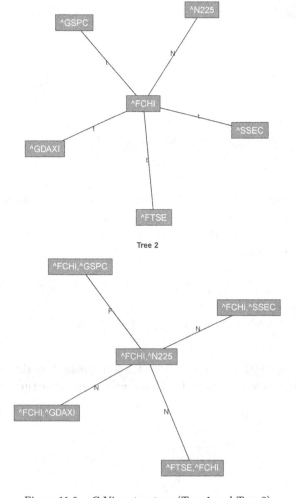

Figure 11.9:   C-Vine structure (Tree-1 and Tree-2)

```
# Copulas selected in the structure
st_rvine$family

#      [,1] [,2] [,3] [,4] [,5] [,6]
# [1,]   0    0    0    0    0    0
# [2,]   1    0    0    0    0    0
# [3,]   6    1    0    0    0    0
# [4,]   2    5    3    0    0    0
# [5,]   5    1    1    2    0    0
# [6,]   1    1    2    2    2    0

# Copula parameters
st_rvine$par   #first parameter

#             [,1]          [,2]        [,3]        [,4]
# [1,]  0.00000000   0.00000000  0.0000000   0.0000000
# [2,]  0.10958688   0.00000000  0.0000000   0.0000000
# [3,]  1.04007234  -0.02937854  0.0000000   0.0000000
# [4,] -0.01260442  -0.22628795  0.1376563   0.0000000
# [5,]  0.80301306  -0.14835617  0.1519013   0.0665243
# [6,]  0.32463376   0.31160843  0.7301567   0.9631197
#             [,5] [,6]
# [1,]  0.0000000    0
# [2,]  0.0000000    0
# [3,]  0.0000000    0
# [4,]  0.0000000    0
# [5,]  0.0000000    0
# [6,]  0.9388581    0

st_rvine$par2   #second parameter

#             [,1] [,2]      [,3]      [,4]      [,5] [,6]
# [1,]   0.00000    0  0.000000  0.000000   0.00000    0
# [2,]   0.00000    0  0.000000  0.000000   0.00000    0
# [3,]   0.00000    0  0.000000  0.000000   0.00000    0
# [4,]  11.42255    0  0.000000  0.000000   0.00000    0
# [5,]   0.00000    0  0.000000  8.660623   0.00000    0
# [6,]   0.00000    0  5.005079 14.054805  13.48021    0

# Tree plots (figure-11.10)
pr1 = RVineTreePlot(x = st_rvine, tree = 1, edge.labels = c("family"),
        P = NULL, type = 1)
pr2 = RVineTreePlot(x = st_rvine, tree = 2, edge.labels = c("family"),
        P = NULL, type = 1)
```

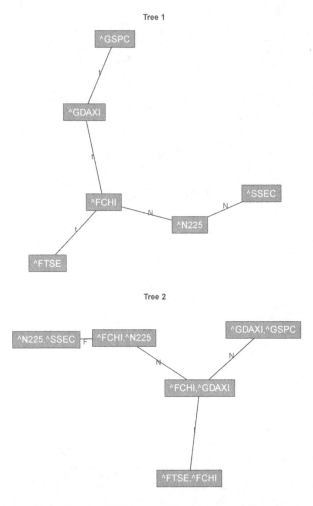

Figure 11.10:   R-Vine structure (Tree-1 and Tree-2)

Figure 11.10 as compared to Figure 11.9 shows a more flexible tree structure from the R-Vine fit which confirms the more flexible structure of an R-Vine copula model.

The *CDVine* and *VineCopula* package also provide several other functions to calculate important statistics for copula like probability density, conditional density, quantile, tail dependence, etc., which are not discussed here for the sake of brevity.

## 11.4 Example: Portfolio VaR Estimation using Vine Copula

As shown in the previous section, the R-Vine approach potentially gives better results than the usual bivariate copula approach as the copulas can be selected from a range of copulas with different underlying distributions and dependence structures. The multivariate dependence structure obtained from R-Vine Copulas can be used for portfolio evaluation and risk modelling such as forecasting portfolio VaR. Allen *et al.* (2013), provide an empirical example which models VaR for an equally weighted portfolio of 10 stocks from the Dow Jones Industrial Average index. We will replicate that empirical exercise in this example and calculate VaR for a portfolio of five stock indices, viz., ASX All Ordinaries, Nikkei-225, Dow Jones Industrial Average, Heng Seng Stock Index and FTSE 100 using R-Vine Copula. We use the *data_ch11.RData* file with daily percentage log returns of these five indices for this example.

### 11.4.1 Data and methodology

We construct an equally weighted portfolio of five stock indices data from the *data_ch11.RData* file. The data used is from July-2013 to June-2014 with a total of 456 returns per index. As the process is highly computationally intensive, we use only the last 300 returns from the data with a 250 days moving window dynamic approach to forecast VaR which results in 51 forecasts. The main steps of the approach (adapted from Allen *et al.* (2013)) are as outlined below:

(1) Convert the data sample to log returns.
(2) Select a moving window of 250 returns.
(3) Fit GARCH(1,1) with Student-t innovations to convert the log returns into an i.i.d. series. We fit the same GARCH(1,1) with student-t in all the iterations to maintain uniformity in the method, and this approach also makes the method a little less computationally intensive.
(4) Extract the residuals from Step 3 and standardise them with the Standard deviations obtained from Step 3.
(5) Convert the standardised residuals to student-t marginals for Copula estimation. The steps above are repeated for all the 10 stocks to obtain a multivariate matrix of uniform marginals.
(6) Fit an R-Vine to the multivariate data with the same copulas as used in Section 11.1.

(7) Generate simulations using the fitted R-Vine model. We generate 1000 simulations per stock for forecasting a day ahead VaR.

(8) Convert the simulated uniform marginals to standardised residuals.

(9) Simulate returns from the simulated standardised residuals using GARCH simulations.

(10) Generate a series of simulated daily portfolio returns to forecast 1% and 5% VaR.

(11) Repeat Steps 1–10 for a moving window.

The approach above results in VaR forecasts which whilst not dependent in time have the advantage of being co-dependent on the stocks in the portfolio. We can also easily generate ES forecasts after generating VaR estimates using the same steps. We use this approach as a demonstration of a practical application of the information about co-dependencies captured by the flexible Vine Copula approach applied to generate a frequently applied risk metric.

### 11.4.2   VaR forecasts using R

We use the *VineCopula, rugarch, sn* and *xts* packages to implement our simulation based VaR procedure. The R code demonstrated here uses easy to understand *for* loops in the recursive procedure.

```
# R-Vine VaR
library(sn)
library(rugarch)
library(VineCopula)
library(xts)
set.seed(100)   #to get consistent results
# load data
load("data_ch11.RData")
# moving window size
window = 250
# take a sample of last 300 returns
data_rv1 = data_ch11[(nrow(data_ch11) - 299):nrow(data_ch11),
    ]
# remove the date column
data_rv2 = data_rv1[, -1]
# remove NAs if any
data_rv2 = na.omit(data_rv2)
# number of assets
n.asset = ncol(data_rv2)
# total number of returns
```

```
n.tot = nrow(data_rv2)
# length of test window
n.test = n.tot - window
# convert log return to simple return for
# portfolio
s.ret = exp(data_rv2) - 1
# equally weighted portfolio returns
data.port.sr = (apply(s.ret, 1, sum))/n.asset
# covert to log return for GARCH
data.port.lr = log(1 + data.port.sr)
# Test data
data.prediction = data_rv2[(window + 1):nrow(data_rv2),
    ]
# Portfolio returns for test window
data.port.pred = data.port.lr[(window + 1):length(data.port.lr)]
# data frame to store VaR predictions
var.pred = data.frame(var1 = rep(0, times = (n.test +
    1)), var2 = rep(0, times = (n.test + 1)))
# data frame to store ES predictions (remove
# comments to generate cvar)
# es.pred=data.frame(es1=rep(0,times=(n.test+1)),
es2=rep(0,times=(n.test+1)))
# ugarchspec object to fit GARCH(1,1) with
# student-t
spec = ugarchspec(variance.model = list(model = "sGARCH",
    garchOrder = c(1, 1)), distribution.model = "std",
    mean.model = list(armaOrder = c(0, 0)))
# initiate loop counters
j = 1
k = 1
l = 1
i = 1
# master loop to itirate 51 times
for (j in 1:(n.test + 1)) {
    dum1.ret = as.matrix(data_rv2[(j):(window +
        j - 1), ])
    dum1.residuals.s = data.frame(matrix(0, nrow = nrow(dum1.ret),
        ncol = ncol(dum1.ret)))
    dum1.marginals = data.frame(matrix(0, nrow = nrow(dum1.ret),
        ncol = ncol(dum1.ret)))
    # data frame to store student-t parameters
    dum1.marginals.par = data.frame(matrix(0,
        nrow = ncol(dum1.ret), ncol = 4))
    # list to store GARCH fits
    dum1.fits = list()
```

```
# loop for filtered residuals and marginals
for (l in 1:n.asset) {
    # fit GARCH
    dum1.fit1 = ugarchfit(spec = spec, data = dum1.ret[,
        l], solver = "hybrid", fit.control = list(scale = 1))
    # Store fit for parameters
    dum1.fits[[l]] = dum1.fit1
    # Store standardised residuals
    dum1.residuals.s[, l] = coredata(residuals(dum1.fit1,
        standardize = TRUE))
    # change residuals to uniform student-t
    # marginals
    dum1.marginals[, l] = pt(dum1.residuals.s[,
        l], df = as.numeric(coef(dum1.fits[[l]])[5]))
}
colnames(dum1.marginals) = c(colnames(dum1.ret))
Marginals = dum1.marginals
# Fit R-Vine Copula
RVMO = RVineStructureSelect(Marginals, familyset = c(1:6),
    type = 0, selectioncrit = "AIC", indeptest = FALSE,
    level = 0.05, progress = FALSE)
# number of simulations
n.simul = 1000   #simulate R-Vine Data
dum1.simul.vine = as.matrix(RVineSim(n.simul,
    RVMO))
# data frame for simulated marginals
dum1.simul.marg = data.frame(matrix(0, nrow = n.simul,
    ncol = ncol(dum1.simul.vine)))
# data frame for simulated series
dum1.simul.series = data.frame(matrix(0, nrow = n.simul,
    ncol = ncol(dum1.simul.vine)))
# other data frames
dum1.simul.sigma = data.frame(matrix(0, nrow = n.simul,
    ncol = ncol(dum1.simul.vine)))
dum1.simul.resid = data.frame(matrix(0, nrow = n.simul,
    ncol = ncol(dum1.simul.vine)))
# inner loop for marginals
for (i in 1:n.asset) {
    # convert simulated data to student-t
    # residuals
    dum1.simul.marg[, i] = qt(p = dum1.simul.vine[,
        i], df = as.numeric(coef(dum1.fits[[i]])[5]))
    res = dum1.simul.marg[, i]
    # type='z' below means that standardized
    # residuals are passed so it doesnt have to be
```

```
# multiplied by sigma
sim = ugarchsim(dum1.fits[[i]], n.sim = n.simul,
    m.sim = 1, startMethod = c("sample"),
    custom.dist = list(name = "sample",
        distfit = as.matrix(res), type = "z"))
dum1.simul.series[, i] = sim@simulation$seriesSim
dum1.simul.sigma[, i] = sim@simulation$sigmaSim
dum1.simul.resid[, i] = sim@simulation$residSim
}
# convert back to simple returns
dum1.simul.sr = exp(dum1.simul.series) - 1
# simulated portfolio returns
dummy.port1 = log(1 + (apply(dum1.simul.sr,
    1, sum)/n.asset))
# calculate VaR
var1 = quantile(dummy.port1, c(0.05, 0.01))
# cvar1=mean(dummy.port1[dummy.port1<var1[2]])
# #remove '#' for ES
# cvar5=mean(dummy.port1[dummy.port1<var1[1]])
# #remove '#' for ES
var.pred[k, ] = var1
# es.pred[k,]=cbind(cvar1,cvar5)#remove '#'
# for ES
k = k + 1
}
```

We can also plot the estimated VaR after some data processing as shown below

```
# data.plot to be used
data.plot = cbind(-1 * var.pred, c(data.port.pred, 0))
data.var = data.plot
dates.plot = data_rv1[(window + 1):n.tot, 1]
data.plot = cbind(dates.plot, data.plot[1:n.test, ])
colnames(data.plot) = c("Dates", "VaR_5%", "VaR_1%", "Port_Returns")


# plot (figure-11.11)
matplot(data.plot[, 2:4], ylab = "", type = "l", axes = FALSE,
    main = "Portfolio VaR (1% & 5%)"), lty = c(1:3))
axis(1, at = c(1:nrow(data.plot)), labels = data.plot[,
    1])
axis(2, at = c(round(min(data.plot[, 2:4]), 2):(round(max(data.plot[,
    2:4]), 2))))
```

```
legend("bottomleft", title = "Series", c("VaR 5%", "VaR1%",
    "Returns"), fill = c(1:3), cex = 0.9), lty = c(1:3))
box()
```

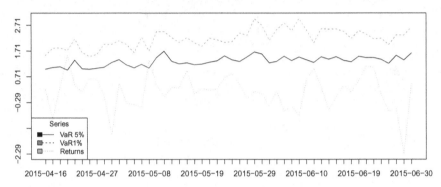

Figure 11.11:   R-Vine VaR forecasts

Figure 11.11 plots the 1% and 5% VaR forecasts along with original portfolio return series obtained from the method. The plot shows that the VaR forecasts closely follow the daily returns with few violations. We can also test the VaR estimates using the backtests introduced in Chapter 9.

## 11.5   Summary

In this chapter, we introduced multivariate modelling using Copula. We discussed some commonly used bivariate copulas as well as recently developed multivariate Vine Copulas which are more flexible than usual bivariate copulas. We discussed various examples of bivariate copulas and vine copulas using R packages. Finally, we concluded this chapter with an example showing how to forecast VaR using R-Vine Copulas which are capable of modelling VaR as well as ES for portfolio returns with multivariate dependence structures. In this last chapter, we concluded our discussion of multivariate analysis using R.

# Bibliography

Aas, K., & Berg, D. (2009). Models for construction of multivariate dependence–a comparison study. *The European Journal of Finance*, *15*(7–8), 639–659.

Aas, K., Czado, C., Frigessi, A., & Bakken, H. (2009). Pair-copula constructions of multiple dependence. *Insurance: Mathematics and Economics*, *44*(2), 182–198.

Agnello, L., Castro, V., Jalles, J. T., & Sousa, R. M. (2015). Fiscal consolidation and financial reforms. *Applied Economics*(ahead-of-print), 1–16.

Alexander, C. (2008). *Market Risk Analysis: Practical Financial Econometrics, Volume 2*. John Wiley & Sons.

Allen, D. E., Ashraf, M. A., McAleer, M., Powell, R. J., & Singh, A. K. (2013). Financial dependence analysis: Applications of vine copulas. *Statistica Neerlandica*, *67*(4), 403–435.

Allen, D. E., Gerrans, P., Singh, A. K., & Powell, R. (2009). Quantile regression and its application in investment analysis. *Finsia Journal of Applied Finance (JASSA)*.

Allen, D. E., Singh, A. K., & Powell, R. J. (2011). Asset pricing, the Fama–French factor model and the implications of quantile regression analysis. I. In G. N. Gregoriou (ed.), *Financial Econometrics Modeling: Market Microstructure, Factor Models and Financial Risk Measures* Palgrave Macmillan.

Alonso-Rodríguez, A. (2001). Logistic regression and world income distribution. *International Advances in Economic Research*, *7*(2), 231–242.

Altman, E. I., & Sabato, G. (2007). Modelling credit risk for SMEs: Evidence from the US market. *Abacus*, *43*(3), 332–357.

Artzner, P., Delbaen, F., Eber, J., & Heath, D. (1999). Coherent measures of risk. *Mathematical Finance*, *9*, 203–228.

Ball, L., Jalles, J. T., & Loungani, P. (2015). Do forecasters believe in Okun's law? an assessment of unemployment and output forecasts. *International Journal of Forecasting*, *31*(1), 176–184.

Baltagi, B. (2005). *Econometric Analysis of Panel Data* (3rd edn.). John Wiley & Sons.

Barnes, M. L., & Hughes, A. T. W. (2002). A quantile regression analysis of the cross section of stock market returns [Working Paper]. Available at http://ssrn.com/abstract=458522.

Bazen, S., Benhayoun, G., Sloane, P., & Theodossiou, I. (1994). The economics of low pay in Britain: A logistic regression approach. *International Journal of Manpower*, *15*(2/3), 130–149.

Bedford, T., & Cooke, R. M. (2001). Probability density decomposition for conditionally dependent random variables modeled by vines. *Annals of Mathematics and Artificial intelligence*, *32*(1–4), 245–268.

Bedford, T., & Cooke, R. M. (2002). Vines: A new graphical model for dependent random variables. *Annals of Statistics*, 1031–1068.

Beirlant, J., Goegebeur, Y., Segers, J., & Teugels, J. (2006). *Statistics of Extremes: Theory and Applications*. John Wiley & Sons.

Bollerslev, T. (1986). Generalized autoregressive conditional heteroskedasticity. *Journal of econometrics*, *31*(3), 307–327.

Bouyé, E., Durrleman, V., Nikeghbali, A., Riboulet, G., & Roncalli, T. (2000). Copulas for finance — a reading guide and some applications. *Available at SSRN 1032533*.

Box, G. E., Jenkins, G. M., & Reinsel, G. C. (1994). *Time Series Analysis: Forecasting and Control* (3rd edn.). Prentice Hall.

Brechmann, E., Czado, C., & Paterlini, S. (2014). Flexible dependence modeling of operational risk losses and its impact on total capital requirements. *Journal of Banking & Finance*, *40*, 271–285.

Brechmann, E. C. (2010). *Truncated and Simplified Regular Vines and their Applications*. Diploma.

Brechmann, E. C., & Czado, C. (2013). Risk management with high-dimensional vine copulas: An analysis of the euro stoxx 50. *Statistics & Risk Modeling*, *4*(30), 307–342.

Breusch, T. S., & Pagan, A. R. (1980). The Lagrange multiplier test and its applications to model specification in econometrics. *The Review of Economic Studies*, 239–253.

Chan, L. K., & Lakonishok, J. (1992). Robust measurement of beta risk. *Journal of Financial and Quantitative Analysis*, *27*(02), 265–282.

Chang, W. (2012). *R graphics cookbook*. O'Reilly Media, Inc.

Cherubini, U., & Luciano, E. (2001). Value-at-risk trade-off and capital allocation with copulas. *Economic Notes*, *30*(2), 235–256.

Cheung, W. (2009). Copula: A primer for fund managers. Available at http://papers.ssrn.com/sol3/papers.cfm?abstract_id=1456980.

Christoffersen, P., Hahn, J., & Inoue, A. (2001). Testing and comparing value-at-risk measures. *Journal of Empirical Finance*, *8*(3), 325–342.

Christoffersen, P. F. (1998). Evaluating interval forecasts. *International Economic Review*, 841–862.

Clayton, D. G. (1978). A model for association in bivariate life tables and its application in epidemiological studies of familial tendency in chronic disease incidence. *Biometrika*, *65*(1), 141–151.

Coles, S. (2001). *An Introduction to Statistical Modeling of Extreme Values* (Vol. 208). Springer.

Coles, S., Heffernan, J., & Tawn, J. (1999). Dependence measures for extreme value analyses. *Extremes*, *2*(4), 339–365.

Cowpertwait, P. S., & Metcalfe, A. V. (2009). *Introductory Time Series with R*. Springer Science & Business Media.

Croissant, Y., & Millo, G. (2008). Panel Data Econometrics in R: The plm package. *Journal of Statistical Software, 27*(2), 1–43.

Diebold, F. X., Schuermann, T., & Stroughair, J. D. (1998). *Pitfalls and Opportunities in the Use of Extreme Value Theory in Risk Management*. Springer.

Dissmann, J. (2010). Statistical inference for regular vines and application. *Diploma the-sis, Technische Universitat Miinchen*.

Dissmann, J., Brechmann, E. C., Czado, C., & Kurowicka, D. (2013). Selecting and estimating regular vine copulae and application to financial returns. *Computational Statistics & Data Analysis, 59*, 52–69.

Drew, M. (2003). Beta, firm size, book-to-market equity and stock returns. *Journal of the Asia Pacific Economy, 8*(3), 354–379.

Embrechts, P., Höing, A., & Juri, A. (2003). Using copulae to bound the value-at-risk for functions of dependent risks. *Finance and Stochastics, 7*(2), 145–167.

Embrechts, P., Klüppelberg, C., & Mikosch, T. (1997). *Modelling Extremal Events* (Vol. 33). Springer Science & Business Media.

Embrechts, P., Lindskog, F., & McNeil, A. (2001). Modelling dependence with copulas. *Rapport technique, Département de Mathématiques, Institut Fédéral de Technologie de Zurich, Zurich*.

Embrechts, P., McNeil, A., & Straumann, D. (2002). Correlation and dependence in risk management: Properties and pitfalls. *Risk management: Value at Risk and Beyond*, 176–223.

Engle, R. (2001). Garch 101: The use of arch/garch models in applied econometrics. *Journal of economic perspectives*, 157–168.

Engle, R. F. (1982). Autoregressive conditional heteroscedasticity with estimates of the variance of United Kingdom inflation. *Econometrica: Journal of the Econometric Society*, 987–1007.

Fama, E. F., & French, K. R. (1992). The cross-section of expected stock returns. *Journal of Finance, 47*(2), 427–465.

Fama, E. F., & French, K. R. (1993). Common risk factors in the returns on stocks and bonds. *Journal of Financial Economics, 33*(1), 3–56.

Faraway, J. J. (2005). *Extending the Linear Model with R: Generalized Linear, Mixed Effects and Nonparametric Regression Models*. CRC press.

Fischer, M., Köck, C., Schlüter, S., & Weigert, F. (2009). An empirical analysis of multivariate copula models. *Quantitative Finance, 9*(7), 839–854.

Frank, M. J. (1979). On the simultaneous associativity off (x, y) and x + y− f (x, y). *Aequationes Mathematicae, 19*(1), 194–226.

Franke, J., Härdle, K., & Hafner, C. (2008). *Statistics of Financial Market: An Introduction*.

Franke, J., Härdle, K., & Hafner, C. (2015). *Statistics of Financial Market: An Introduction* (4th edn.). Springer-Verlag.

Georges, P., Lamy, A.-G., Nicolas, E., Quibel, G., & Roncalli, T. (2001). Multivariate survival modelling: A unified approach with copulas. Available at SSRN 1032559.

Ghalanos, A. (2014). Introduction to the rugarch package.(Version 1.3-1) (Tech. Rep.). Technical report.

Giesecke, K., & Goldberg, L. R. (2005). Forecasting extreme financial risk. In M. Ong (Ed.), *Risk Management: A Modern Perspective* (pp. 609–536). Elsevier Academic Publishing.

Gilli, M., et al. (2006). An application of extreme value theory for measuring financial risk. *Computational Economics, 27*(2–3), 207–228.

Greene, W. H. (2008). *Econometric Analysis*. Granite Hill Publishers.

Grunfeld, Y. (1958). *The Determinants of Corporate Investment: A Study of a Number of Large Corporations in the United States.* Unpublished doctoral dissertation, Department of Photoduplication, University of Chicago Library.

Gujarati, D. N. (2012). *Basic Econometrics*. Tata McGraw-Hill Education.

Gumbel, E. J. (1960). Distributions des valeurs extrêmes en plusieurs dimensions. *Publications de l'Institute de Statistique de l'Université de Paris, 9*, 171–173.

Hauser, R. P., & Booth, D. (2011). Predicting bankruptcy with robust logistic regression. *Journal of Data Science, 9*(4), 565–584.

Hausman, J. (1978). Specification tests in econometrics. *Econometrica*.

Heffernan, J. E. (2000). A directory of coefficients of tail dependence. *Extremes, 3*(3), 279–290.

Heffernan, J. E., & Tawn, J. A. (2004). A conditional approach for multivariate extreme values (with discussion). *Journal of the Royal Statistical Society: Series B (Statistical Methodology), 66*(3), 497–546.

Heinen, A., Valdesogo, A. et al. (2009). *Asymmetric CAPM Dependence for Large Dimensions: The Canonical Vine Autoregressive Model.* CORE.

Hilal, S., Poon, S.-H., & Tawn, J. (2011). Hedging the black swan: Conditional heteroskedasticity and tail dependence in s&p500 and vix. *Journal of Banking & Finance, 35*(9), 2374–2387.

Hilbe, J. M. (2009). *Logistic Regression Models*. CRC Press.

Hsiao, C. (2001). Economic panel data. In N. J. S. B. Baltes (ed.), *International Encyclopedia of the Social & Behavioral Sciences* (pp. 4114–4121). Oxford. Available at http://www.sciencedirect.com/science/article/pii/B0080430767004113.

Huang, H.-C., & Yeh, C.-C. (2013). Okun's law in panels of countries and states. *Applied Economics, 45*(2), 191–199.

Joe, H. (1996). Families of m-variate distributions with given margins and m (m − 1)/2 bivariate dependence parameters. *Lecture Notes–Monograph Series*, 120–141.

Joe, H. (1997). *Multivariate Models and Dependence Concepts*. Chapman & Hall, London.

Jondeau, E., & Rockinger, M. (2001). Conditional dependency of financial series: An application of copulas. *HEC Working Paper*.

Kleiber, C., & Zeileis, A. (2008). *Applied Econometrics with R*. Springer Science & Business Media.

Koenker, R. (1994). Confidence intervals for regression quantiles. In *Asymptotic Statistics* (pp. 349–359). Springer.

Koenker, R. (2005). *Quantile Regression* (No. 38). Cambridge University Press.

Koenker, R., & Bassett Jr, G. (1978). Regression quantiles. *Econometrica: Journal of the Econometric Society*, 33–50.

Kurowicka, D. (2011). *Dependence Modeling: Vine Copula Handbook*. World Scientific.

Kurowicka, D., & Cooke, R. M. (2006). *Uncertainty Analysis with High Dimensional Dependence Modelling*. John Wiley & Sons.

Kwiatkowski, D., Phillips, P. C., Schmidt, P., & Shin, Y. (1992). Testing the null hypothesis of stationarity against the alternative of a unit root: How sure are we that economic time series have a unit root? *Journal of Econometrics*, *54*(1), 159–178.

Ledford, A. W., & Tawn, J. A. (1996). Statistics for near independence in multivariate extreme values. *Biometrika*, *83*(1), 169–187.

Ledford, A. W. et al. (1998). Concomitant tail behaviour for extremes. *Advances in applied Probability*, *30*(1), 197–215.

Lintner, J. (1965). The valuation of risk assets and the selection of risky investments in stock portfolios and capital budgets. *The Review of Economics and Statistics*, 13–37.

Ljung, G. M., & Box, G. E. (1978). On a measure of lack of fit in time series models. *Biometrika*, *65*(2), 297–303.

Loretan, M., & Phillips, P. C. (1994). Testing the covariance stationarity of heavy-tailed time series: An overview of the theory with applications to several financial datasets. *Journal of Empirical Finance*, *1*(2), 211–248.

Low, R. K. Y., Alcock, J., Faff, R., & Brailsford, T. (2013). Canonical vine copulas in the context of modern portfolio management: Are they worth it? *Journal of Banking & Finance*, *37*(8), 3085–3099.

Mancini, L., & Trojani, F. (2011). Robust value at risk prediction. *Journal of Financial Econometrics*, *9*(2), 281–313.

Manganelli, S., & Engle, R. F. (2001). Value at risk models in finance.

Maroney, N., & Protopapadakis, A. (2002). The book-to-market and size effects in a general asset pricing model: Evidence from seven national markets. *European Finance Review*, *6*(2), 189–221.

Marsh, T. A., & Wagner, N. (2004, January). *Return-Volume Dependence and Extremes in International Equity Markets* (Finance No. 0401007). EconWPA. Available at http://ideas.repec.org/p/wpa/wuwpfi/0401007.html.

Matyas, L., & Sevestre, P. (eds.) (1996). *The Econometrics of Panel Data-Handbook of Theory and Applications*. Kluwer.

McNeil, A. J. (1999). Extreme value theory for risk managers. *Departement Mathematik ETH Zentrum*.

McNeil, A. J., & Frey, R. (2000). Estimation of tail-related risk measures for heteroscedastic financial time series: An extreme value approach. *Journal of Empirical Finance*, *7*(3), 271–300.

McNeil, A. J., Frey, R., & Embrechts, P. (2005). *Quantitative Risk Management: Concepts, Techniques and Tools: Concepts, Techniques and Tools.* Princeton University Press.

McNeil, A. J. (1998). *Calculating Quantile Risk Measures for Financial Return Series Using Extreme Value Theory.* Departement Mathematik, Eidgenössische Technische Hochschule Zürich Zürich, Switzerland.

Meneguzzo, D., & Vecchiato, W. (2004). Copula sensitivity in collateralized debt obligations and basket default swaps. *Journal of Futures Markets, 24*(1), 37–70.

Michou, M., Mouselli, S., & Stark, A. (2007). *Estimating the Fama and French Factors in the UK: An Empirical Review.* Manchester Business School Manchester.

Mossin, J. (1966). Equilibrium in a capital asset market. *Econometrica: Journal of the Econometric Society*, 768–783.

Neftci, S. N. (2000). Value at risk calculations, extreme events, and tail estimation. *The Journal of Derivatives, 7*(3), 23–37.

Nelsen, R. B. (1999). *Introduction to Copulas.* Springer-Verlag.

Ohlson, J. A. (1980). Financial ratios and the probabilistic prediction of bankruptcy. *Journal of Accounting Research*, 109–131.

Okun, A. M. (1962). Potential gnp: Its measurement and significance. *Cowles Foundation Paper.* Available at http://cowles.econ.yale.edu/P/cp/p01b/p0190.pdf.

Onour, I. A. (2010). Extreme risk and fat-tails distribution model: Empirical analysis. *Journal of Money, Investment and Banking*, (13).

Özel, H. A., Sezgin, F. H., & Topkaya, Ö. (2013). Investigation of economic growth and unemployment relationship for g7 countries using panel regression analysis. *International Journal of Business and Social Science, 4*(6).

Palaro, H. P., & Hotta, L. K. (2006). Using conditional copula to estimate value at risk. *Journal of Data Science, 4*, 93–115.

Patton, A. J. (2006a). Estimation of multivariate models for time series of possibly different lengths. *Journal of Applied Econometrics, 21*(2), 147–173.

Patton, A. J. (2006b). Modelling asymmetric exchange rate dependence. *International Economic Review, 47*(2), 527–556.

Poon, S.-H., Rockinger, M., & Tawn, J. (2003). Modelling extreme-value dependence in international stock markets. *Statistica Sinica, 13*(4), 929–954.

Poon, S.-H., Rockinger, M., & Tawn, J. (2004). Extreme value dependence in financial markets: Diagnostics, models, and financial implications. *Review of Financial Studies, 17*(2), 581–610.

Ramsey, F. L. et al. (1974). Characterization of the partial autocorrelation function. *The Annals of Statistics, 2*(6), 1296–1301.

Reiss, R., & Thomas, M. (2007). *Statistical Analysis of Extreme Values: With Applications to Insurance, Finance, Hydrology and Other Fields.* Springer.

Ruppert, D. (2011). Statistics and data analysis for financial engineering. In (Chapter 8). Springer.

Said, S. E., & Dickey, D. A. (1984). Testing for unit roots in autoregressive-moving average models of unknown order. *Biometrika, 71*(3), 599–607.

Sanders, C. K., & Scanlon, E. (2000). Mortgage lending and gender. *Affilia*, *15*(1), 9–30.

Schirmacher, D., & Schirmacher, E. (2008). *Multivariate Dependence Modeling Using Pair-Copulas* (Tech. Rep.). Technical report.

Sharpe, W. F. (1964). Capital asset prices: A theory of market equilibrium under conditions of risk*. *The Journal of Finance*, *19*(3), 425–442.

Sheather, S. (2009). A modern Approach to Regression with R. In (Chapter 8). Springer Science & Business Media.

Shumway, R. H., & Stoffer, D. S. (2013). *Time Series Analysis and Its Applications*. Springer Science & Business Media.

Singh, A. K., Allen, D. E., & Powell, R. J. (2013). Extreme market risk and extreme value theory. *Mathematics and Computers in Simulation*, *94*, 310–328.

Singh, A. K., Allen, D. E., Powell, R. J., & Reddy, K. (2014). Multivariate financial dependence analysis of Asian markets using vine copulas.

Sklar, M. (1959). *Fonctions de répartition à n dimensions et Leurs Marges*. Université Paris 8.

Stărică, C. (1999). Multivariate extremes for models with constant conditional correlations. *Journal of Empirical Finance*, *6*(5), 515–553.

Stock, J. H., & Watson, M. W. (2012). *Introduction to Econometrics: Global Edition*. Pearson Education.

Swamy, P., & Arora, S. S. (1972). The exact finite sample properties of the estimators of coefficients in the error components regression models. *Econometrica: Journal of the Econometric Society*, 261–275.

Taylor, S. J. (2007). Modelling financial time series. S. J. Taylor (ed.), In *Modelling Financial Time Series* (Second Edition), World Scientific Publishing.

Treynor, J. L. (1961). Market value, time, and risk. *Unpublished Manuscript*, 95–209.

Treynor, J. L. (1962). *Toward a Theory of Market Value of Risky Assets*. (Unpublished manuscript. Subsequently published as Chapter 2 of Korajczyk (1999))

Tsay, R. S. (2010). *Analysis of Financial Time Series* (3rd edn.). John Wiley & Sons.

Tsay, R. S., & Tiao, G. C. (1984). Consistent estimates of autoregressive parameters and extended sample autocorrelation function for stationary and nonstationary ARMA models. *Journal of the American Statistical Association*, *79*(385), 84–96.

Wickham, H. (2009). *ggplot2: Elegant Graphics for Data Analysis*. Springer.

Wickham, H. (2010). A layered grammar of graphics. *Journal of Computational and Graphical Statistics*, *19*(1), 3–28.

Wooldridge, J. M. (2010). *Econometric Analysis of Cross Section and Panel Data*. MIT press.

Zaghdoudi, T. (2013). Bank failure prediction with logistic regression. *International Journal of Economics and Financial Issues*, *3*(2), 537–543.

# Index

**A**

Autoregressive Moving Average
  Model (ARMA), 159
  armaFit, 163
    predict, 164
    summary, 163
  arma, 162
  auto.arima, 163

**C**

Copula, 195, 212
  Clayton copula, 218
  Gaussian copula, 213
    normalCopula, 213
  Gumbel copula, 220
  Student-t copula, 215
  BiCopSelect, 222
  fitCopula, 214
  persp, 213
core packages, 9
CRAN, 3

**D**

Data Structures, 20
  arrays, 23
  data frames, 25
  lists, 27
  matrices, 21
  vector, 20
Data transformation
  reshape2
    melt, 101, 144
  dcast, 145

Data Types, 15
  character, 17
  complex, 16
  date & time, 18
  double, 16
  factor, 18
  integer, 16
  logical, 17

**E**

Expected Shortfall (ES), 191, 204
Extreme Value Theory (EVT),
  183
  excess distribution, 186
  Generalized Pareto Distribution
    (GPD), 185
    gpdFit, 187
    gpd, 187
  Mean Excess Function,
    186
  Mean Excess Plot, 186
    meplot, 186
  Peak Over Threshold (POT), 185
    dynamic VaR, 204
  Tail Dependence, 195
    asymptotic dependence,
      197
    asymptotic independence,
      198
    coefficient of tail
      dependence($\eta$), 202
    Fréchet marginals, 196
    chiplot, 199

chi, 199
taildep, 199
tcplot, 203

**G**

Generalised Autoregressive
Conditional Heteroskedasticity
(GARCH), 166, 204
*rugarch*, 167
    plot, 173
    report, 180
    ugarchfit, 168
    ugarchforecast, 172
    ugarchroll, 178
    ugarchspec, 167
generalised linear models (glms),
140
Getting Help, 10
Graphics
bar plot
    barplot, 80
    legend, 82
Histograms, 57
    hist, 57
line plot, 71, 78
multivariate scatter plot
    pairs, 85
parameters, 88
    margins, 89
    par, 88
pie chart
    labels, 83
    pie, 83
quantile–quantile plot, 58
    chart.QQPLOT, 177
    qqline, 59
    qqnorm, 206
    qqplot, 58
scatterplot, 76
*ggplot2*, 91
    facet_grid, 96, 146
    facet_wrap, 96
    geom_bar, 95, 98
    geom_line, 96
    ggplot, 93, 145

ggtitle, 98
qplot, 92
plot.zoo, 80
plot, 71, 76
title & labelling
    main,xlab,ylab, 77

**I**

integrated development environment
(IDE), 3–4
if-else, 46

**L**

Linear Regression, 103
ordinary least squares (OLS), 104
*formula*, 104
    abline, 107
    lm, 104
        generic functions, 105
        summary, 105
Logistic Regression, 139
    summary, 141
longitudinal data, 131
Loops
    for, 48
    repeat, 49
    while, 48

**M**

Matrix Manipulations, 22
Missing Data, 20
Multivariate Analysis, 211

**P**

Panel Data, 131
Panel Regression, 132
    Fixed Effects Model, 132, 134
    Random Effects Model, 132, 136
    *plm*, 133
        pdata.frame, 145
        pFtest, 137, 150
        phtest, 139
        plmtest, 138, 150
        plm, 133, 148

**Q**

Quantile Regression, 107
  *quantreg*, 110
    latex, 128
  rq, 110
    summary, 111

**R**

R Package
  *CDVine*, 222, 224
  *copula*, 213
  *evd*, 199, 203
  *evir*, 187
  *extRemes*, 199, 206
  *fArma*, 163
  *fExtremes*, 186, 192
  *fExtreme*, 207
  *fGarch*, 207
  *forecast*, 163
  *foreign*, 34
  *ggplot2*, 91
  *pastecs*, 67
  *PerformanceAnalytics*, 177
  *plm*, 133
  *psych*, 66
  *quantreg*, 110
  *R.matlab*, 37
  *reshape2*, 101
  *rugarch*, 167, 230
  *sn*, 230
  *Stargazer*, 123
  *texmex*, 199
  *texreg*, 123
  *tseries*, 156, 162
  *VineCopula*, 222, 224, 230
  *xts*, 230
R Packages, 7
Reading Data, 29
  load, 31
  read.csv, 32
  read.dta, 36
  read.spss, 34
  read.table, 29
  readMat, 37
RStudio, 4

**S**

Sklar's Theorem, 195, 212
Summary Statistics, 53
  Shapiro–Wilk test, 177
    shapiro.test, 177
  describe, 66
  stat.desc, 67
  summary, 56, 62

**T**

Task Views, 9
apply, 52
cbind, 39
function, 50
rbind, 39
switch, 47
Time Series
  autocorrelation function (ACF),
    157
  Ljung-Box test, 159
    acf, 157
    Box.test, 159
  stationarity, 154
    adf.test, 156, 162
    kpss.test, 156
  stochastic process, 153
  white noise, 159
type inference, 2

**V**

Value at Risk (VaR), 175, 191, 204
  Portfolio VaR, 229
Vine Copula
  R-vine, 223
    RVineStructureSelect, 224
    RVineTreePlot, 225
Vine Copulas, 222

**W**

Writing Data
  write.csv, 32
  write.table, 31

Printed in the United States
By Bookmasters